THE VICTORIAN SUMMER
OF THE CLYDE STEAMERS
(1864-1888)

The *Adela* in Rothsay Bay (from a painting by Victor Welch)

THE
VICTORIAN SUMMER
OF THE
CLYDE STEAMERS
(1864-1888)

by

ALAN J. S. PATERSON

This edition published in 2001 by
John Donald, an imprint of
Birlinn Limited
West Newington House
10 Newington Road
Edinburgh
EH9 1QS

www.birlinn.co.uk

First published in 1972 by
David & Charles, Newton Abbot

ISBN 0 85976 550 4

British Library Cataloguing-in-Publication Data
A catalogue record for this book is available
from the British Library

Printed and bound by
Antony Rowe Ltd., Chippenham, Wiltshire

CONTENTS

FOREWORD

In 1812 a small steamship called the *Comet* started to voyage between harbours in the Firth of Clyde which had until then only seen vessels moved by oar or sail. This first Clyde Steamer was rapidly followed by many more of her type. The demand for reliable transport across the waters of the Firth, the relatively sheltered and short voyages, and the skills of the Clyde ship-builders and engineers resulted in a unique combination of circumstances which produced a fleet of world fame.

The Clyde Steamer was more than a means of transport for the islands and mainland outposts of the Clyde, and more too than a source of relaxation, fresh air and pleasure for a population many years away from television, the car and flights abroad. The Clyde Steamer was a West of Scotland institution. The names of the vessels—evocative names like *Jupiter*, *Ivanhoe*, *Queen Empress* and *Columba*—were known to all and each new building was widely discussed in terms of speed, appearance and passenger comfort.

The Clyde Steamer in classic form continued until well after the Second World War. As a young boy in the 1950s I became very familiar with steamers such as the *Duchess of Hamilton*, *Glen Sannox* and *Caledonia*. The trip from Glasgow's Bridge Wharf 'doon the watter' to view the docks, shipping and shipyards which at that time seemed to extend for miles downstream was undertaken at least twice each year. Along with thousands of others the summer holiday in Whiting Bay started with the taxi to St Enoch Station, the train to Fairlie and that long awaited steamer trip to far off Arran.

Times have changed and so have Clyde Steamers: the diesel engine is now supreme and the requirement to carry cars, lorries and buses has produced what might be unkindly described as highly functional floating garages. At the start of the twenty-first century only the paddle steamer *Waverley* shows a new generation what was commonplace, although the piers this last Clyde Steamer visits are still those which welcomed the *Comet* all those years ago.

While the traditional Clyde Steamer has long vanished, interest in the genre remains strong, if perhaps somewhat changed from the past. I suspect that there are now very few who will be keen to learn that the *Benmore* was built in Rutherglen in 1876, while the nominal horsepower of the first *Lord of the Isles* may not be high among today's points of discussion. However, should such detail be of importance, the classic books of James Williamson and Duckworth and Langmuir provide the answers.

What Alan Paterson set out to do in *The Victorian Summer of the Clyde Steamers*, as with his earlier companion volume, *The Golden Years of the Clyde Steamers*, was to go beyond the bald facts relating to hulls, engines, builders and owners. Following more in the style of Williamson and McQueen, Mr Paterson's extensive research has produced stories and tales which allow the reader to move easily back in time to that Victorian Summer period when private owners dominated the Clyde's steamer trade and the railway to Gourock was not yet complete. Piers and storms, captains and crews, accidents and mishaps, fares and races, all feature in the history of the Clyde Steamer in that period. Some will read this volume with nostalgia, remembering the Clyde Steamer of the mid twentieth century, if not the early nineteenth. Other readers will have no direct memories and will never have seen the Clyde cris-crossed by trails of smoke on a summer Saturday. All will be absorbed by Mr Paterson's enthusiasm and depth of knowledge.

John Riddell, Fairlie, Ayrshire
September 2001

PICTURE CREDITS

ABERDEEN UNIVERSITY LIBRARY
(G. W. Wilson collection)

The *Hero* at the Broomielaw (p. 51); the *Undine* at the Broomlielaw (p. 52); the *Marquis of Lorne* and *Carrick Castle* at the Broomielaw (p. 52); Glasgow fair in 1885 (p. 141); the *Victoria* on trials (p. 159); the *Eagle* at Brodick Fair (p. 160)

W. J. ANDERSON, MBE, CAMPBELTOWN
On board the *Davaar* (p. 141)

ANNAN, GLASGOW
The *Venus* at Glasgow (p. 33)

THE BAILIE
Captain John McGraw of the *Iona* and *Columba* (p. 87); Captain William Barr, of the Lochgoil Company (p. 87); Captain Alexander Campbell, of the Wemyss Bay Fleet (p. 124); Captain William Buchanan (p. 124)

G. E. LANGMUIR COLLECTION
The *Iona* at Ardrishaig (p. 33); the Campbeltown steamer *Kintyre* (p. 34), McLean's *Marquis of Bute* (p. 34); the ill-fated *Lady Gertrude* at Rothesay (p. 69); Shearer's *Glen Rosa* (p. 70); the Duke of Hamilton's *Heather Bell* (p. 70); the *Viceroy* of the 'Turkish Fleet' (p. 88); the *Lord of the Isles* (p. 88); the *Guy Mannering* (p. 159)

IAN SHANNON COLLECTION
The *Columba* (p. 105); the *Ivanhoe* at Rothesay (p. 106); the *Diana Vernon* at Mambeg (p. 123); the *Chancellor* of 1880 at Arrochar (p. 123)

VICTOR WELCH
The *Adela* in Rothesay Bay (frontispiece)

'Who shall say that paddles are prosaic, and that there is no poetry in the steamboat? Nay, there have even been times when from Ardrishaig Pier, on a brilliant day in August, we have watched the *Iona* steam in, a thing of life and beauty, crowded with animation, graceful in all her lines and motions, with her every spar and plank white like snow, and gleaming in the intense sunlight, that we have thought her the finest realisation we had ever seen of poetry in motion—a very epic, in short, of swiftness and steam.'

Anonymous Victorian writer

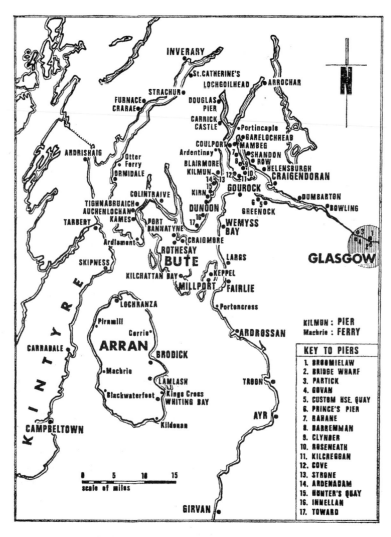

Map of the River and Firth of Clyde

INTRODUCTION:
THE RIVER AND FIRTH OF CLYDE

IN few other parts of the British Isles can there be found a city of the size of Glasgow situated so closely to an area of such surpassing scenic beauty and variety as the Firth of Clyde. Within a distance of but a few miles from the industrial and commercial heart of Scotland are to be found quiet sea lochs, popular holiday resorts, peaceful villages, secluded islands; within the broad expanse of the relatively sheltered waters of the estuary, protected from the Atlantic Ocean by the long barrier of the Mull of Kintyre, the scene ranges from the busy industrialism of Glasgow, Greenock and Port Glasgow to the remote stillness of Loch Striven, from the bustling gaiety of Rothesay and Dunoon to the subtler attractions of Campbeltown and Inveraray, and from the lowland expanses of the Ayrshire coast to the Highland grandeur of Arran and Lochfyne.

Industry, expanding rapidly in the early years of the nineteenth century, found in the River Clyde a natural highway to the markets of the world. Schemes proposed by imaginative and far-sighted men converted the shallow tidal waterway into a wide, deep, ship canal to the heart of Glasgow. Trade flourished, industry grew, and in a few decades the city became the undisputed commercial capital of Scotland with an importance acknowledged in due course by the proud title of the 'Second City of the Empire'.

When Henry Bell's little *Comet* first ventured timidly down from the Broomielaw to Greenock in 1812, her owner could scarcely have foreseen the unbelievably rapid development of steamboats. Within ten years, every corner of the firth resounded to the beat of paddles, and a veritable fleet of ships linked the city to the quiet communities of the estuary. Glasgow had discovered the Clyde and in the abiding affections of generations of her citizens for the scenic glories of the firth there began a love affair that has lasted into modern times. Nourished by frequent and cheap services, traffic to the coast expanded mightily; quiet villages such as Rothesay and Dunoon grew into prosperous towns, to which thousands were glad to escape from the claustrophobic background of Victorian Glasgow. The well-to-do early appreciated the advantages of living at the coast and travelling daily to the city on business, and took their families to Clyde resorts for the summer. Ground was feued in many places, and imposing villas built for the successful businessmen whose employees must needs be content with day trips from up river. There came the cult of the coasting 'season', and the annual ritual of the Glasgow Fair when the whole population, or thus it seemed, made for the Clyde.

Alongside the river shipbuilding grew rapidly, spurred on by the development of iron ships and steam propulsion. There appeared famous yards—Tod & McGregor, at Partick; James & George Thomson, at Govan; Henderson, at Renfrew; Blackwood & Gordon, at Port Glasgow, and many others stretched along the coast from Rutherglen to Ayr—and in the heat of their competition was evolved the classic Clyde paddle steamer, designed and built for passenger service in the shallow waters of the firth, usually good-looking, often very beautiful, and above all, speedy and manoeuverable. Development of the type reached a high point in the late fifties and some of the better known shipyards produced vessels which were intended primarily as advertisements for their builders. These were the great years of Clyde steamer racing, but as economic propositions many of the best ships were ruinous. Then came the American Civil War of the early sixties, and Clyde owners found it lucrative to dispose of their beautiful but expensive thoroughbreds to agents of the secessionist southern states for blockade running out of Nassau carrying munitions of war into Confederate ports, returning with cargoes of cotton. The

Clyde, for several seasons, was annually stripped of its best boats, to the chagrin of the travelling public, but the process had the unexpected result of producing a brand new, modern fleet of steamers on the firth after 1865.

Thereupon commenced a period of about twenty-five years during which private owners controlled steamboat traffic on the river, all competing fiercely for trade. Some prospered, others failed, fleets were built up by purchase and amalgamation, and slowly the traffic pattern evolved throughout the seventies and eighties. Eventually came a demand for better ships, faster services, improved standards of comfort, which only the richer proprietors could meet. The river route fell into disfavour as Victorian sewage provisions failed to keep pace with a rapidly growing city, and the railways began to build new lines to the coast allowing substantial parts of through journeys to be made by train. The period closes with the Caledonian Railway extension to Gourock approaching completion, and the entire pattern of Clyde steamer services on the verge of the greatest changes for over half a century.

CHAPTER ONE

THE CLYDE FLEET AND SERVICES IN 1864

IN America the Confederacy was dying in the spring of
1864, slowly but surely strangling in the grip of Federal
armies. In the west, southern troops fell back on Atlanta,
able only to delay the inexorable advance of Sherman's hard-
ened veterans; in the Wilderness of northern Virginia, despite
bloody repulses, Grant pressed Robert E. Lee mercilessly
back on Richmond. The end of a dream was plainly in sight,
if not to the defiant Confederates, then certainly to men elsewhere. Political realities had strange effects in unexpected
quarters, and one of the places directly affected was the Firth
of Clyde and its steamboat services. Gone at last were the
mysterious Americans who bought the finest and swiftest
Clyde vessels 'for the Nassau trade'. It was again possible to
expect that the best steamers of one season would reappear in
the following year. Despite the inroads made in the fleet in
the early sixties for blockade running, the ultimate effect was
to the good of the river boats and services. There came a resurgence of building and a modern fleet evolved rapidly of
ships built on the finest principles, superior to anything of
their kind in the world at that time. These were concentrated for the time being on the upper firth; down river, the
ageing McKeller fleet maintained an uncertain and much-
criticised service as the public waited eagerly for the opening
in 1865 of the Wemyss Bay Railway and the arrival of newer
steamers sailing in connection with that line.

ANOTHER IONA

The guests who appeared at the Govan shipyard of James and

17

B

George Thomson on the afternoon of Tuesday 10 May 1864 to watch the launch of a fine new paddle steamer for the brothers Hutchesons' fleet of Clyde and West Highland Royal Mail steamers must have been forgiven for thinking that the event was to become an annual one, for this, the latest flagship, was the third to appear on the Glasgow and Ardrishaig route in as many years. As the long, slim, beautifully-modelled hull began to leave the ways she received from Master William Hutcheson the honoured name *Iona*, borne also by her two predecessors, and glided smoothly into the river which was to know her comings and goings for no less than seventy-two years.

The first *Iona* was built by the Thomsons in 1855 and was for her time about the finest Clyde steamer afloat. Long of hull, flush-decked, and graced by two well-raked red and black funnels fore and aft of her handsome paddleboxes, she represented the best practice of the earlier Victorian period and remained a great favourite during her time on the Clyde. It was too much to expect that a vessel of her type would avoid the attention of Confederate blockade runners; in the summer of 1862 the Hutchesons accepted what was doubtless a generous offer for her disposal, and she was made ready for sea. Painted dull grey, stripped of her furnishings, she came down river without lights one evening in October to avoid the vigilant eyes of Federal agents. Unhappily, the precautions were her undoing and she never left her native river. The steamship *Chanticleer*, too well deceived, ran her down off Gourock and the *Iona* foundered in thirteen fathoms.

The second *Iona*, also a Thomson steamer, appeared in 1863 and embodied the latest improvements in construction. Her design was based on that of the earlier vessel but she was longer and was fitted with full deck saloons fore and aft, a major advance in passenger accommodation. Like her predecessor she was driven by oscillating machinery and was capable of $17\frac{1}{2}$ knots. A worthy successor of the first *Iona*, she might well have achieved the same life span as the third of the name, but again American politics intervened and, after only one

season on the Ardrishaig mail run, she too was snapped up
for blockade running. Her departure from the Clyde was recorded on 19 January 1864 when she was observed to be
schooner-rigged and deeply laden with coals and cargo, steaming fast down channel. She was more fortunate than the first
Iona in getting clear of the Clyde, and headed down the Irish
Sea to Queenstown, where she re-coaled in readiness for the
Atlantic voyage. Her crew was uneasy, and thirteen hands refused to work the ship. They were arrested, and stood trial for
mutiny. Captain Chapman put out from Queenstown, but
soon ran into heavy weather. The *Iona's* hull had been greatly
strengthened for the voyage, but hours of pounding by a head
sea damaged the light plating and she began to leak. The master decided to run for Milford Haven, but on 2 February the
Iona ran under the lee of Lundy Island making water so rapidly that the fires were put out. The pumps failed and the
engines stopped, leaving the ship helpless. Fortunately the
Bristol pilot boat No 32 was at hand to take the crew off, and
half an hour later the *Iona* foundered.

The third *Iona* inherited not only the name of her immediate forerunner, but also her fine deck saloons, which that ill-
fated ship did not require in her intended career as a blockade
runner. She was slightly longer than the 1863 steamer, and her
overall length of 255 feet exceeded that of any other Clyde
steamer of the day. The hull was built with five watertight
bulkheads, a precaution not then mandatory, but the adoption
of which, in the words of a contemporary writer, spoke volumes for the owners' anxiety to secure the comfort and safety
of their passengers. The layout of hull and machinery followed
that of the two earlier *Ionas*. Oscillating engines were installed
by the builders, in company with the then standard jet condenser, but the boilers were of the horizontal, or navy, type
instead of the haystack pattern generally employed in other
contemporary Clyde steamers. The funnels were short and
stubby, rather marring the ship's appearance in her early
years, but this apart she was a magnificent vessel and rightly

commanded admiration as the most splendid example of her class afloat. The *Glasgow Herald* reported:

> As in the last *Iona*, the great feature in the present boat consists in the introduction of spacious deck saloons, with promenade above extending nearly from stem to stern. The cabin saloon, occupying the after part of the vessel ... is elegantly decorated in white and gold, is provided with cushioned seats of the most luxurious description, and is fitted all round with plate glass windows, which slide up and down like those of a railway carriage. At the extreme end next the stern, a small space is partitioned off, and most tastefully and commodiously fitted up as a ladies' retiring room. Beneath this saloon is the first cabin, a spacious apartment, admirably lighted and ventilated, and affording all the comfort of a well-furnished dining room. Immediately adjoining are the steward's pantry and a gentlemen's retiring room, provided with wash-hand basins and all other needful conveniences. On the forward part of the deck is a second saloon ... comfortably fitted up, and affording equally with the other the advantages of shelter from foul weather, abundant light, and perfect ventilation.

The *Iona's* official trial took place on 18 June when an invited party accompanied her from Lancefield Quay to Greenock, picking up more guests, before proceeding to the classic Clyde trial grounds, 'running the lights' from the Cloch to Cumbrae. The weather was boisterous, a south-westerly gale blowing up the firth so that it was practically impossible for a man to stand on the promenade deck, but the steamer maintained a speed of $19\frac{2}{3}$ statute miles an hour in the adverse conditions, and she was thereby judged at least the equal of her predecessor.

The *Iona* was much in the limelight during her first season. It was recorded that on one occasion she had sailed between Ardlamont and Ardrishaig in over four minutes less time than the second *Iona*, which bore out the opinion of her speed formed by those attending the official trial. At the Fair Holiday, in mid July, she carried immense crowds from Glasgow; a Greenock observer noted that her appearance on arrival there was a sight rarely witnessed. No proper estimate was ventured as to the crowds she carried, but on Fair Saturday she was filled to capacity long before her departure hour from the Broomielaw and had to sail early. In August she came into her own as the annual rush of English tourists came north, conveying many shooting parties to West Highland estates. The tourist influx to Greenock was larger than ever previously known, all of the local hotels being full up every night with travellers waiting to join the *Iona* next day.

The vessel's undoubted popularity had occasional drawbacks, as a passenger to Dunoon found out to his dismay one Saturday in August. Attracted by cheap excursion fares, a huge complement was aboard the steamer as she came down river, and first class passengers found to their irritation that their accommodation was over-run by steerage travellers. The correspondent wrote:

All the first-class passengers were thus being crushed by this excursionist party. Still, although ladies were rather rudely pushed about, and in many cases had their beautiful dresses destroyed by the tobacco spittles which were squirted about in all directions, no one complained—such small inconveniences as an occasional rude knock or a spoiled dress being as nothing, if only we were otherwise comfortable and happy, favoured by the appearance of a continuation of fine weather... Having taken tickets for Dunoon, I had my children collected in readiness to disembark them there as soon as we reached the pier, but keeping at a reasonable distance from the gangway, for fear of my young charges getting into danger. No sooner, however, had the *Iona* been made fast to the quay, than we were carried by the tremendous pressure of the excursionists... completely off our feet; and, but for the merciful hand of Providence, some of my children would have been trampled on and crushed to death. Fortunately, however, I and my young charges got out in safety; but the shrieks of women and children behind us told too plainly of the dreadful crushing and disorder in getting to the gangways. But the scene at Dunoon quay, when the excursionists were getting on board the *Iona* about five o'clock, on her return trip to Glasgow, baffles description. During the day a large proportion of the excursionists had become intoxicated, the result of which was that, as the hour approached when the steamer was expected, many were quarrelling and fighting, and bleeding faces and torn clothes were almost universal. At the entrance to the quay many refused to pay the penny of dues, and tremendous fighting ensued... In a state of madness a number of fellows got on the quay, which was crowded with about 1000 people. ... The drunken brutes attempted to force a passage for themselves by knocking down all before them. Women, with infants in their arms, were mercilessly knocked down and trampled over; husbands and fathers, protecting their wives and children, were likewise knocked down and abused, and probably not a few seriously injured.

Such scenes were all too common in 1864, and a leader in the *Glasgow Herald* took up the matter at some length, pointing out the dangers of overloading steamers and dwelling on the evils of intemperance:

Travellers who are paying handsomely for their transit to and from the Highlands have good reason to complain if the vessel is inundated with a swarm of excursionists or others who pay a shilling or eightpence to get a sail in the *Iona* to or from a place like Dunoon. The disgraceful scene described by a correspondent is the natural consequence of the present arrangement. Such spectacles must give the English and other strangers travelling by the steamers concerned a most humiliating idea of Glasgow life and Glasgow morality... The plain fact is, that before they reach their destination great numbers are drunk and riotous, and pour themselves, like a horde of Goths, over the quiet watering place where the steamer stops, filling the roads, shores, and quays with brawling, fighting, and every kind of drunken excess...

THE ARROCHAR ROUTE

Far removed from the hurly-burly of the Rothesay route was the service up the fjord-like Loch Long, to Arrochar. From early years ships on this station had afforded a connection with excursion steamers on Loch Lomond, permitting a tour of outstanding scenic attraction to be undertaken comfortably within a day from Glasgow. By 1864 commercial interests on the Arrochar and Loch Lomond sections were closely associated, and several shareholders of the Lochlomond Company formed a new concern for which, on 10 May in that year, Blackwood & Gordon launched a new excursion paddle steamer named *Chancellor* to maintain the Clyde sailings

from Glasgow. The new boat was of unusual design, having
the sponsons carried round the hull from bow to stern, thus
affording excellent deck space, but giving the ship a rather
bulky appearance from certain angles. She was closely modelled on a Loch Lomond vessel, the *Prince Consort*, and like
her had deck saloons fore and aft. Both vessels were driven by
twin crank diagonal engines, steam being supplied by the haystack type of boiler, then becoming widely employed for new
boats. The *Chancellor* was ready for service on 1 June, sailing
on that date from Glasgow to Arrochar with a party of directors and guests who, on arrival, made their way across the narrow neck of land separating Loch Long from Loch Lomond
to Tarbet pier to join the loch steamers *Prince Consort* and
Prince of Wales for a cruise to Balloch, where the excursionists joined the Glasgow train. Steamboat provision on Loch
Lomond over a century ago strikes a modern observer as lavish,
but in the middle years of the Victorian period the reputation
of Sir Walter Scott was at its height and his novel *Rob Roy*
had established Loch Lomond as an area which no tourist
would willingly miss. Royal patronage by the Queen herself,
Prince Albert, and other members of the Royal Family had
given the accolade to the steamer service, and for years it continued to operate profitably, justifying the construction not
only of successive new steamboats for the loch itself, but also
for the Glasgow and Arrochar trade with which it was so
closely associated.

'DOON THE WATTER'

For the great majority of Glaswegians, however, going 'doon
the watter' meant a sail from the Broomielaw to Rothesay,
and on that route was concentrated the bulk of the river fleet
of 1864. Several owners operated almost exclusively on it,
amongst the best known of whom were William Buchanan
and Alexander Williamson, former partners who had gone
their separate ways some years earlier. Captain Buchanan got

a new steamer for his Rothesay service early in June, the second *Eagle*, built as a replacement of her predecessor which had gone to Nassau. She was a great, black, two-funnelled boat from Charles Connell & Co, their solitary production for the river trade, and the powerful double diagonal engine which propelled her was supplied by the Anchor Line, once well known in the Finnieston district of Glasgow. The *Eagle* was one of the first Clyde steamers of the raised quarter deck class, in which head room in the first class saloon aft was increased by the expedient of raising the deck to the level of the main rail, so allowing much improved ventilation. 'The *Eagle*', ran a newspaper report, 'has been elegantly fitted up and every modern improvement introduced for the comfort of passengers. In this respect the *Eagle* is certainly not excelled by any steamer on the river. Her spacious saloon is decorated in a neat and chaste manner, and passengers who are musically inclined can enjoy themselves at a fine-toned piano ... Altogether great taste has been displayed in fitting up the *Eagle*, and there is little doubt that she will prove a favourite on the Rothesay route, with which her owner has been so long connected.' The *Eagle* was unusual in having both funnels placed forward of her strikingly-designed paddleboxes, steam coming from two haystack boilers. She was quite fast by the standards of the time, although never regarded as a record breaker; nevertheless, an enthusiastic traveller noted that she had sailed from Rothesay to Glasgow in just under two and a half hours, exclusive of time at piers, shortly after entering service.

Captain Alexander Williamson's family was to become more influential in Clyde steamer history than any other, three of his sons holding important managerial posts with the railway and turbine fleets in later years, but he himself seemed content to operate an efficient, profitable, but relatively featureless service between Glasgow and Rothesay, becoming identified in the seventies and eighties with the Kyles of Bute trade. Williamson's boats were the great reliables of the Clyde fleet, seldom reaching the headlines, but always earning a steady livelihood for their cautious, if perhaps unimaginative, owner. Nevertheless, they provided a splendid training ground for James, Alex (junior) and John, each of whom rose to command his father's steamers before moving on to greater things. The only Williamson vessel in 1864 was the *Sultan*, a rather small steamer built in 1861 and acquired second hand in the following year. A flush-decked boat, with haystack boiler and steeple engine thriftily inherited from an older ship of 1853, the *Sultan* had nothing remarkable about her, but she was useful and enjoyed a long career under successive owners. Her daily run in the summer of 1864 involved a six o'clock morning sailing from the Kyles of Bute to Glasgow, returning at two o'clock in the afternoon.

Captain 'Sandy' McLean was one of the great 'characters' of the Firth of Clyde. He and his brother, who managed the steward's department, were proprietors of a neat little steamer called the *Vulcan*, built in the middle fifties, a ship very much of her time with funnel abaft the paddleboxes. She had oscillating engines and an old fashioned square boiler. Sailing out of Rothesay at 7.20 every morning, she left from the Broomielaw at one o'clock. Stories told of the brothers were legion and testified to their popularity with the travelling public. The late Andrew McQueen described Sandy McLean as 'a rough diamond, but a diamond all the same'. Captain James Williamson, who knew him well, records that his generosity was taken advantage of, and indeed his open-heartedness was a byword. It was one of the tragedies of Clyde steamer history that in later life the old man's affairs went into decline and he was obliged to give up in 1888. A resident of Rothesay, McLean was an enthusiastic member of the 1st Buteshire Artillery Volunteers, a councillor and bailie of the Royal Burgh, a Justice of the Peace of the County of Bute, and an office bearer in a local church. It was his annual custom to entertain the local Volunteers to a free pleasure excursion on board his steamer, and on 23 May 1864 they returned the compliment by presenting the captain with a 'very handsome and valuable telescope, or field-glass, in token of the high estimation in which he is held by them'.

One of the more fortunate private steamboat owners of the period was Captain Duncan Stewart, whose commercial success appeared to have been due to his ability to sell ships at a good profit as opportunity arose. In 1863 he had taken delivery of rather a good looking boat, the *Victory*, a flush-decked steamer with haystack boiler and steeple engine. As a good, modern example of her type, it was surprising that she had not been sold for blockade running, but it is quite possible that her owner realised the advantage of retaining her in his service during a period when the firth services as a whole were at a low ebb. She did not remain long with Stewart, but in 1864 he ran the *Victory* on the Glasgow and Rothesay station apparently as a consort to Captain Buchanan's *Eagle*, for the two ships were advertised during the summer to sail on alternate days on the same complementary runs. There was no formal partnership between the two owners, although both used the one-time popular funnel colours of black with a broad white band, which was intended to avoid fruitless competition.

THE OUTER FIRTH

The longest sailings on the Clyde were those of David Hutcheson & Co, to Ardrishaig and Inveraray, and the Campbeltown & Glasgow Steam Packet Joint Stock Company's service to the southern end of the Kintyre peninsula. The *Iona* maintained Hutchesons' mail service to Ardrishaig during the summer months only, for traffic in the off-season did not justify the employment of a vessel of her size; consequently, throughout the winter her place was taken by the *Mountaineer*, a two-funnelled, flush-decked steamer which had been built for the route in 1852 but had suffered relegation to West Highland services on the appearance of the first *Iona*. Also a production of J. & G. Thomson's Govan yard, she had a steeple engine and locomotive-type boilers.

The Inveraray service was in the hands of two elderly ships, the *Inveraray Castle* and the *Mary Jane*, built in 1839 and 1846 respectively by Tod & McGregor. Both were driven by steeple engines. With one funnel abaft the paddleboxes, a fiddle bow and square stern, each vessel was of the older school. They were employed as consorts on a distinctly leisurely service between Glasgow and Loch Fyne, sailing out to Inveraray and back on alternate days with cargo and passengers. Acquired second hand with the goodwill of the Glasgow & Lochfyne Steam Packet Company in 1857, both ships had nevertheless served other owners previously.

The Campbeltown Company's service was carried on by two paddle steamers called *Celt* and *Druid*, dating back to 1848 and 1857. Here, too, cargo was an important part of the trade and times for the journey from Glasgow to Campbeltown were very slow. These vessels served the west Arran villages of Lochranza and Pirnmill as well as Carradale, in Kintyre, none of which had steamboat piers at that period, but ferries were employed to ship passengers and goods ashore, a process that was usually time consuming, often uncomfortable, and sometimes dangerous. In 1864 the Campbeltown and Inveraray services were generally regarded as being rather beyond the scope of the main Clyde steamer orbit, and the areas served had more of a Highland atmosphere than anywhere else on the Clyde estuary. Gaelic was widely spoken, crofting extensively practised, and fishing from Campbeltown, Carradale, Tarbert, Lochgilphead and other places was an important feature of the local economy. Campbeltown was the largest town, then and for years afterwards famous for its whisky distilleries. Tourism was in its infancy, and apart from occasional excursions no pleasure steamers penetrated to these remoter corners of the firth.

MORE NEW STEAMERS

One of the earliest Clyde steamboat services connected Glasgow with the town of Dumbarton, some fifteen miles down river, but the opening of a direct railway in 1858 had caused river traffic to lapse by 1864. Nevertheless, the service offered by the Edinburgh & Glasgow Railway on this westerly outpost of its system left something to be desired and early in January 1864 it was reported that a new company was about to resume steamer services to Dumbarton Old Quay, with two vessels then building. The first of these, named *Leven*, was launched on 29 April, her sister ship, the *Lennox*, following her into the water on 5 May. Both ships were small flush-deckers with oscillating engines and haystack boilers. The *Leven* was the first to take up service, under Captain A. Lang, on 31 May when it was noted that she carried considerable numbers of passengers. The initial service consisted of two return runs from the Broomielaw to Dumbarton, one of which was extended to Port Glasgow and Greenock, these sailings being augmented when the *Lennox*, Captain John Price, joined her consort in June.

Another newcomer of 1864 was a steamer built on a speculative basis for blockade running by Kirkpatrick, McIntyre of Port Glasgow, but left in the builders' hands in an unfinished state. She was completed for joint owners, Captain Alexander Watson, of Glasgow, and Captain William Brown, of Bangor, her launch taking place on 20 July when she was named *Arran Castle* by Miss Watson. One of the best Clyde ships of her class, she was very finely modelled for speed and unusually strongly constructed in view of the trade for which she had originally been intended. Of flush-decked pattern, the *Arran Castle* had two haystack boilers and was driven by oscillating machinery installed by Rankin & Blackmore. She was completed rapidly and went on trials on 17 August, taking up regular service on the Rothesay station at the end of the month.

ROUND THE LOCHS

Communities on the northern shores of the Clyde were much

remoter in 1864 than in later years and had to rely almost exclusively upon steamers for access to Glasgow. Thus, places such as Kilmun, on the Holy Loch, and the Gareloch piers, as well as Lochgoilhead, enjoyed daily steamboat services from the city throughout the year.

Traffic to Lochgoilhead was handled by the Lochgoil and Lochlong Steamboat Company with two vessels, the older of which was the appropriately-named *Lochgoil*, of 1853, a flush-decked steamer of the older type with funnel abaft the paddle-boxes, a haystack boiler, and steeple engine. Her younger sister, the *Loch Long*, had entered service in 1859 and was a smaller ship of rather more modern appearance, with funnel forward. Her boiler was also a haystack, but the machinery was of oscillating pattern. Both vessels wore the striking Lochgoil Company funnel colours, red, with black and white bands under a black top.

The *Nelson*, owned by A. McKellar, provided a ferry service between Greenock and Helensburgh, as well as serving the Gareloch piers of Row, Roseneath and Garelochhead. She was not a remarkable steamer, although adequate enough for the traffic. Her steeple engine was salvaged from an earlier steamer, the *Eclipse*, whose short career had ended ingloriously on the Gantocks, off Dunoon, in 1854.

The Holy Loch trade was in the hands of the Campbell family, of whom Captain Robert Campbell was to become one of the best known owners on the river. They took delivery of a new steamer, the *Vivid*, in 1864. She was a smart, flush-decked boat, conventionally equipped with steeple engine and haystack boiler. Her consort was a vessel called the *Express* which had appeared in 1854 and had an unusually short life, being broken up at the end of the season of 1864. That summer had not gone far before the new *Vivid* was in the news. Coming down the river one day in July she encountered the *Victory* in charge of her owner, Duncan Stewart, who 'did strive or race with her upon a voyage from Greenock to Kilmun, whereby the passengers on board both steamers were greatly alarmed, and placed in danger', as the charge ran in the Glasgow River Bailie Court a fortnight later. For that escapade, Stewart was duly fined £5 or, failing payment, 20 days' imprisonment but he and his fellow skippers appeared to treat such penalties as an incidental hazard of the trade and as deterrents they had little effect, to judge by the annual procession of steamboat masters before the magistrates.

VARIOUS STEAMERS

Purchases for blockade running denuded the Clyde of the most modern steamers, built for the most part in the late fifties and early sixties, and such older ships as remained in 1864 were built in some instances during the forties. One of the best of these was the *Petrel*, which appeared in 1845 to run in connection with the Glasgow, Paisley & Greenock Railway. Of decidedly old-fashioned appearance, she had two funnels abaft the paddleboxes, was driven by a steeple engine, and had paddle floats of the non-feathering type rapidly being displaced by 'patent' or feathering floats in new vessels. Of approximately similar vintage and dimensions was the *Cardiff Castle*, said to have been the first Clyde steamer to be fitted with double diagonal engines. She had fallen into the disreputable Sunday trade by 1864 and appeared to sail during the week on the Broomielaw and Millport route. The *Hero*, a somewhat larger vessel built by Wingate in 1858 had a very long life in Scottish waters, passing through the hands of several owners before ending her days as a West Highland tourist steamer early in the present century. She was advertised variously on the Rothesay and Arran routes in the 1864 summer, in some form of association with the *Petrel*, *Arran Castle*, *Eagle* and *Victory*, from which it may be deduced that the owners of all these boats had an arrangement as regards competition and fares, but it was evidently a temporary understanding and did not last.

Of the handful of older ships still in the trade, the *Aquilla* of 1843 under her original name of *Emperor* had gained notoriety in 1853 by being the first steamboat to break the Sabbath peace of the firth. Two of the McKellar fleet, the *Lady Brisbane* and the *Lady Kelburne*, were her contemporaries, having been launched respectively in 1842 and 1843. Both were distinctly old-fashioned, slow, and inadequate as regards accommodation. With the larger *Venus*, a two-funnelled steamer of 1852, they were the survivors of a once well-run fleet on the Millport station. Their larger, faster consorts had all gone blockade running and the trio remaining on the river kept up a reduced service which drew justified public criticism in 1864 not so much on account of its slowness but rather because of the condition of the boats themselves, for they had fallen on evil times. The McKellars knew that their connection would scarcely hope to survive the competition of the new Wemyss Bay Railway, then in an advanced state of construction, and its associated company's new steamboats when the whole route opened in 1865. There was no incentive to undertake other than minimum maintenance to keep the boats in traffic; as a natural result, breakdowns occurred frequently enough to excite public alarm, the service was chronically late, and dissatisfaction general.

Traffic from Ardrossan to Arran was in the hands of the Ardrossan Steamboat Company, whose *Earl of Arran*, a paddle steamer built in 1860, maintained a rather slow service to Brodick and Lamlash, perfectly adequate for the very sparse trade. Neither village at this period had a proper pier and ferry boats were needed to convey passengers and goods ashore at certain states of the tide.

Two other steamers justifying reference were the *Alma*, built for Captain Duncan Stewart in 1851, and the *Vesta*, launched two years earlier for Henderson & McKellar's Glasgow and Helensburgh trade. The *Alma* was a poor thing, nearly at the end of her tether in 1864. Her owner finally lost patience and had her broken up at the close of the season, retaining the machinery for use in a new ship in the following year. The

Vesta was a better steamer in every respect, although never outstanding, and enjoyed a much longer career on the firth.

All these steamers competed for the patronage of a society which presented as many contrasts as the Clyde fleet itself. The student of social history cannot fail to be impressed by the extremes of poverty, the lack of public concern for the unfortunates who in a later and more enlightened age are rightly supported by the state, and an astonishing indifference to such matters as hygiene and sanitation which nowadays are taken for granted. Life was a grim struggle for a majority of the population in an industrial city like Glasgow in the middle years of Victoria's reign. Disease, drunkenness, poverty, malnutrition, accidents—all took their toll. Small wonder that a day at the coast offered a man and his family a welcome if brief chance to escape from a daily round which was all but intolerable, an opportunity to be grasped with an enthusiasm hardly credible to our later generation. Glasgow Fair Saturday of 1864 saw thousands leaving the Broomielaw for the coast in a veritable fleet of pleasure steamers, nothing daunted by the awful state of the Clyde and undeterred by the gross overcrowding of so many boats. The richer citizens with their wives and children poured down to the coast too, for it was a notable feature of that period that rich and poor alike went to the same places, although the better-off could afford to stay at Rothesay or Dunoon all summer. These people came up to the city in huge numbers each morning, often to the embarrassment of the railway officials at Greenock—'Yesterday morning' ran a *Herald* report of July, 1864, 'the number of passengers from the coast by the several steamers was in excess of any previous Monday morning ever remembered. The whole resources of the Caledonian Railway Company's plant were brought into requisition to meet the large increase of passengers who demanded means of transit. Upwards of 3,000 persons left in four trains, within 45 minutes. Fifty-three carriages were required, together with eight of the best engines employed on this branch railway...'

Page 33. *(above)* The Royal Route: the Hutcheson flagship *Iona* lies at Ardrishaig in her first season while fishermen mend nets on the quay in the foreground; *(below)* Rothesay of Yester-year: the former McKellar steamer *Venus* lying inside the old harbour in 1869. The boatyard was closed soon afterwards. The *Argyle* lies at the main quay, then in course of enlargement

Page 34. Steamers of the Later Sixties: *(above)* the beautiful *Kintyre* passing Greenock, outward bound for Campbeltown; *(below)* Sandy McLean's popular *Marquis of Bute* on the Rothesay run, also passing Greenock

These were some of the features of a way of life that is now dead and forgotten. A later age spurns coastal shipping and the citizens of Glasgow now largely neglect the river and firth which were the pride and joy of their great-grandparents, but the story of how the steamboat service developed, expanded, and altered to serve the requirements of its patrons is too fascinating to be allowed to drift into the realm of things forgotten. The year 1864 was a turning point in that story and the succeeding quarter of a century saw the zenith of private enterprise on the river before changing economic patterns brought an inevitable transition to more impersonal control of the traffic by the Scottish railway companies.

Paddlebox of the *Sultan*

C

CHAPTER TWO

THE WEMYSS BAY FIASCO
(1865-1869)

FEW Scottish railways opened with such favourable prospects as the Wemyss Bay Company. Linking one of the most important coast routes to a strategically situated railhead on the lower firth, the new line appeared ready to attract to itself the bulk of the through traffic to Rothesay and Millport. A fleet of new, well designed steamboats sailing in connection with trains from Glasgow would sweep aside competition from established owners and in time create a comfortable monopoly. So it was believed, even by the railway's opponents, of whom there were many amongst the steamboat proprietors of the day. But a combination of over-confidence, bad management and ill fortune dashed the bright hopes of 1865 and by the close of the decade a more modest, but realistic, service operated from Wemyss Bay under private owners in association with the railway.

The Greenock and Wemyss Bay Railway Company led an independent existence as a protegé of the Caledonian Railway for just over a quarter of a century, but for most of that time it was a child of sorrow. For a number of reasons it never quite achieved the traffic potential envisaged by its promoters. Its early months were disastrous, its middle years interrupted by disputes with the Caledonian, and the end of its separate career clouded by widespread criticism of train services and steamer accommodation. Not until the parent company assumed full control in 1890 and embarked upon wide-ranging improvements did the line finally achieve the popularity with the travelling public that its commanding position had always promised. Leaving the original Greenock main line at a junction just west of Port Glasgow, the new railway climbed steeply on a gradient of 1 in 65 into the hills behind Greenock before reaching relatively level ground on the bleak uplands of north-west Renfrewshire. The line then swung southwards towards the quiet village of Inverkip, cut through a short tunnel and descended sharply to the terminus on the shore at Wemyss Bay. Although the railway was single throughout, enough land was acquired to allow doubling of the route at a later stage, but in the event this was not done until the end of the century, and then only partially. Share capital of the Wemyss Bay Company was £120,000, of which £30,000 was allocated to the Caledonian Railway, and authority was obtained to borrow a further £40,000 if required. The Caledonian agreed to work the new route, the Wemyss Bay Company undertaking to maintain the railway and pier at Wemyss Bay to the satisfaction of the Caledonian civil engineer. The Caledonian also undertook to appoint and pay the running and managing staff, the secretary and directors being appointed by the Wemyss Bay Railway.

The new railway company had no authority to run steamers on the Firth of Clyde. It was therefore in order to ensure a proper service to coast resorts in connection with trains from Glasgow that a meeting was held in the city early in 1864 for the purpose of forming a steamboat company to operate through traffic in conjunction with the Wemyss Bay Railway while nevertheless remaining a separate entity in the legal sense. Progress was rapid, and Parliamentary authority was received under Act of 25 & 26 Vict Cap 89 for the formation of the Wemyss Bay Steamboat Company, Limited, incorporated in terms of the provisions of the Companies Act, 1862. The objects were stated to be 'the Conveyance of Passengers, Goods, Cattle, and other Articles in Steamships or Boats between such places as the Directors of the Company may from time to time determine...' and the Articles empowered the directors specifically 'to enter into such Contracts, Agreements, and Arrangements with Railway Companies... as they may think proper.' Capital of the new company was £40,000 in 4,000 shares of £10 each, 360 of which were taken up by the nine subscribers. Orders were placed immediately with Caird & Co for two large excursion saloon paddle steamers for summer traffic, and a smaller, flush-decked boat for all-the-year-round service was ordered from Thos. Wingate & Co of Whiteinch.

THE COMING OF THE RAILWAY

Throughout the summer of 1864 navvy gangs laboured to push the single line of railway across the Renfrewshire hills to Wemyss Bay. Like most of their kind these were rough, hard men, well accustomed to prodigies of physical exertion in all conditions of weather. Many, perhaps the majority, were Irish, driven from their native Donegal or Wexford by extremes of poverty unknown elsewhere in Britain, and a famine which only a few years earlier had decimated the population. Unsympathetic Scots saw only the wilder side of these men descending, as often happened, upon Port Glasgow, Greenock and Gourock to drown their sorrows in cheap whisky and forget, however briefly, the almost unrelieved toil and misery amid the mud and spoil of new railway works. Drunkenness, fights and assaults were so commonplace as to excite little remark; rebukes from local bailies and prison sentences had no obvious effect; and the citizens of coast towns eventually came to look forward to the completion of the Wemyss Bay Railway not only as an improvement of their transport service but also as a delivery from a social scourge.

Down in Caird's shipbuilding yard in Greenock activity was no less intense. The cacophony of riveters' hammers continued unabated as two slim hulls took shape on the stocks. They were noted with interest by travellers, who knew that these were the ships intended to take up service from the new railhead at Wemyss Bay. Both of them would have deck saloons, and that would be an improvement on any ship sailing to

Largs, Millport or Arran. Of the entire river fleet, only the *Iona* and *Chancellor*, two of the newest up-river boats, had deck saloons, and, in specifying similar accommodation for their own steamers, it was plain that the directors of the Wemyss Bay Steamboat Company, Limited, intended their new service to be of the highest standard.

If the public at large interested itself in the two Caird steamers, so also did a number of American visitors to Greenock during the early summer of 1864. In the fine lines of the new ships they saw what was wanted for 'the Nassau trade'— speed and manoeuverability to outrun Federal warships enforcing the blockade of Charleston, Wilmington, and other ports on the Carolina coast. The Americans like what they saw on Cairds' stocks and offered to buy the steamer nearer completion. So it was that on 13 July the press reported that one of the river steamers building by Messrs Caird 'has been disposed of by private bargain'. Secrecy in respect of such sales had been paramount in the early days of the American Civil War, to prevent steamers being identified by Federal agents in Britain, but although a certain reticence still prevailed in newspaper reports nobody was deceived in 1864. No attempt at concealment was made when the new boat was launched as the *Hattie* on 17 August, and the papers stated bluntly that she was destined for blockade running. Running the lights on 1 November the vessel achieved 19 miles an hour, and eight days later sailed for Nassau. Her sale probably came at an opportune moment for her Wemyss Bay owners, for the railway was then far from complete and the new boat would have had to be laid up during the winter. After her launch, work started immediately on a replacement vessel of identical type.

MR BURNS'S DILEMMA

John Burns was one of the most influential shipowners of his time. Not only did his ships carry the lion's share of the traffic from Scotland to Ireland, but his interests also extended to the transatlantic trade of the Cunard line. He was well known as a loyal defender of fellow shipowners against unjust attack from government or public, and generally acknowledged as a redoubtable champion of the legitimate interests of the shipping lobby. His own fleet was maintained to high standards of safety, and it was therefore with feelings of personal embarrassment that he contemplated the run-down state of the Largs and Millport steamers of the McKellar fleet during the summer of 1864. These elderly steamers, most of whose faster and larger sisters had been disposed of for blockade running, continued to trudge up and down the river in various conditions of decrepitude, to the alarm of all who sailed in them. The impending completion of the Wemyss Bay Railway and the introduction of modern steamers inhibited the McKellars from spending money on their own ships other than the absolute minimum necessary to keep them sailing. Their attitude was understandable, but it savoured of gross neglect to Mr Burns and his friends.

Partly through loyalty to colleagues and also, no doubt, to avoid the accusation of adopting a 'holier than thou' attitude, John Burns refrained from public comment until, late in August, 1864, a series of accidents involving the *Lady Kelburne* drove him to write a strongly-worded letter of protest to the *Glasgow Herald*. Twice within a few days boiler accidents occurred, filling the engine room with steam and water. On the first occasion, due to carelessness on the part of the engineer, the sludge hole door under the boiler blew off, and on the second, a feed pipe fixing bolt was blown out. Fortunately the low pressure at which the machinery worked in the old ship avoided a major explosion, but the incidents not unnaturally caused considerable alarm. Burns wrote:

> I have refrained from drawing attention to the state of the Largs steamers from the fact of my being myself so much engaged in steam navigation, but the time has arrived when public safety demands that a protest should be made against the scandalous manner in which the service is conducted... I fail to discover what benefit is de-

rived from the Board of Trade having surveyors at this port, if it is not for them to watch from time to time the state of the steam vessels plying upon the river... I have seen the steamers upon the Largs station so crowded that if an accident occurred no prudence on the part of those in charge would be of any use; and I have seen at such a time the captain leave the deck and collect the tickets in a cabin so filled with people that it was with difficulty he could extricate himself and return to the deck; and all this time the human freight left in charge of a solitary 'hand', who had alike to steer the vessel and command the engines...

Burns's letter was accompanied by a copy of another which had been sent to the engineer surveyor of the Board of Trade in Glasgow, signed by himself and twenty-one other people, some of whom were prominent public figures. The surveyor was not amused, and took the part of the McKellars, stating that the *Lady Kelburne* had been withdrawn for examination, and observing icily that the kind of accidents cited might just as well have happened on Mr Burns's own ships. It was the latter's turn to take offence, expressing astonishment at the surveyor's attitude and repudiating the suggestion that such mishaps could take place on board a Burns steamer. There was a broad hint that the *Lady Kelburne's* boiler was worn out, and the reply concluded with a final condemnation of the unsatisfactory condition of the McKellar fleet. Their poor standards were in fact widely acknowledged and generally deplored.

THE WEMYSS BAY FLEET

All these accusations and recriminations could only favour the new rail and steamer service through Wemyss Bay. Late in 1864 the railway was still largely unfinished, but the steamboat company's first vessel was launched at Wingate's yard on 17 September, being named *Largs* as she took to the water. She was a small, two-funnelled, flush-decked steamer propelled by a new type of diagonal oscillating engine, and her boilers were of the haystack type. Her large paddleboxes were out of proportion to the short hull but although the ship was hardly a beauty she was sturdily built for summer and winter service and 'fitted up in a superior manner for the comfort and accommodation of passengers'.

The second of the original Caird boats was launched on 15 October by Miss Jane Miller, who named the ship *Kyles* as she left the ways. Of considerably larger dimensions than the *Largs*, the new steamer had oscillating machinery and haystack boilers, with funnels fore and aft of the paddles. The deck saloons, although comfortably furnished, were nevertheless rather short. Her completion was not hurried in view of the winter season and she did not run her trials until April 1865. The newspaper report of her maiden trip was unusually guarded and no speed was quoted although it was said that the result was very satisfactory and that the *Kyles* would be able to run at twenty miles an hour. Somewhat unwisely, in the light of subsequent events, it was claimed that the *Kyles* and her sister were 'built to surpass every river steamer afloat'. On 29 April the *Kyles* ran the lights and, to the chagrin of all concerned, achieved only 17½ miles an hour. 'It is but right to state, however,' ran an official account, 'that the pressure of steam on the boilers was only 27 lbs. We understand that the builders...were bound in the contract to produce a speed equal to 19 miles per hour on a given consumpt of fuel, and on Saturday we learn that the consumpt was considerably below the maximum quantity'. The *Kyles* was taken back to Greenock for alterations to her boilers—it may be inferred that her steaming was unsatisfactory—and on 8 May ran another trial, achieving on that occasion a speed of 18½ miles an hour which was an improvement on her earlier performance but still a disappointment to the owners.

In the meantime the *Largs* had been placed in service on 1 April, not, as expected, from Wemyss Bay, but from the Broomielaw, sailing to Largs and Millport in competition with McKellar's steamers. A month later the service was extended to Arran where the *Largs* lay overnight at Lamlash, taking the 5.45 am up run to Glasgow, calling intermediately at Invercloy (Brodick), Corrie, Millport, Fairlie, and Largs, and returning from the Broomielaw at 3 o'clock in the afternoon. She came into immediate rivalry with McKellar's *Venus*, a much superior and more modern steamer than the luckless *Lady Kelburne* which had drawn John Burns's displeasure on the Millport station, and to the embarrassment of the Wemyss Bay people the *Venus* proved more than a match for their fine new steamboat.

THE RAILWAY OPENS

By mid-April 1865 the Greenock and Wemyss Bay Railway was nearly complete and on the 13th of that month the first locomotive, hauling a first class carriage carrying Caledonian Railway directors and officials, ran through from Port Glasgow to the terminus. On 27 April Captain Reid of the Royal Engineers inspected the line on behalf of the Board of Trade and expressed satisfaction at the condition of the works, and authority was given for its formal opening to traffic. A thirteen-coach excursion train ran to Wemyss Bay on 12 May, conveying 600 passengers, and on the following day the directors, with a party of friends, travelled over the line and sailed in the *Kyles* to Lamlash in what appears to have been the very first rail and steamer excursion by the Wemyss Bay route. The *Glasgow Herald* reported the occasion very fully:

The Glasgow portion of the company left Bridge Street Station shortly before nine in the morning, accompanied by the band of the 19th L.R.V.*, whose services had been bespoken for the occasion. The train, consisting of brand new first-class carriages, and forming by the way an excellent sample of the Wemyss Bay rolling stock, arrived in due time at Greenock, where the number of excursionists received a considerable accession. A pleasant ride, affording at intervals charming glimpses of rural scenery, and towards the close a magnificent view of the Firth of Clyde, brought the party to Wemyss Bay about two minutes after ten—the journey from Glasgow, including several stoppages, having been got through in an hour and a

*Lanarkshire Rifle Volunteers

quarter. At the railway pier the handsome and commodious steamer *Kyles* was in waiting, with steam up, to convey the excursionists to sea. The embarkation was speedily effected, and after some little delay, due apparently to the shipment of commissariat stores, the vessel started for the Kyles of Bute... The morning was dull, and a cold wind blew from the north-west, so that those who had brought thick shawls and greatcoats found reason to congratulate themselves on their foresight. Fortunately, however, the day kept fair, and as creature comforts were liberally provided below, the voyage on the whole proved a thoroughly enjoyable one. On her way to the Kyles the steamer called at Rothesay to pick up some passengers, her appearance there attracting a large crowd on the quays. She then threaded her way through the Kyles, after clearing which, the day being yet young, she was headed for Arran. Corrie and Brodick were successively passed, and it was still early in the afternoon when the vessel steamed into the beautiful bay of Lamlash. While coasting along under the Arran hills the company were invited to partake of luncheon, which was served in sumptuous style in the fore cabin. As may be supposed, full justice was done to the viands, and it is scarcely necessary to add that the toast of 'Prosperity to the Wemyss Bay Railway and Steamboat Company' was pledged with right good will. Throughout the voyage the band played in capital style a variety of musical selections, and in the course of the afternoon some of the younger members of the party joined in a quadrille. On leaving Lamlash Bay the *Kyles* was steered for Millport, where she met with a hearty reception from the people assembled on the pier. Making next a brief call at Largs, she reached Wemyss Bay so long before the hour appointed for the starting of the return train that it was found necessary to fill up the time by a supplementary cruise to Innellan. At length, about a quarter to five, the party was once more on the rail, and in due time the Glasgow excursionists were safely deposited at Bridge Street, highly gratified with the day's proceedings.

The Wemyss Bay route was opened to traffic on Monday, 15 May, the inaugural service consisting of four trains each way daily between Bridge Street and the coast. All trains were advertised to include first class carriages and '3d with Seats'(!), no doubt to emphasize the superiority of the Wemyss Bay trains over those running to Greenock, on which carriages without seats were still employed in the middle sixties.

STEAMBOAT CONNECTIONS

The Wemyss Bay Steamboat Company's temporary service to and from Glasgow was withdrawn on the opening of the railway, and the *Largs* and the *Kyles* were based on Lamlash and Tighnabruaich respectively, where both lay overnight to take early morning runs in connection with the 8.10 train from Wemyss Bay. The *Kyles* spent her day on the Rothesay and Kyles of Bute service, working in three return trips to Rothesay and two to Tighnabruaich. The omission of Innellan from her timetable in favour of Toward was an instant cause for complaint; it was pointed out that not only was the existing service to Innellan via Greenock faster than by Wemyss Bay and Toward, but the fares by the new route were substantially higher. The *Largs* commenced the day with her up run from Lamlash, thereafter working in three return trips to Millport and one to Largs before returning to Arran in connection with the 5 o'clock train from Bridge Street.

These schedules left both steamers very fully employed and it was not long before their lack of speed caused lateness, with resultant complaint by travellers. Running of trains on the new railway was no better. These had frequently to be detained to await arrival of late steamers at Wemyss Bay, and consequently lost their paths on the Greenock line east of Port Glasgow, and more especially on reaching the joint line with the Glasgow & South Western Railway between Paisley and Glasgow, where traffic of two companies shared a double line into Bridge Street. Late trains from the coast had to take their turn, with deplorable effects on punctuality. 'Up to Time' wrote to the newspapers to complain of the 5.30 pm up train from Wemyss Bay. 'This train, we are informed in the time-bills, is due in Glasgow "about" 6.43 p.m. Now, what can this mysterious word "about" mean? Surely the directors cannot construe it into 7.32 p.m. . . . Had the train been ten or fifteen minutes late it might have been excusable, but a delay of three-quarters of an hour is surely quite unwarrantable.'

'A.B.C.' wrote a few days later, citing the departure of the same train forty-seven minutes late due to the lateness of the *Largs,* and the eventual arrival at Bridge Street sixty-five minutes behind time. The late running caused a corresponding delay to the 5.20 down train, held at Port Glasgow for an hour until the up train had cleared the single line section. 'Really there is some gross miscalculation in the timing of the steamers,' wrote this correspondent, 'and if they are so irregular as to time in fine weather, what can be expected of them in heavy weather?'

Complaints rained upon the railway directors and the steamboat owners. The purchase of Captain Duncan Stewart's useful vessel, the *Victory,* at the end of May, however, seemed to hold out the prospect of improvement. The transaction cost the steamboat company £5,000 and, after repainting, the new acquisition joined the fleet on 1 June. Her arrival was the signal not for a consolidation of the service but for further extensions. The *Kyles* now lay overnight at Ardrishaig, the Rothesay sailings were extended to Port Bannatyne, and Innellan and Dunoon were added to the list of calls. Most of the day sailings were given to the *Victory,* while the *Kyles* set off on a pleasure cruise via the Kyles of Bute to Lamlash in connection with the 9.30 am train from Glasgow, returning to connect with the 5.30 up train from the coast.

The timetable would have taxed any fleet to its limits, but punctuality on the Wemyss Bay route virtually was thrown to the winds. The chorus of complaints was now swelled by the rare event of a leader in the *Glasgow Herald* in June:

> During the last ten days we have published a number of letters from various gentlemen regarding the management or mismanagement of the Wemyss Bay Railway, and we have received at least double the number on the same subject, which we have not thought it necessary to print. It is abundantly evident that the travelling public have good reason to complain... The steamers, in the first place, do not keep time; the trains are kept waiting until the steamers arrive, and are then despatched at any hour whether suitable for the traffic on the main Greenock line or not... The only effectual remedy is to

start the trains punctually ... whether the steamers have arrived or not; and if a regulation such as this was rigidly enforced the steamboat company would either require to study punctuality, or to move their present vessels out of the way altogether, and make way for better...

The steamboat owners seemed unable to learn from experience, nor did they heed the rebuke. The arrival of the second saloon steamer, the *Bute*, late in June might have saved the situation for them, but motivated seemingly by a death wish the proprietors promptly announced a double service between the Broomielaw and the coast, calling at Wemyss Bay in each direction. The *Kyles* ran from Ardrishaig to Glasgow, while her sister ship sailed to Lamlash daily from the city. The results were chaotic. Letters poured into the offices of the *Glasgow Herald*, to be printed under such headings as 'Relapse of the Wemyss Bay Railway', 'The Wemyss Bay Railway Company Again', and 'Joys of Travelling on the Wemyss Bay Line'. 'There is something radically wrong about the general management somewhere,' said one writer, and he spoke for everyone. By mid July the directors were forced to come to grips with reality, and the *Kyles* ceased calling at Tarbert and Ardrishaig; while the up river sailings to Glasgow were abandoned at the end of August.

RAILWAY TROUBLES

As if operating problems were not enough for the unhappy management, the railway service was completely disrupted on 7 July by the partial collapse of a cutting to the north of Wemyss Bay station. Driven through red sandstone, it had required the provision of retaining walls during construction but during a spell of dry weather in early July fissures had opened in the earth above it. Heavy rain loosened the soil, and shortly after the passage of a down train, some 1,500 cubic ft of earth and rock fell on the permanent way. The driver of the 12.30 up train was able to stop just in time to avoid running into the obstruction. Gunpowder had to be used to clear the line, new track was laid, and the line was re-opened in the evening. The Ardrishaig and Lamlash sailings were delayed by no less than five hours as a result of the accident.

The unhappy summer of 1865 closed with a buffer stop collision in Wemyss Bay station on 16 September when the driver of a down train misjudged his braking power. Fortunately there were few injuries, but to judge by a *Herald* report of a few days later, the incident affected at least one passenger adversely:

> On Saturday last, shortly after the passengers, who had been wounded at Wemyss Bay Station, had been landed from the Largs steamer at Millport, a young woman, with a pale and anxious face, entered the surgery of Dr McGown, and said, 'Oh, Doctor, will you give me a pennyworth of pills?' 'What kind of pills, my girl?' asked the Doctor. 'Railway Accident Pills, if you please,' responded the lass, 'for I was up there at Wemyss Bay and I'm terribly shook.' Dr McGown had not any 'Railway Accident Pills' in his stock, but we understand that instead of them he supplied some other medicine, which, it is to be hoped, proved satisfactory and salutary to the patient.

RETRENCHMENT

The opening season had been a disaster, as both rail and steamboat managements had to admit, and the latter made drastic economies in time for the summer of 1866. After withdrawal at the end of September 1865, the *Kyles* and the *Bute* were disposed of for service on the Thames where they were renamed *Albert Edward* and *Princess Alice* respectively. No steamer history would be complete without reference to the sinking of the latter early in September 1878 by the collier *Bywell Castle*, with an appalling death roll, a disaster quite without parallel in British coastal steamer history.

The disposal of two large steamers allowed the Wemyss Bay Steamboat Company to acquire, on 2 April 1866, the almost new steamer *Argyle* from Captain Duncan Stewart, for whom she had sailed only a fortnight. She was a flush-decked steamer of practically the same size as the company's earlier acquisition from the same owner, the *Victory*, and like her was fitted with a haystack boiler and a steeple engine. The *Argyle* was just as economical as the *Victory*, and a fine sea-boat, and these two, in company with the *Largs*, maintained a much more sensible service than that of the over-ambitious timetable of 1865, abandoning the Arran section and concentrating on the Rothesay, Largs and Millport sailings. The withdrawal from Port Bannatyne drew complaints, but on the whole the revised arrangements met with approval and criticism was rare in the second season. Nevertheless, the Wemyss Bay Steamboat Company's affairs did not prosper, even with the rationalisation of its sailings. The imposition of a surcharge for pier dues on through bookings from Glasgow to coastal resorts caused much ill feeling, which the company would have done well to avoid.

By 1868 its affairs were on the point of collapse. In December of that year it was reported to a joint committee of the railway and steamer proprietors that the steamboat company was in arrears of debt to the Caledonian Railway to the amount of £1,810 and that this sum could not be paid 'in spite of urgent remonstrances and applications for payment'. The steamers were reported to be held by the company's bankers as security for advances, and all calls on the shareholders had been made and paid up. Clearly, it was time to call a halt, and arrangements were made for a statement of affairs to be laid before the shareholders. The company, inevitably, went into liquidation early in 1869.

Faced with the urgent necessity of maintaining adequate steamer connections, the Wemyss Bay Railway entered into agreements with various owners for the continuance of sailings. These were not mutually satisfactory, and the steamboat proprietors apparently felt that they could take advantage of the situation to crush the opposition of the new railway. Realising the need for a permanent arrangement, therefore, the railway directors entered into fresh negotiations with two newcomers to steamboat ownership, James Gillies, and his son-in-law, Alexander Campbell, and concluded an agreement with them in August 1869 under which they acquired the *Largs* and the *Argyle* from the liquidator of the Wemyss Bay Steamboat Company, Limited, paying the purchase price of £5,100 by a cash deposit of £100 and financing the balance by a loan from the National Bank of Scotland. They already owned the old McKellar steamer *Venus* and all three ships were mortgaged to the bank in security for the advance, which was repayable in five annual instalments of £1,000 commencing on 1 October 1870, four of the Wemyss Bay Steamboat Company's directors personally guaranteeing £2,000 of the loan to the bankers as additional security.

With this fleet, Gillies and Campbell ran an economical service in association with the railway for the following two decades. It was essentially a 'round-the-year' affair, with few expensive frills; these could not be afforded by men with their livelihood at stake. On the whole, it was a good service, regarded with respect and affection by regular patrons and casual excursionists alike who sailed in the austere little black and white paddle steamers to Rothesay and Millport. There was little of the panache and gaiety of some of the larger excursion steamers further up the firth, but their steady and dependable service to the coastal communities was widely appreciated in their time.

Paddlebox of the *Victory*

Page 51. Broomielaw Set Piece: an early morning view at Glasgow in about 1877. The *Hero* lies nearest the camera, moored alongside the *Windsor Castle*. Ahead of the latter lies the *Undine*, forward of her the *Vesta*, with the *Eagle* moored outside, and in the distance lies the *Iona*

Page 52. Scenes of the Later Seventies: *(above)* Duncan Stewart's *Undine* loads passengers at the Broomielaw, ahead of her lie the *Windsor Castle* and *Elaine*; *(below)* the *Carrick Castle* embarking Fair Holiday passengers at Glasgow, ahead of her lies the then new *Benmore*, and astern the *Marquis of Lorne*

CHAPTER THREE

THE LATER SIXTIES
(1865-1869)

THE end of the American war was followed by a resurgence of Clyde steamboat traffic and a large number of new ships entered service in the second half of the sixties, most of them to the order of private owners. The North British Railway, undeterred by the misfortunes of its Wemyss Bay counterpart, also came upon the scene with grandiose plans to capture the West Highland trade, only to encounter immediate disaster. The Campbeltown Company's comfortable monopoly was challenged by a powerful competitor who was driven off at the cost of expensive new construction. The whole pattern of services was in the melting pot as new owners appeared and older ones withdrew. Graham Brymner, of Greenock, was prominent in a plan to rationalise the trade and improve standards but he, like so many before and after, found only frustration and disappointment. The failure of some ventures saw several vessels sold off the river and in some instances the merciless waters beyond the firth exposed the flimsiness of construction of those lightly-made ships, the loss of the *Arran Castle* with all her crew being a tragedy that shocked the West of Scotland. The decade closed with virtually a new Clyde fleet in being and river trade settling into the general pattern which prevailed for nearly twenty years.

THE HELENSBURGH ROUTE

The North British Railway was a newcomer to the Clyde coast, having gained access to Helensburgh by amalgamating with the Edinburgh & Glasgow Railway on 31 July 1865. The

D

latter had similarly absorbed the Glasgow, Dumbarton & Helensburgh Railway as recently as August 1862; and as that concern had only opened its single line to the coast in 1858 the railway connection with Glasgow along the northern shores of the firth was still a comparative novelty in the middle sixties. Compared with the Caledonian route to Greenock the North British line was lightly used, Dumbarton and Helensburgh offering nothing of the industrial traffic which was such a profitable feature south of the river. Thus, the Helensburgh railway meandered through the sparsely populated northwestern environs of Glasgow and amidst unspoiled country to Dalmuir and Bowling, running thence within sight of the Clyde to Dumbarton and on by way of Cardross to the fashionable watering place which Sir James Colquhoun of Luss had named in honour of his wife on its founding in 1774.

From Helensburgh the railway directors planned to introduce an ambitious coast service in the summer of 1866 with two splendidly equipped, modern paddle steamers. An inkling of the scheme reached the newspapers in March; steamers were to be run to Greenock, Rothesay, and Ardrishaig, a fleet of five ships at least being implied; a new harbour was to be built at Ardmore, near Helensburgh, and a line of screw steamers would convey goods traffic from Greenock to the North British route in competition with the Caledonian Railway. Certainly, such grandiosities were not beyond the imagination of Richard Hodgson, the company's chairman, whose railway career, then at its zenith, was devoted to an unceasing battle with the 'auld enemy'. Was the Caledonian at Carlisle? Then to Carlisle went the North British also, over the Border hills in a spectacular attempt to attract trade from Irish Sea ports. Was the Caledonian at Perth and Dundee? There also went Hodgson's North British. And what of the Clyde, and its lucrative seasonal traffic to the West Highlands? Here too came Richard Hodgson, and the first North British Clyde steamers.

Afterwards, and with all the advantages of hindsight, the

venture could be seen to be over-extravagant. The Ardmore project came to nothing, but, as with many rumours, the scheme hinted at in this newspaper was founded on hard fact —the attraction of the Ardrishaig trade. Under the aegis of the North British Steam Packet Company—which was really the railway company operating in the names of some of its directors to avoid Parliamentary restrictions on direct ownership—two steamers were ordered from A. & J. Inglis, of Pointhouse. These were sister ships, considerably smaller than the *Iona*, but finished to the same high standards as that notable vessel. The first to be launched was the *Meg Merrilies* on 27 March 1866, her consort, the *Dandie Dinmont*, following her into the water on 11 April. Both ships were fitted fore and aft with deck saloons 'of the most luxurious description' and were driven by two-cylinder diagonal oscillating engines, steam being supplied by haystack boilers. The funnels, placed fore and aft of the machinery, were of the currently fashionable short pattern, similar to those of the *Iona* and other contemporary steamers. The *Meg Merrilies* went down-river on 28 April, running the lights at a speed of eighteen miles an hour, well over the contract speed. Thus far, all was well, and the new steamer took up her sailings from Helensburgh Quay on 1 May under command of Captain McKinlay.

The North British made a strong feature of the connections between Edinburgh and the Clyde coast, and advertised a day excursion from the Capital to Ardrishaig, allowing two hours ashore, admittedly at the cost of a very early start. Through coach connections between Ardrishaig and Oban were also advertised, so that the North British service was in direct competition with Hutchesons' *Royal Route*. This was emphasized by a clash with the *Mountaineer* on the first day of the railway service; a large crowd on Rothesay pier watched with interest as the *Meg Merrilies* rounded Toward Point in company with the Hutcheson steamer and reached Rothesay ahead of her. This promising start, was, however, offset by the almost immediate withdrawal of the *Meg* because of mechanical trouble and it was not until 21 May that the Ardrishaig service could be resumed by her consort, the *Dandie Dinmont*, which had completed her trials three days earlier. The *Meg Merrilies* was unable to join her until 6 June when the full North British service came into operation, but ill luck continued to dog the Steam Packet Company when the *Dandie Dinmont* in turn suffered a machinery breakdown on 23 June. It was made good within a few days and the Helensburgh traffic was noted as improving during the following week but no sooner had the *Dandie* returned to her station on 29 June than she broke down again, more seriously, and had once more to be withdrawn. On this occasion the newly renovated *Petrel* was chartered to take her place for a week until the necessary repairs had been undertaken.

After these early adventures the railway service appears to have settled down reasonably enough and certainly with none of the mismanagement which had caused so much public offence in the case of the Wemyss Bay Company in 1865. Nevertheless, the Ardrishaig steamers were withdrawn at the end of the summer season, victims of a financial crisis which shook the North British Railway to its foundations, led to the most searching inquiry by a committee of shareholders and caused the enforced resignation of the chairman. The fact was that the company was stretched well beyond its financial means and was to all intents and purposes bankrupt. Hodgson, zealous in his company's interests in the constant feud with the Caledonian, was discovered to have resorted to questionable accounting practices to maintain public confidence in the North British; revenue expenditure had been transferred to suspense accounts and the annual profits thereby fictitiously enhanced, while dividends were paid out of steadily mounting bank overdrafts. Sooner or later a crash was inevitable, and Hodgson had to go. He went, feeling that his efforts on behalf of the company had been scantily rewarded. It is doubtful if any personal advantage resulted from his activities, but modern company legislation would certainly have led to his prosecution and all things considered he was fortunate in getting away unscathed.

Severe retrenchment was the inevitable outcome of the committee's investigation. The Clyde steamer venture was unprofitable and it was hardly surprising when the two fine paddlers were withdrawn at once. With them went a smaller, less imposing vessel named *Carham*—after Richard Hodgson's mansion—which had been built in 1864 to sail on the company's services out of its Cumberland port of Silloth, and in 1866 had kept up short distance connections from Helensburgh. Both of the larger steamers were advertised for sale in April 1867 but the *Carham* returned to Silloth. The *Meg Merrilies* was 'sold foreign' in April 1868 and her sister spent some time on the Forth before returning to the Clyde in 1869 to resume services from Helensburgh to the Holy Loch and Dunoon. Although sadly attenuated in comparison with the original sailings, the service with which the *Dandie Dinmont* thereafter became identified was much more in accordance with reality, and manifestly more profitable than the heroic scheme of 1866.

THE ARRAN CASTLE DISASTER

When the American Civil War was at its height, several Clyde shipbuilders had found it rewarding to build paddle steamers on a speculative basis for sale to the men who carried on the dangerous but profitable blockade-running trade into Confederate ports from Nassau, in the Bahamas. When the end of hostilities approached, some firms were left with ships on their hands, among which we have already noted the *Arran Castle*, launched in 1864. By contemporary standards, the *Arran Castle* was a large steamer, not of the size of the *Iona*, but a good deal longer and broader than most vessels on the river. Her speed was not as great as had been hoped, and during the winter of 1864-5 she was returned to Rankin & Blackmore for alterations to the machinery. That these were effective was borne out on 27 April 1865 when the steamer ran the lights in forty-eight minutes, proving herself about as speedy as the *Iona*. She was accompanied on this occasion by her owners and guests who, after the trial, sat down to a 'substantial and elegant *déjeuner*' in the saloon. Amongst the usual toasts 'Those South of the Tweed' was significant in the light of after events for, as early as this, the owners were involved in negotiations for starting a river steamboat service on the Thames. For the time being, however, the *Arran Castle* remained in Scottish waters, spending the season of 1865 on the Broomielaw and Rothesay route.

Nevertheless, the Thames prospects lured Watson and Brown into a scheme for taking the *Arran Castle* south early in 1866 to run between London and Gravesend. The steamer was flush-decked as built, for deck saloons were of no value for blockade running purposes and now, with a view to improving passenger accommodation, a proper saloon was added on the quarter deck. Thus altered, the *Arran Castle* left the Clyde on 21 March and headed down the Irish Sea. Besides her crew she had on board her two owners, two stewards, and Captain Watson's eleven-year-old son, in all about twenty people. It was expected that the vessel would complete the journey to the Thames in sixty hours.

There was no further news of the ship for over a week, until 30 March, when readers of the *Glasgow Herald* were appalled to read that 'from circumstances which came to light at Greenock yesterday, there is every reason to believe that the handsome paddle-steamer *Arran Castle* has foundered at sea, and that all on board have perished.' Behind the stark announcement lay one of the mysteries of the sea, a tragedy that was never fully explained, although the basic facts could be surmised with fair accuracy. Briefly, the *Arran Castle* had set out in good weather, and was observed by the master of the Cork and Waterford steamer *Saltee* about ten o'clock on the morning of 22 March, being then about four hours' sail from Dublin. It was believed that the steamer was making for Kingstown, and she was making normal progress in fine conditions. Later on the same day she was sighted off Wicklow Light, and that was the last time she was seen. Then came a gap of several days until the afternoon of 28 March, when three Greenock tugs came across large quantities of wreckage floating in the channel between the Copelands and Portpatrick. One of them brought to the Clyde a piece of mast, a sparred seat, and some broken timber, and another arrived with half of a ship's wheel and other wreckage; the matter was put beyond doubt when a lifeboat with the name *Arran Castle* painted on the stern was put ashore at Maryport. Of survivors, or even bodies, there was not a sign.

Eye witnesses unanimously agreed that the ship's boilers must have exploded, for the sheer quantity of small wreckage allowed of no other logical explanation. The mystery was, why was the steamer so far north when she had last been seen well south of Dublin? Captain Ward, of the Glasgow and Dublin steamer *Lord Gough*, gave the first clue to the circumstances that had driven the *Arran Castle* to her doom. Going south on the same day, the *Lord Gough* had reached Dublin on Thursday, 22 March and the weather had remained fine until late in the same evening, when the wind came round to the north-east and freshened. It was the prelude to a furious gale which prevented the *Lord Gough* from leaving port until early on 24 March and it is certain that the *Arran Castle* had run into what was then a south-westerly gale, had been forced to turn and run for shelter back to the Clyde, and was overwhelmed off Corsewall Point. Why, though, had the vessel foundered so dramatically? Evidence was not lacking of the soundness of her construction, and it was clear that she had not simply been swamped by the waves. Some authorities supported the view that she had broken her back, but others pointed out that the ship had quite obviously been blown to pieces.

'Observer', writing in the *Glasgow Herald*, advanced the most likely explanation: 'The vessel, it appears, was running back for shelter nearly before the wind. No doubt all were disheartened, probably some of them sea-sick, and all the engineers were strangers to the vessel. From the construction of the boilers, twenty minutes' neglect would bring the water below the inside dome, or tube plate; if cold water were pumped in when this was the case she would blow up like powder; and I believe this is the only way to account for the quantity of wreck seen in the Channel.'

The *Herald* published a leading article on the disaster, summing up the universal horror occasioned by the fate of a ship in which so many of its readers had sailed:

> It must, at the very least, be said that the voyage on which the *Arran Castle* was despatched was for her an extremely perilous one. There was, of course, a possibility of smooth weather; but considering the vicious spaces over which she had to pass, and the uncertain season of the year, the probability of a rose-water voyage was reduced almost to the throw of a dice. We utter no blame against those who sent or took the steamer on a trip too unsuited to her build. The penalty of the adventure has been paid with twenty precious lives. There, however, stands the tragic fact—another testimony, it may be, to the daring character of British seamanship—but, nevertheless, a solemn warning against the temerity, the rashness, if not the utter folly of venturing forth in a vessel not exactly fulfilling the conditions demanded by the season and the nature of the seas to be navigated. To sail in the very middle of the equinox was an adventure attempted at the peril of human life, in which the forfeit has been exacted to the letter.

In all the history of Clyde steamboat navigation, there is no more ghastly picture than that of the doomed *Arran Castle* blowing to pieces amidst the awful fury of a storm in the Irish Sea.

THE ROTHESAY ROUTE

Captain Duncan Stewart's star was in the ascendant during the middle sixties. That shrewd and competent owner had the happy knack of knowing when to sell his ships and—equally important—when not to do so. With the *Victory* he had reaped the benefit of being one of the few to operate an up-to-date service on the firth during the early part of the decade. Having disposed of that vessel to the harassed Wemyss Bay Steamboat Company, he used the money to order two new ships. Of these, the *Argyle* was of much the same style and dimensions as the *Victory*, and inherited the steeple engine of the *Alma*. The *Argyle* sailed for Stewart for only about a fortnight before she too was snapped up by the Wemyss Bay Company, leaving him with the *Athole*, a larger and finer boat launched by Barclay, Curle & Co in March 1866. Fitted with a haystack boiler and steeple engine, the *Athole* was a thoroughly dependable steamer of the raised quarter deck type, with slanting bow in the older style; she was typical of the best practice of her time and although never in the limelight to the same extent as some of her contemporaries she nevertheless put in a remarkable amount of good, steady work.

But of all Stewart's steamers, the *Undine* was perhaps best known. Built by Henderson, Colbourne & Co in 1865, this was a finely-modelled, fast vessel with a Scotch boiler and a powerful diagonal engine. Owned at first by her builders, she passed early into Duncan Stewart's hands and became well known as his 'crack' steamer. For her length—200 feet—she was narrow in the beam and lay over at the slightest excuse, listing heavily with a crowd on board. When in trim, however, she was a redoubtable racer and twice in August 1865 was reported to have sailed from the Broomielaw to Rothesay, calling at four intermediate piers, in as short a time as two hours, thirty-five minutes.

Captain Buchanan's *Eagle* underwent drastic alterations early in 1866. Her double diagonal engine was too heavy and powerful for the hull which was therefore lengthened by sixteen feet abaft the paddleboxes to improve her performance. Her first outing after this surgery took place on 30 March when a party of guests accompanied her on trials in the Gareloch. The improvement in the *Eagle's* speed was marked, nearly nineteen miles an hour being attained over the measured mile. In the following year her owner purchased a consort, the *Rothesay Castle*, a two-funnelled steamer of 1865. She was the last Clyde steamer to carry that celebrated name, the least distinguished in the matter of speed, but none the less a good ship. Her machinery was of the steeple type and, being smaller and less powerful than the *Eagle*, she was doubtless a more economical boat as far as her owner was concerned.

The practice of laying the *Iona* up in Bowling Harbour during the winter months, and handing over the Ardrishaig mail service to smaller steamers has already been remarked. In 1866, the brothers Hutcheson took delivery of a new steamer from J. & G. Thomson, intended to sail between Crinan and Corpach during the tourist season and to maintain the Ardrishaig sailings as deputy to the *Iona* during the off-season. The new steamer was a smaller version of the *Iona*, with full deck saloon aft, short promenade deck forward (afterwards enclosed at the sides), two funnels, and oscillating machinery and, although not having the superb lines of her larger sister, was nevertheless one of the most attractive members of the river fleet. She received the name *Chevalier* at her launch on 12 April. Her reputation was made rather in West Highland waters, but her many seasons of winter duty on the Clyde were just as useful to her owners as the years of summer sailings in the Firth of Lorne.

THE CAMPBELTOWN RUN

The two paddle steamers engaged in the trade between Glasgow and Campbeltown were past their best in 1865. The *Druid* and the *Celt* enjoyed a monopoly and appeared likely to remain on the station for years to come, but the complacency of their owners was badly shaken in the following year by the arrival of a notable competitor. On 3 March 1866 Caird & Co launched 'a very handsome paddle steamer, named the *Herald*, intended for the Glasgow, Greenock and Campbeltown trade... with oscillating engines of 150 horse-power, fitted with Caird's patent expansion valves and feathering floats. From the high character of her builders, and her beautiful model, the *Herald* is expected to attain a high rate of speed and will, no doubt, be a welcome acquisition to the travelling public and the trade of Campbeltown.' So ran the newspaper report, and the Campbeltown Company's directors were obviously worried by the arrival of such an impressive vessel. Captain Robert Young, one of the most capable skippers on the river, was appointed as her commander. The *Herald* was advertised to take up her public sailings on 7 May but two days earlier she went on a trial run to Campbeltown with a party of invited guests, performing splendidly, and pleasing everyone with her superior accommodation and facilities. The comparison with the Campbeltown Company's steamers was very much to their disadvantage, the *Herald's* superiority being emphasized in no uncertain manner on 2 June when she left the Kintyre port a few minutes after the *Druid* and reached Greenock precisely one hour ahead of her.

Something obviously had to be done quickly to counter the threat posed by the *Herald* and as a short term measure the fares to Kintyre were slashed to well below those of the newcomer. The excursion rates for the *Druid* and *Celt* came down to two shillings (cabin) and one shilling (steerage) as against five and three shillings by the *Herald*. It was a ruinous business, but desperate cases require desperate remedies, and in the event the price war paid off for the Campbeltown Company. Their long term interests demanded new ships, however, for the public would have had no time for the older vessels after the experience of the *Herald*. As early as July 1866, therefore, it was announced that Robertson & Co, a new firm of shipbuilders, had undertaken to build a new paddle steamer, to be ready in time for the summer season of 1867, and it was stated that the new boat would be built with a view to great speed, the estimated journey time from Greenock to Campbeltown being under four hours. A second new ship was promised if the trade should warrant its construction.

The new paddle steamer was named *Gael*. Her first trial

took place on 5 April 1867 when she attained a speed of nineteen miles an hour, vastly superior to anything achieved by her older consorts. Twelve days later, with a special party on board, the *Gael* ran to Campbeltown in just over three and a half hours, setting up a new record time for the passage. She was a heavily-built steamer in view of her work in the open waters of the lower firth and it has been truly remarked that she had more in common with the average channel steamer of the day than with Clyde steamers. She looked very smart, with two well-raked funnels fore and aft of the paddles, which were driven by powerful oscillating machinery. As in the case of all ships on the Kintyre route, there was accommodation for cattle and cargo, but her passenger cabins were 'beautifully fitted up and tastefully decorated.' As early as 6 May the *Gael* was setting up new records on the Campbeltown to Glasgow run and, faced with her formidable competition, the owners of the *Herald* accepted defeat, withdrew their steamer and sold her off the firth for service between Barrow in Furness and the Isle of Man.

Not content with their victory the Campbeltown directors then decided to order a consort for the *Gael* in time for the 1868 season, returning to Robertson & Co, whose first venture had been so successful. That firm now built a no less famous and successful boat, the beautiful steamer *Kintyre*. Her launch took place on 10 June 1868. In many respects she broke new ground, not least in being a screw-propelled vessel. Blackwood & Gordon provided her two-cylinder simple expansion vertical machinery which gave her a speed of fourteen knots, not in the same category as the *Gael* but much superior to the older ships, both of which were quickly sold.

THE GREEN BOATS

In an age which has witnessed the despoliation of the lovely little Gareloch by military and industrial installations, not to mention the gradual extension of outer suburbia to its very shores, it is difficult to visualise a time when it was one of the most peaceful, beautiful, and sought-after parts of the whole Clyde coast in summer and winter alike, justifying for many years a daily service between Garelochhead and the Broomielaw and regular connections with the railheads at Helensburgh and Greenock. By 1865, however, increasing traffic appeared to justify a radical improvement in existing services between Greenock Steamboat Quay and the Gareloch piers, and there were complaints about the Helensburgh ferry service in particular, which then stopped too early in the afternoon to permit return connections with the incoming Ardrishaig steamer. Prospects of a large increase in traffic based upon speculative building plans on the northern shores of the firth led to the formation of a new limited company in the summer of 1865, one of the most ambitious ventures during the whole period with which this history is concerned. The Greenock and Helensburgh Steamboat Company, Limited, was formed by 'a party of influential gentlemen' of whom Sir James Colquhoun, Bart., of Luss, was appointed chairman. Aiming at a frequent, cheap service between Greenock, Helensburgh, and the Gareloch, the company placed orders with local builders for four small paddle steamers and also bought in the old Henderson & McKellar steamer *Nelson*, then maintaining a service from Glasgow to Garelochhead. With a view to reducing fares the company also acquired the rights to the Helensburgh pier dues, which were cut to a halfpenny per passenger, the fares on the boats themselves being adjusted by corresponding amounts.

The four steamers ordered by the new company were certainly the smallest built during the period, and appeared during the spring of 1866, the *Ardencaple* and *Rosneath* from Robert Duncan & Co, the *Levan* from Kirkpatrick McIntyre & Co, and the *Ardgowan* from Lawrence Hill & Co, all of Port Glasgow. Rankin & Blackmore provided haystack boilers and oscillating machinery for all these vessels, which were uniformly of raised quarter deck type.

Under the managership of Graham Brymner, a Greenock tug manager and a prominent citizen and magistrate of the town, the Greenock and Helensburgh Company seemed set fair for a successful and prosperous career. In April 1867 its capital was increased by an issue of £5,000 of preference stock, the guaranteed rate of interest to its existing shareholders who invested being no less than ten per cent. Truly a money-making company, it may well have been thought, but within only two years of that event the concern was wound up and its steamers disposed of by the disillusioned owners. What went wrong? Captain James Williamson later stated* that the crews of the company's steamers had been the most undisciplined in his own long experience of the Clyde steamboat services, and his explanation can probably be accepted as a hint that the managership was not as firm as it should have been, and that general slackness led to the failure of the new venture. The *Nelson* was the first boat to go, being sold to T. B. Seath for £500 in April 1868, and one year later it was announced that the *Ardgowan*, *Levan* and *Rosneath* had all been sold by private offer. The last-named went to Cork, but it appears that Graham Brymner may have assumed direct ownership of the others on the dissolution of the Greenock and Helensburgh Company. The *Ardencaple* was sold in May 1869 to Keith and Campbell, by whom she was thereafter employed on the Broomielaw and Gareloch route.

Although not strictly germane, the brief and unfortunate history of the Brymner connection with the Gareloch service may conveniently be dealt with at this stage. A fifth steamer, named *Craigrownie*, similar to the original quartet of 1866 but on a larger scale, was launched in May 1870, intended for the Gareloch section. The *Craigrownie* in fact entered service on the Largs station under Captain Charles Brown, but Brymner's luck there was no better and in October 1871 his remaining fleet was sold en bloc. Keith and Campbell got

The Clyde Passenger Steamer

the *Craigrownie,* together with the *Levan* and *Ardgowan* but these, together with the *Ardencaple,* were disposed of to London owners at the close of the 1875 season, bringing to an unexpectedly speedy conclusion the short, unhappy story of the Greenock and Helensburgh Steamboat Company and its ships.

GRAHAM BRYMNER

Graham Brymner had entered the river traffic on his own account with the launch of a handsome little vessel, the *Elaine,* on 6 April 1867. Built by Robert Duncan & Co, and engined by Rankin & Blackmore, this was a raised quarter deck steamer, fitted with square ports in her first class cabin, but this useful improvement did not generally supersede conventional practice on the Clyde until a much later period, when circular ports gave place to large observation windows in the full deck saloons. The paddleboxes were very small, but larger ones were fitted under Buchanan ownership at a later stage in the *Elaine's* career. For Graham Brymner, the steamer plied between Glasgow and Millport under command of Captain Robert Young who had been out of a job since the sale of the *Herald.* In his competent hands the *Elaine* became popular and was widely recognised as one of the best-managed boats in the trade.

She was joined by her larger consort, the *Lancelot,* in the following year, a vessel similar in every respect to the *Elaine,* and from the same builders and engineers. On trial in April 1868 in a gale and heavy sea, the *Lancelot* ran the lights in 50 minutes 40 seconds, not a remarkable speed but more than satisfactory for a ship of her class in rough conditions.

Brymner's largest steamer appeared in 1869, being named *Guinevere* at her launch on 14 April. Robert Duncan & Co were again responsible for the hull, while Rankin & Blackmore fitted their patent double piston rod oscillating machinery and two haystack boilers, placed conventionally fore and aft of the engine space. Two funnels distinguished the *Guine-*

vere from all the other Brymner steamers although, like them, she had a raised quarter deck. Her station, on which she remained for most of her life under successive Clyde owners, was between Glasgow and Arran, via Rothesay and Kilchattan Bay. Her preliminary trial trip, run on 22 May, took place in 'delightfully fine' weather, when she recorded a speed of about nineteen statute miles per hour, not really much faster than the *Lancelot*, but the 'select party of gentlemen' on board were well satisfied with the *Guinevere*'s performance and her elegant internal furnishings.

Once again there has to be recorded the collapse of a venture which began with high hopes of success; by the middle of the seventies the three steamers had all been sold, and Graham Brymner retired from passenger steamboat ownership for good. The *Elaine* passed to Captain Duncan Stewart, a careful owner with an eye for an economical steamer; the *Lancelot* entered the Gillies & Campbell fleet, sailing for many years in connection with the Wemyss Bay Railway; and the *Guinevere* was purchased by Hugh Keith.

VARIOUS NEW SHIPS

Several Clyde owners during this period took delivery of new steamers, none of which fell into the luxury category, all being intended for general service throughout the year. The *Sultana*, built for Alexander Williamson as a consort to the *Sultan*, ran her trials on 24 April 1868. This was one of the neatest ships on the river, with a beautifully-modelled hull, a short, smartly-raked funnel, and well-designed paddleboxes. Of flush-decked design, she was fitted with a single diagonal engine and haystack boiler and, as well as being fast, she was a very manoeuvrable vessel, a factor which stood Captain Williamson and his sons in good stead as they successively commanded the attractive and popular little ship.

The *Marquis of Bute*, built and engined by Barclay, Curle & Co for Captain McLean, was an exact contemporary of the

Page 69. Summer Afternoon at Rothesay: a rare view of the ill-fated *Lady Gertrude* moored at Rothesay Quay in the early seventies

Page 70. Under Goatfell: *(above)* a rare photograph of the *Glen Rosa* lying at Brodick Pier; *(below)* the powerful *Heather Bell* lying alongside the iron pier at Brodick, Isle of Arran

Sultana, although a little larger and more powerful than that vessel. Like her, she was flush-decked and equipped with similar types of boiler and machinery. Her reputation, like that of her owner, stood high for many years and she was undoubtedly one of the best-run Clyde steamers of the privately owned type, much of the credit for this state of affairs being due to McLean himself who personally commanded the ship.

A well-known steamer on the river for many years, in various guises, was the *Dunoon Castle,* launched by Wingate in 1867 for a consortium of Dunoon and Rothesay carriers who felt it necessary to have a ship of their own in order to avoid what they regarded as excessive freight charges imposed by the existing steamboat owners. The vessel which entered their service in due course was something of an anachronism. Into a long, slim, and shapely hull there was fitted the last single steeple engine of the classic type used widely in the early Clyde steamboats, while the funnel, also for the last time in a Clyde steamer, was placed abaft the paddleboxes. This arrangement, strange to modern eyes accustomed to funnels placed forward of the paddles, nevertheless presented a very beautiful outline, and the *Dunoon Castle* was an attractive steamer, but reconstruction with two funnels aft at a later date was less happy, and she looked bizarre until restored to her original condition during the later eighties. The experience of the carriers was unfortunate and in the end strong competition led to the early sale of the *Dunoon Castle.* Her subsequent career was varied, and in the hands of Sunday operators the vessel achieved notoriety before finally joining the railway service in the early eighties.

Of the older steamers still in service the *Petrel* gained a new lease of life at this point in her career. When it was reported in July 1865 that she had broken a paddle shaft off the Cloch Lighthouse on her outward sailing to Arran it might have been thought that such a mishap would be fatal to an outmoded steamer. However, she was repaired and resumed service but at the end of May 1866 was advertised for sale, the

E

upset price being eventually reduced to £1,600 'in order to insure a Sale'. She apparently changed hands at that price and was advertised to sail from 25 June from the Broomielaw to Arran, leaving Glasgow at eight o'clock in the morning. The *Petrel* had been given a very comprehensive overhaul and, indeed, had been practically rebuilt at a cost of almost £3,000. She was reboilered and equipped with new paddle wheels with feathering floats, her machinery was considerably improved and a new hurricane deck fitted. On trial a day or two before taking up the Largs and Arran service she ran with a party of guests to the Holy Loch, 'her performance throughout thoroughly satisfying all on board'.

The old McKellar steamer *Lady Brisbane* entered Hugh Keith's fleet in 1868 but on the evening of 18 April she was involved in a serious collision at Bowling with the tug *Flying Cloud*, as a result of which both vessels sank and the tug's pilot was drowned. The *Lady Brisbane* was raised and refurbished, but entered service after renewal as the *Balmoral*, sailing on the firth for well over twenty years more before going to Newry as a coal hulk in the early nineties. She was a sturdy old vessel, one of the best examples of older Clyde shipyard construction, and her long life bore testimony to the excellent craftsmanship which had gone into her building in the forties.

PRINCE'S PIER

Almost at the close of the sixties, in December 1869, a new railhead was completed on the upper reaches of the Clyde. The Greenock & Ayrshire Railway, a protégé of the Glasgow & South Western Company, obtained powers to build a new line from Johnstone to Greenock, ostensibly to connect Kilmarnock and other Ayrshire towns with the coast, but too late the Caledonian Railway saw that the provision of a short connection would permit through running from Glasgow, in direct competition with their own line from the city to Greenock. So it turned out, and within a few years, after the opening of the South Western's splendid new Glasgow terminal station at St Enoch Square, the rival company's trains were providing a service to the coast which was much superior to the Caledonian connections. Bridge Street station, shared by both companies, was inconveniently situated south of the river in Glasgow, and most people preferred the South Western line from St Enoch for this reason alone. At Greenock, however, the new railhead at Albert Harbour (soon to be better known as Prince's Pier) was down river from the Steamboat Quay, and passengers by the newer route were spared the necessity of traversing the noisome East Quay Lane to the Caledonian terminus at Cathcart Street. The bulk of the coast traffic gradually drifted to the new line, and for a few years Prince's Pier provided severe competition even for the Wemyss Bay route, until the Caledonian Railway eventually drove its line on to Gourock and effectively by-passed Greenock. But all this lay in the distant future, and at the close of the sixties the stage was set for a decade of competition and expansion of the steamboat services to a level hitherto unheard of by passengers and operators alike.

Paddlebox of the *Eagle*

CHAPTER FOUR

THE MIDDLE YEARS
(1870-1879)

INCREASING emphasis on tourism was a feature of the seventies, a decade in which the affairs of the old-established Lochgoil Company reached high-watermark. Gillies and Campbell rapidly established a good service at Wemyss Bay, in spite of a serious setback resulting from the total loss by stranding of their newest steamer. Strong competition was offered by the 'Turkish Fleet' sailing from Prince's Pier in connection with the Glasgow & South Western Railway and gradually the importance of the Caledonian route through Greenock waned as other railheads gained popularity. In the outer firth the Duke of Hamilton made a brief attempt to work the Arran service while, on the Kintyre route, the Campbeltown Company modernised and improved its fleet and services. Keith and Campbell emerged as a force on the upper river, while the North British Railway maintained a sensible, if unspectacular, service to the Holy Loch, Dunoon, and the Gareloch.

THE LOCH GOIL ROUTE

The Lochgoil steamer service was an early victim of competition and from its significance as an interchange point on a tourist route to the Western Highlands, Lochgoilhead gradually came to be regarded in later years as something of a backwater. In 1870, however, prospects were bright for the Lochgoil and Lochlong Steamboat Company and its capable and energetic manager, M. T. Clark. The tourist trade was expanding and the company felt that the time was opportune to

74

replace the outdated *Lochgoil* with a larger passenger steamer.

The new vessel, launched at Paisley on 30 April 1870, received the name *Carrick Castle* after the old fortress dominating the entrance to Loch Goil. She was to be the only product of John Fullerton & Co's yard in Clyde passenger service, but her builders made of her a handsome steamer, very similar in style to the *Sultana*, flush-decked and propelled by a single diagonal engine. The *Carrick Castle* was commanded by Captain William Barr, a man of considerable ability, who had not only planned the steamer but also superintended her building. Having begun his career in 1835 he was by 1870 one of the senior men on the firth. The new boat went out on an opening excursion to Lochgoilhead on 23 May, 'gaily decorated with evergreens and flags, the latter having been presented the company by General Douglas of Glenfinnart, who, in a letter of congratulation, hoped great prosperity would attend the future of the *Carrick Castle*... The sail up Loch Goil was greatly enjoyed by all on board. At every pier and ferry a little demonstration was got up by the natives, while their welcome greeting was acknowledged by the firing of the steamer's cannon and the stirring strains of the bagpipes.' After the inaugural trip the steamer was returned to the builders for finishing and decorating to be completed and by early June she was ready for service—'equal to any boat of her class in speed, elegance, and commodiousness'. Her advent allowed the institution of a twice-daily service between Inveraray and Glasgow via St Catherine's and Lochgoilhead, passengers being conveyed by the Inveraray and St Catherine's Ferry Company Limited in its steamer *Fairy* across Loch Fyne, and thence to Lochgoilhead in a handsome new 20-seater coach.

Increasing traffic demanded the provision of another new steamer in 1875, a ship in all essentials similar to the *Carrick Castle*, but slightly larger than her predecessor. She was named *Windsor Castle*, and differed from every other vessel on the Clyde at that period by having her bridge and steering wheel placed on the hurricane deck immediately forward of the

funnel. While having the obvious advantage of an uninter-
rupted view forward, this position was not generally liked, as
it interfered with navigation at piers.

Construction of the *Windsor Castle* as a flush-decked steamer as late as 1875 was a decision hard to justify in the light of
increasing demand for better accommodation, and the Lochgoil management caused little surprise by having her extensively remodelled in time for the season of 1878, when she re-
appeared with a saloon and a number of other improvements.
She was turned over to her builders, T. B. Seath & Co, to be
altered and the Rutherglen firm, as well as providing the
saloon, converted the original first class cabin into a dining
room for eighty passengers, besides enlarging and improving
lavatories, ladies' cabins and retiring rooms. On trial early in
March the *Windsor Castle* proved herself as good a sea boat as
ever and her unqualified success after rebuilding made it even
more difficult to understand her having been turned out originally in what was virtually an obsolete form.

In the following year a third new steamer entered the Lochgoil fleet, the *Edinburgh Castle*, by Robert Duncan & Co, 'on
whose taste and workmanship', ran a newspaper report, 'she
reflects great credit'. Despite the comment the new boat owed
much to the ideas of Captain William Barr who was responsible for several of the features which distinguished this ship
from her contemporaries. Designed as a saloon steamer on the
lines of the altered *Windsor Castle*, the new vessel however
was designed to have an 'awning deck' carried forward nearly
to the mast over the steerage accommodation on the main
deck. No great shelter was thus provided, for the space underneath was not closed in with plating. Unfortunately, this deck
caused the ship to be 'tender' and it was soon cut back.

The dominating feature of the *Edinburgh Castle* was her
enormous paddle wheels, no less than 22ft in diameter, provided on the recommendation of Captain Barr who was a firm
believer in their supposed advantages. Whatever these may
have been, the steamer's appearance suffered from the huge

paddleboxes which were out of proportion to her slim hull, while a more practical drawback was the obstruction caused by the paddle shaft in the ship's engine room alleyways.

The *Edinburgh Castle* took an invited party on an excursion from Greenock to Lochgoilhead on 31 May 1879, sailing afterwards to Ormidale where lunch was served and a lengthy toast list gone through, it being recorded that the steamer had nearly arrived back at Greenock before it had been completed! The ship was much admired for her excellent accommodation. The *Glasgow Herald* noted that:

> She has spacious and good space below decks. Extending nearly the entire length of the vessel is a saloon deck, having aft and immediately beneath a handsome cabin comfortably fitted up and from which a view of the scenery through which the steamer's journey passes can be commanded. On the lower deck is one of the finest dining saloons to be met with in any of the craft that sail the river. Accommodation is furnished for sitting 100 persons. The apartment is furnished in the most luxurious style, and is decorated in excellent taste, all the side panelling being filled in with coloured glass, on which is represented a number of views familiar to the tourist eye... The whole arrangements are of the most complete description, and speak volumes for the sound judgment as well as the enterprise of the owners.

The *Edinburgh Castle* spent her whole career on the Lochgoilhead route, remaining a firm favourite despite the decline of her owners' fortunes in the early years of the present century. In the superb Wotherspoon collection of shipping records in Glasgow, there is a charming description of the ship and her crew, a paragraph summing up perfectly the character of the Lochgoil route of older times, and well worth repetition here:

> No reference to the *Edinburgh Castle* would be complete without reference to its genial skipper, Captain Barr, who had charge of the steamer from the year in which it was launched, until his death in 1906. Latterly he was always accompanied on the bridge by his faithful Scotch collie. Next there was Ferguson, the stout Steward, good conservative he was, and popular with the travelling public. He latterly became lessee of Ardentinny Hotel. In the prosperous days

of the concern the officials, during the summer, were dressed in uniform, and so careful were the Captain and Ferguson of their gold laced caps, that if they appeared on deck with the glazed cover on them, it was a sign that wet weather might be expected! Then there was Sandy the pilot, burly in form, with a superabundance of red hair on his face, and Highland to the core. Lastly the poor blind fiddler, a daily passenger on the steamer, who, when the vessel departed from a pier, invariably struck up 'The girl I left behind me!' All are gone, and the old steamboat, which must have carried many thousands of delighted tourists every season as it sailed by the shores of the everlasting hills and on the deep waters of Loch Goil, is now also among the things which were.

WEMYSS BAY STEAMERS

The seventies saw steady expansion of Gillies & Campbell's steamboat service in connection with the railway at Wemyss Bay. All their early steamers were second-hand, the oldest being the *Venus* of 1852, but the *Argyle, Largs* and *Victory* were relatively new. During 1870 the last-named was advertised for sale, but it was not until the spring of the following year that she was disposed of to the egregious Duncan Dewar for employment in the Sunday trade. By him she was renamed *Marquis of Lorne* but the change did the ship no good and for several years she was unquestionably looked down upon as one of the tramps of the river. To replace her at Wemyss Bay, the *Lady Gertrude* was ordered from Blackwood & Gordon in 1872, the first new ship in the Gillies & Campbell fleet. Named in honour of the only child of the Earl and Countess of Glasgow, the *Lady Gertrude* was a typical Clyde steamer of her period. Flush-decked, she resembled the *Marquis of Bute, Sultana* and other contemporary vessels in general outline and, like them, was equipped with a haystack boiler and single diagonal engine.

In 1875 the old *Venus* was broken up and there was brought in to replace her Graham Brymner's useful and attractive *Lancelot*. Not a fast ship, she was nevertheless one of those exceptionally useful craft which every now and then appeared on the river and put in a great deal of hard work with a minimum of fuss.

Quite the most remarkable year in the whole history of Gillies & Campbell's connection with Wemyss Bay was 1877. These owners, who took a close personal interest in their steamboats, suffered an unexpected blow in January when their flagship, the *Lady Gertrude*, was totally lost by stranding on the beach at Toward. The year started with a succession of gales which interfered considerably with ordinary services. On 3 January, for example, passengers coming down from Glasgow in the late train, due at Wemyss Bay at seven o'clock, discovered to their disgust that conditions on the firth prevented the *Argyle* from sailing until much later in the evening. Captain Campbell, however, took them aboard and 'entertained them to an excellent tea. The passengers at first discomfited and disappointed, soon found themselves at home in the commodious and well-furnished cabin of the *Argyle*, and soon song, toast, and sentiment prevailed. By 12 o'clock the wind and snow had somewhat moderated, and the *Argyle* setting out, landed her passengers at Rothesay in safety about 1 o'clock in the morning.' Such was the personal attention which a private owner found it possible to give his passengers.

On Saturday 13 January the *Lady Gertrude*, newly returned to service after overhaul, left Wemyss Bay at midday on the down run to Rothesay. The weather was rough, with a strong south-easterly breeze blowing. As the *Lady Gertrude* approached Toward Pier, the signal was given on the engine room 'knocker' to reverse the engine, but to the dismay of Captain McDonald there was no response. The machinery refused to answer, and in a few moments the steamer ran past the pier, the wind caught and blew her shorewards, and as her stern quarter struck the pierhead the bow swung round and grounded on the rocks. There was some alarm amongst the passengers but it was eventually found possible to land them from the stern. Unhappily for the *Lady Gertrude*, she had gone ashore at high water and in a short time the ebb tide left her hopelessly stranded. The *Inveraray Castle* was passing when the accident occurred and her captain at once attempted to tow the *Lady Gertrude* clear, but to no avail. Two tugs made a further attempt to pull her off during the afternoon but the stricken vessel had then filled with water and settled. Her stern remained afloat and the ship was under such stress in the strong swell that it soon became evident that she would be a total loss. Further salvage operations later in the day were unsuccessful and on the next day the steamer had sunk. The only hope of salving her during the ensuing week was unfortunately frustrated when another gale set in, during which the *Lady Gertrude* broke in two and went to pieces. All that could be salved was her machinery which was recovered in good order and set aside for use in a new steamer. The boiler lay for many years afterwards on the shore as a reminder that even within the relatively sheltered waters of the firth, a ship could be destroyed by stress of weather. The loss of the *Lady Gertrude,* in itself a blow to her owners, was aggravated by the fact that she was uninsured, but no doubt they, and other owners, were prepared to weigh the outside chances of disaster against the real economies to be realised by not paying insurance premiums. On this occasion, they were unlucky.

Without their newest steamer, and having by then disposed of the *Largs,* the Wemyss Bay owners were in a predicament but took immediate steps to order new tonnage from Caird & Co, of Greenock. The launch of one of two new ships for the fleet so soon after the *Lady Gertrude* disaster as April 1877 suggests that she had probably been ordered at an earlier date, perhaps as a replacement for the *Largs,* and this would be a perfectly reasonable explanation were it not for the fact that the new Wemyss Bay boat was one of a pair of 'twins', the other being intended for the Arran route under the ownership of Shearer Brothers, of Gourock. Now, it is at least *possible*—no more, in the absence of corroborative evidence—that Gillies & Campbell, urgently requiring a new ship as soon as possible, went to Caird & Co and the Shearers and asked them to sell the new vessel already building in the Greenock yard, and that to save time and expense the shipbuilders at once laid down a duplicate steamer for the Shearers. The explanation fits the facts, but unless further details come to light it must remain an interesting speculation.

The new Wemyss Bay steamer was named *Sheila*, and it is hardly too much to say that she was perhaps the best boat that Gillies & Campbell ever owned. She was of the raised quarter deck type, with a turn of speed far above the average, in appearance much superior to the unlucky *Lady Gertrude*. On trial on 18 May she attained a speed of twenty statute miles an hour, but it is likely that she was capable of something better than that when well handled, for, under the very competent Captain Duncan Bell, she immediately won a reputation as a racer.

The Wemyss Bay route sorely needed a fast boat in 1877, for the Glasgow & South Western route via Prince's Pier had gained considerable popularity amongst regular coast travellers, drawing away much of the traffic which had previously gone by the Caledonian line. The new St Enoch station of the South Western, conveniently situated in the heart of Glasgow, offered many advantages in comparison with Bridge Street on the south side of the river, where Wemyss Bay trains terminated. The South Western route was longer, but the *Sultana* of the Williamson fleet, running in connection with the 4.5 pm express from St Enoch, offered a service which was just as fast as the Wemyss Bay route, and many passengers preferred it. So serious was the erosion of traffic that determined efforts were made to recover it in the summer of 1877. A new express from Bridge Street was provided at 4.35 pm, stopping only at Port Glasgow for ticket collection, and no luggage was permitted. The *Sheila* was put on the Rothesay run in connection with the express and gave a very fast service to the newly opened pier at Craigmore, to Rothesay itself, and to Port Bannatyne, the last-named being thus brought to within ninety minutes of Glasgow.

Competition between the *Sheila* and *Sultana* was inevitable, and these two well-matched steamers engaged in a hammer-and-tongs contest each summer for the remainder of the seventies. Interested readers are referred to Mr Andrew McQueen's classic description of a race between the two ships, in which the whole excitement and atmosphere of those contests are beautifully caught.* But this was the best known part of the *Sheila's* daily round, most of which was spent on the Rothesay route in connection with slower services from Glasgow during the day, while on Wednesdays she sailed to Lamlash. In 1878 the Arran run was made a daily service, the *Sheila* sailing from Wemyss Bay in connection with the 10.30 train from Bridge Street, returning from Arran at 2.45 and calling at Millport and Largs on the up run.

The second Caird steamer for the Wemyss Bay fleet was the direct successor of the *Lady Gertrude* and inherited the machinery from that unfortunate ship. Towards the end of May 1877 it was reported that the new boat was in an advanced state of completion but the Clyde shipyard lock-out of that summer delayed her entry into service. In fact, the steamer was wholly constructed by apprentices in view of the labour troubles then bedevilling Clyde yards. The launch took place on 13 August, when Mrs Campbell christened the vessel *Adela* as it entered the water. In view of the prowess of the *Sheila*, and the very ordinary reputation of the *Adela*, it is surprising to note that the latter was marginally the longer ship of the two, but not as 'beamy' as her more celebrated sister. The *Adela* was the last Clyde steamer of the flush-decked type, all subsequent vessels having raised quarter decks or full saloons, and the *Adela* herself was later improved by the addition of rather short, narrow deck saloons fore and aft. Like the *Lancelot*, she was a useful vessel for regular, all-year-round work, attracting scant attention and certainly having none of the glamour of the famous excursion steamers which were so much

*Clyde River Steamers of the Last Fifty Years.

in the public eye during the summer season. Nevertheless, she was a pretty little steamer, not unattractive in a douce, Presbyterian way, and it is as a tribute to her class of Clyde steamer, the real backbone of the firth services, and in acknowledgment of the long forgotten service of her owners that your author has chosen her as the subject of his frontispiece rather than one of the more obvious claimants for this position.

THE LAND O' BURNS

In the early years of Clyde steam navigation the route from Glasgow to Ayr had been one of the most important on the river, but railway competition after 1840 made the steamboat owners' position untenable. By the middle sixties it had become an excursion service in the summer season only and from then until 1881, when it was abandoned, it was associated with steamers built and partly owned by Mr T. B. Seath of the Rutherglen shipyard. The oldest of these was the *Vale of Clwyd,* originally built for passenger service on the north coast of Wales, and the significance of her name was lost on most Glaswegians, who insisted on referring to her as *Vale of Clyde.* However, as her owner so advertised her in the local press from time to time, it was hardly surprising that many people were misled. She was old-fashioned in build, with funnel abaft the machinery. Her consort of 1866, the *Vale of Doon,* was a larger and more powerful vessel, equipped with haystack boiler and steeple engine.

But the steamers which became so well known on the Ayr service during the seventies were the *Bonnie Doons,* built respectively in 1870 and 1876. The first vessel of the name was sold abroad after only a short period and her successor was much better known. Launched on 27 April 1876, she sailed on her maiden voyage to Ayr on 14 June, leaving the Broomielaw at 7 o'clock in the morning and arriving at Ayr at half past twelve. Her sailings were usually advertised to 'The Land o' Burns' and waggonettes awaited her arrival at Ayr Harbour to convey tourists to Burns' Monument at Alloway. In the early summer of 1876 the *Bonnie Doon* offered some unusual afternoon and evening excursions from Ayr, Irvine and

AYRSHIRE EXCURSION.

GRAND PLEASURE EXCURSION
TO
LOCHLONG AND LOCHLOMOND,
On WEDNESDAY, 14TH AUGUST,
Per Saloon Steamer "BONNIE DOON,"
SAILING FROM

AYR for ARROCHAR at 8.15 A.M.
TROON   „   „ 8.45 „
ARDROSSAN „   „ 9.30 „
Reaching Arrochar about 12.30 P.M.

Arrochar is situated at the Head of Lochlong, and distant about 1½ miles from Tarbet on Lochlomond, where a Special Steamer will be in waiting to convey the Excursionists down the Loch; Returning to Tarbet about 3.30, in time for Passengers to reach Arrochar for Sailing of "BONNIE DOON" at 4 P.M.

The Scenery of this Route opens up the Gems of the far-famed Firth of Clyde, the Mountain Ranges of Arran, the Verdant Island of Bute, the Wooded Shores of Cowal, and the magnificent Alpine Scenery of Lochlong; Lochlomond, "The Queen of Scottish Lakes," surrounded with its majestic and precipitous mountains, and studded over with its green islands reposing in fairy loveliness, all combine to form a scene of grandeur and variety which cannot be surpassed.

FARES—
		Cabin.	Steerage.
To ARROCHAR	{ including Fare for Loch- lomond Steamer }	5s	3s 6d
To ARROCHAR	....	3s	2s

Passengers from Kilmarnock by the 8.44 A.M. Train for Ardrossan will be in time to connect with Steamer there, and Steamer is expected to return in the Evening before departure of the 7.15 Train.

A Bonnie Doon excursion in 1878

Ardrossan to Ailsa Craig, Turnberry Point, and round the Cumbraes, but such sailings were out of the ordinary. In 1877, however, she had taken part in an ambitious experiment promoted in connection with the Glasgow & South Western Railway. On 1 June, the *Bonnie Doon* sailed from Ayr to Campbeltown with a party of 400 passengers bound for the Kintyre Agricultural Show. This excursion was undertaken to explore the possibility of starting a regular passenger and goods service from Ayrshire to Kintyre, with a view to captur-

ing the export market in sheep, cattle, fish, and whisky—
Campbeltown in those days boasting no fewer than twenty-
two distilleries!

Two trains left Glasgow at seven o'clock and a quarter past
eight in the morning, and as well as the Glasgow traffic, bookings were made from as far south as Carlisle. The *Bonnie
Doon* left Ayr Harbour at 10.5 and reached Campbeltown in
just under two and a half hours. Allowing her passengers $4\frac{1}{2}$
hours ashore, she left again for Ayr at five o'clock and reached
her destination in two hours, twenty minutes. It had been a
pleasant day but evidently the results were not sufficiently
favourable to justify the projected service on a permanent
footing.

The *Bonnie Doon* was a smart-looking steamer, fitted with
a deck saloon aft, and was noted for her comfortable passenger
accommodation. With a haystack boiler and diagonal engine,
she was of conventional construction, but the unfortunate
steamer acquired an unenviable reputation for breaking down
which dogged her throughout her Clyde career. It was a pity,
for she was in many respects a fine vessel and, in her owners'
unusual colours, quite a striking ship.

THE ARRAN RUN

When the *Earl of Arran* was sold in the later sixties, the
steamboat service between Ardrossan and Arran was taken
over by the Duke of Hamilton's trustees, who ran *The Lady
Mary* and the *Heather Bell* on it successively between 1868
and 1874. The former was an unremarkable steamer, but the
Heather Bell, launched on 2 May 1871, was rather a different
proposition. Her double diagonal machinery was unusually
powerful, and steam was supplied by two horizontal boilers,
leading up into a single funnel. She was fast, but some trouble
was experienced in the first months of her career and she had
to be withdrawn for a time during the summer of 1871 for
repairs. She was in fact unsatisfactory in her original state

and a number of improvements and alterations to the machinery were carried out during May and June 1872.

The *Heather Bell* returned to service just as the first pier in Arran was opened to traffic on 17 June 1872. The Duke of Hamilton's policy of discouraging land development of the kind seen in Cowal and on the upper reaches of the firth had long delayed the provision of proper landing facilities, and it is nothing short of astonishing that Arran depended upon ferryboats and inadequate tidal jetties for fully sixty years after the *Comet* first paddled downstream from Glasgow. Nevertheless, the new pier at Brodick was a very fine structure, unusually constructed of wrought iron, a material thought to offer certain advantages over the normal wooden type of Clyde coast pier, but apart from a few similar examples—at Skipness, Carradale, and Craigmore—wrought iron never challenged the traditional wooden quays on the river and firth.

The *Heather Bell* maintained the Arran service only at a considerable cost in coal, for she was really too powerful a steamer for the route. Early in 1874, therefore, the Duke's trustees sold the ship and made arrangements with Captain William Buchanan to place his *Rothesay Castle* on the Arran run, which she maintained satisfactorily for four seasons.

Late in 1877 it was announced that H. McIntyre & Co, of Paisley, had been given a contract to build a paddle steamer for the Arran route and, intriguingly, she was to be fitted with the machinery from Buchanan's Rothesay steamer *Eagle*. That otherwise fine craft had been over-engined from the first, and it will be recalled that radical hull alterations were carried out quite early in her life. Now, in 1878, she was completely rebuilt and emerged with one haystack boiler instead of the original two, and a new single diagonal engine in place of the powerful double engines which had driven her since 1864. One funnel thereafter sufficed and the *Eagle* returned to service not only improved and rejuvenated, but looking immeasurably more attractive than in her former condition.

Buchanan's new Arran steamer was launched on 18 April

Captain John McGaw, for many years master of the *Iona* and *Columba*

Well-known Skippers:

Captain William Barr, of the Lochgoil Company

Page 88. (above) Williamson Flagship: the *Viceroy* shows the elegant lines of the classic Clyde steamer of the seventies; *(below) Lord of the Isles*: the Inveraray Company's beautiful excursion steamer arriving at Rothesay in the later eighties

1878. She was no beauty; on a long, heavy hull two thin funnels were placed closely together forward of the large paddleboxes, giving an impression of imbalance to the vessel's outline which a large forecastle and a short saloon on the main deck aft did nothing to improve. The *Brodick Castle* looked exactly what she was—a robust, well-made ship for service all the year round in every kind of weather, with no frills about her. The main saloon was described as being 'a spacious and elegant apartment' and, indeed, no criticism could be made of her internal accommodation, but in an age of good-looking ships she was one of the ugly ducklings of the firth. The *Brodick Castle* inherited the *Eagle's* healthy appetite for coal along with that vessel's machinery, and it is possible that her extravagance in that respect caused her sale to owners in the South of England only eight years later. Nevertheless, in her day the *Brodick Castle* was a good ship, well thought of by the regular travellers, and a distinct advance on the *Rothesay Castle*, which was sold out of the Buchanan fleet in the following year.

THE CAMPBELTOWN TRADE

The *Kintyre* was generally regarded as one of the most graceful ships in the Clyde coastal trade, but she was economical and handy as well as beautiful and her owners came to the conclusion that she was superior to a paddle steamer for the special requirements of the Campbeltown traffic. It was no surprise, therefore, when it was announced that a second screw steamer was to be built to take the place of the *Gael*. The order was placed with A. & J. Inglis, of Pointhouse, who launched the new vessel on 30 May 1878. She was named *Kinloch* as she left the ways by Miss McTaggart, of Campbeltown, who performed the ceremony. The design, a larger and improved version of the *Kintyre*, was the work of Duncan Robertson, son of the designer of the *Gael* and *Kintyre*. Once again a beautiful ship resulted. The *Kinloch* was longer and

F

broader than her older sister and was well described as a more robust version of the *Kintyre*. For the first time in Clyde service compound machinery was employed, giving the ship a speed of almost fourteen knots, well above the contract requirements. It was a technical advance for which credit has seldom been accorded the Campbeltown Company. The first class cabin, 'tastefully fitted up', accommodated 150 passengers, and there was room in the steerage for 650 people. The hold took 200 tons of cargo, and the ship was fitted with steam steering gear, steam windlasses and 'every modern improvement tending to the safety of navigation and the rapid loading and discharge of cargo.'

On the advent of the *Kinloch* a new daily service for excursionists was started between Greenock and Campbeltown by the *Gael*. It was a tour that became popular at once and the company planned to expand the existing facilities by speeding up the journey, providing waggonette trips from Campbeltown to Machrihanish, and arranging connecting tours in Arran. Another new steamer was originally contemplated but ultimately it was decided to have the *Gael* thoroughly modernised and improved, as she was still relatively new. Duncan Robertson was responsible for the alterations, which were carried out by Inglis at a cost of £14,000.

The *Gael* was practically stripped down at Pointhouse. Her original boilers were replaced by two new haystacks, new paddle wheels were fitted, and the machinery was taken down, overhauled and re-assembled, a surface condenser replacing the original one of the jet type. The ship's decks were wholly renewed, and improved lifeboats provided, while a saloon was built on the main deck aft. The old saloon below the main deck was enlarged, converted into a dining room, and 'wholly and luxuriously refurnished, and entirely decorated afresh and elaborately ornamented'. The additional accommodation allowed provision of improved galleys, lavatories, and side cabins, and the *Gael's* steerage was entirely re-fitted.

Completely renovated, more imposing than ever, the *Gael*

went out on a trial trip on 27 June carrying the usual party of invited guests. A summer gale raged as she forged her way down the firth towards Arran but in spite of very rough seas the vessel behaved splendidly. She then ran up the Kyles of Bute, meeting and racing the *Iona* on the way, but that lovely ship showed the *Gael* a clean pair of heels. Nevertheless, the directors were well satisfied with the *Gael's* performance and accommodation and for several years she remained a firm favourite on the Campbeltown day excursion route.

RAILWAY CONNECTIONS

When the financial collapse of 1866 led to abandonment of the ambitious North British Railway attempt to capture the Ardrishaig and West Highland traffic, the possibility of a resumption of services from Helensburgh appeared remote. However, the company found itself able to introduce a much less pretentious service in 1869, connecting Helensburgh with Dunoon and the Holy Loch, utilising the *Dandie Dinmont* whose superior accommodation and high standard of passenger facilities quickly won for her owners a profitable trade. The lesson was not lost on the railway company, whose subsequent operations on the firth were marked by a carefulness conspicuously lacking in some other circles. In 1870 the service was extended to the Gareloch piers by recalling the *Carham* from her haunts at Silloth and stationing her again at Helensburgh. The *Dandie Dinmont*, newly reboilered, took up an extended timetable of four up and down sailings daily between Helensburgh and Dunoon, and new express trains were provided to give fast connections from Glasgow. The introduction of second class carriages to all Helensburgh trains, reduction of third class fares to the coast, and a reciprocal arrangement for interavailability of return tickets with the Glasgow & South Western Railway route via Greenock were imaginative improvements which attracted much fresh traffic to the North British line.

The *Carham* was used as a stopgap and a steady improvement in traffic soon required the provision of a new steamer for the Gareloch service. Accordingly, in March 1872, Henry Murray & Co launched the appropriately named *Gareloch*, a charming little raised quarter deck vessel fitted with a haystack boiler and oscillating machinery, capable of carrying 600 passengers. Her performance on trials early in May delighted the owners and builders and within her limits the *Gareloch* proved a remarkably successful steamer.

On the whole the seventies marked a time of slow consolidation by the North British Steam Packet Company, a policy amply justified by the traumatic experience of 1866, and by sensible working the company built for itself a soundly based trade which was later used as a springboard for expansion during the eighties.

Meanwhile the convenience of the new Glasgow & South Western route to the coast via Prince's Pier, Greenock, soon attracted a steady traffic which gradually increased throughout the seventies, consolidating further on the opening of St Enoch Station, Glasgow, in 1876. The South Western now commanded the upper firth and bid fair to snatch the advantage even from the Wemyss Bay route. Captain Alexander Williamson entered into an arrangement to maintain steamboat connections from Prince's Pier to Rothesay and the Kyles of Bute, a relationship which continued amicably until the early nineties. The two existing steamers, *Sultan* and *Sultana*, were joined by a larger consort in 1875, the *Viceroy*, launched by Miss M. Williamson on 6 May from the yard of D. & W. Henderson & Co, of Partick. The new ship was of raised quarter deck type, and was one of the earliest Clyde steamers to be built with steam steering gear. She was by no means as fast and handy as the *Sultana* but with the passage of years the *Viceroy* was much rebuilt and modernised and generally could be regarded as one of those useful vessels, the maids of all work, which the Clyde fleet threw up every now and again. Her modern fittings and standard of furnishing made her a favourite and compensated for what her owners must have looked upon as a disappointing sluggishness.

Racing prowess apart, the Williamson fleet was popular with travellers. Not only were the steamers well managed, but they were run punctually and with the interests of the public very much in the minds of the owners. The names which they bestowed on their ships soon led to the affectionate nickname of 'the Turkish Feet', by which these boats were best known, reinforced by the star and crescent of Islam which was their house flag. The reputation of the Williamsons stood very high on the Clyde, none more so than that of Captain James Williamson, the oldest of the three brothers whose influence on the later history of Clyde services was to be so profound. The *Glasgow Herald* reported a pleasant occasion during September 1878, which was eloquent of the high regard in which the young captain was held:

A short time ago a movement was inaugurated among the regular travellers travelling with the *Viceroy*... to present Captain James Williamson with a testimonial, in order to mark their appreciation of the ability with which he discharges his duty, and as a testimony of his courteous attention and care of his passengers while on board his steamer. A large sum was readily subscribed, when the committee decided on presenting the captain and his wife with their portraits in oil, besides giving him a valuable and unique timepiece in the form of a capstan, having a compass, barometer, and thermometer surrounding it. The presentation took place on board the *Viceroy* on Saturday. About 100 gentlemen belonging to Glasgow, Greenock, Dunoon, Rothesay, &c., made up a very enjoyable party, and the steamer proceeded through the Kyles of Bute and across Loch Fyne to Skipness pier, where she was moored. Dinner was served in the main saloon... In making the presentation, the Chairman in appropriate terms spoke of the admirable service provided by the Messrs Williamson... and the great satisfaction felt by the travelling public owing to the careful and skilful way in which their guest handled his well-appointed steamer... Captain Williamson, who on rising to reply was greeted with much applause, said... he was possessed with feelings of intense satisfaction when he found that the little efforts he had made towards the pleasure and comfort of his passengers had been so highly appreciated. He did not flatter himself that this compliment was given entirely on his own account, as it would ill become him to take credit for the position the steamers belonging to them held on the Clyde. He was only following in the footsteps of his father, who had borne the burden and the heat of the day in establishing what is sometimes humourously called the 'Turkish Fleet' (laughter and applause). These handsome gifts, however, would only stimulate him to further exertions on behalf of the passengers who may be pleased to travel with their steamers... Thereafter the engineer and the pilot of the *Viceroy* were presented by the chairman with gold Albert chains and appendages... A number of appropriate toasts followed, and Greenock was reached about nine o'clock, all on board having spent a most enjoyable day. The band of the Greenock Rifles... accompanied the steamer and discoursed excellent music.

KEITH AND CAMPBELL

The combined fleet of Hugh Keith and Captain Robert Campbell became something of a force on the river during the seventies. These owners worked in a loose form of partnership, Campbell operating principally between Glasgow, the Holy Loch and Lochgoilhead while Keith concentrated largely on the Gareloch and Arran stations. Different funnel colours were used for the two groups of ships, Campbell employing the all-white livery so well known at Kilmun, while Keith's funnels were distinguished by a most unusual scheme of all-red, with thin white hoops. Now and again a ship would be transferred from one route to another, changing colours in the process.

In the middle of the decade Keith bought in the old *Hero* of 1858 to join the *Balmoral* on the Gareloch route, where they were joined in 1877 by the *Vesta*, displaced from Kilmun service by a new steamer. The only remaining Brymner vessel, *Guinevere*, entered Keith's ownership in 1876 and was retained on the Broomielaw-Arran service where, during the following seasons, she suffered severe competition from the magnificent new *Glen Rosa*, the twin of the Wemyss Bay *Sheila*, and fully that vessel's equal in performance. Fortun-

TO GARELOCHHEAD FOR 3D.
CHEAP TRIPS
TO-DAY (THURSDAY).
SAILS AT 11.30 A.M.

The Steamer "LOCH FOYLE" Sails from Bridge Wharf
TO-DAY (THURSDAY), 5TH. at 11.30 A.M., for PARTICK,
RENFREW, BOWLING, DUMBARTON, GREENOCK,
HELENSBURGH, ROW, ROSENEATH, CLYNDER, and
GARELOCHHEAD; Returning from Garelochhead at 3 P.M.
FARES—Steerage, 3d; Cabin, 6d.   ?

What for will you be wand'ren here, says Tonall to me
Ugh! says I, my Chief, I cam' to see
THE CLASSIC KOOLIMOOCHT.

NOTE.—Passengers will have nearly One Hour Ashore at
the New Pier at Carrick Castle, being sufficient time to see
the classic lands of Koolimoo'ht.

THE THIRTEENTH POPULAR
SATURDAY AFTERNOON
EXCURSION,
TO LOCHGOILHEAD AND BACK FOR 1s.
SAILS AT 3 P.M.

The fine Steamer "HERO" Sails on SATURDAY First,
7TH JULY, from Bridge Wharf, at 3 P.M., for PARTICK,
RENFREW, DUMBARTON, GREENOCK, KILCREG-
GAN, BLAIRMORE, ARDENTINNY, CARRICK CASTLE,
and LOCHGOILHEAD; Returning in the Evening, arriving
in Glasgow about 9.30 P.M.

Capt. M'Pherson has kindly consented to exhibit his Patent
Boat-lowering Apparatus during the Trip.   Passengers will
thus have an opportunity of judging its efficiency for saving
life at sea.

RETURN TICKETS—Steerage, 1s; Cabin, 1s 6d.

Excursions of the later seventies

ately for Keith, the *Guinevere* had by then established herself
as a general favourite and was able to survive an onslaught
that might well have caused the withdrawal of a lesser boat. A
cut-throat price war developed, during which Keith advertised day return fares to Arran as low as sixpence and four-
pence, cabin and steerage class respectively, but it was clear
that such tactics offered no future to himself or the Shearer
brothers. The inevitable rapprochement took place in time
for the summer season of 1880, when the *Glen Rosa* and
Guinevere sailed by arrangement on alternate days to Arran,
while on the other days of the week the two vessels attempted
to start a regular passenger connection with the remote Kintyre village of Skipness. No profit derived from that unlikely
experiment and after a brief, brilliant career the *Glen Rosa*

ELEVENTH SEASON.

FIFTH POPULAR SATURDAY
AFTERNOON EXCURSION.

CHOICE OF EITHER ROUTE.

RETURN FARES—STEERAGE, 9D; CABIN, 1s.

SAILS AT 3.5 P.M.	SAILS AT 3 P.M.
The fine Saloon Steamer "VIVID" Sails TO-DAY (SATURDAY) 18TH MAY, for PARTICK, RENFREW, BOWLING, DUMBARTON. GREENOCK, GOUROCK, DUNOON, and LARGS; Returning from Largs at 6.30 P.M., arriving in Glasgow about 9.30 P.M.	Fine Steamer "HERO" Sails TO-DAY (SATURDAY 18TH MAY, for PARTICK, DUMBARTON, GREENOCK. HELENSBURGH, ROW, ROSENEATH (Passengers go ashore here for the Yew Tree Avenue) CLYNDER MAMBEG, and GARELOCH-HEAD ; Returning from Garelochhead at 7 P.M. Passengers have about One Hour ashore at Garelochhead, and reach Glasgow about 10 P.M.

NOTE.—There will be a grand Musical Promenade on Dumbarton Pier, at which the Dumbartonshire Battalion Band will be in attendance, and play selections of their choicest Music. There will also be several Races and other Land Sports, commencing at 4 P.M. Admission to the Pier from the Steamer is One Penny.

Return Tickets to Dumbarton, ... 9d.

Passengers may return by Steamer "Vesta" from Dumbarton about 5.45 P.M.

SATURDAY AFTERNOON
EXCURSIO
18TH MAY.

The splendid Saloon Steamer "WINDSOR CASTLE" Sails on SATURDAY, at 2.30 P.M., Direct for KILCREGGAN, BLAIRMORE, ARDENTINNY, and LOCHGOILHEAD ; Returning in the Evening. Passengers can have about an hour ashore.

RETURN FARES—Saloon, 1s 6d ; Steerage, 1s.

Campbell afternoon excursions of 1878

was sold off the river in 1881, leaving her less attractive but more economical rival undisturbed.

In 1876 Robert Campbell took delivery of a famous steamer from Seath, of Rutherglen. Neither a racer in the grand tradition, nor yet a tourist vessel in the luxury category, the *Benmore* was however the epitome of Clyde practice of the mid seventies, a reliable steamer ideally suited to the trade. Named for the well known mountain and estate near Kilmun, the *Benmore* was a handsome, raised quarter deck ship, destined to outlive all other steamers of her type. She was provided with the usual haystack boiler and jet condensing, single diagonal machinery—all absolutely typical of the period. What she lacked in knots she made up for in good looks. She was a 'bonny' ship, a good Clydeside description admitting to gracefulness not, perhaps, up to the highest aesthetic standards, but in Campbell's striking colours the *Benmore* was a most attractive vessel and under command of the popular and respected owner she rapidly became an institution on the Holy Loch.

DUNCAN STEWART

The close of the seventies brought to an end the interest of the Stewarts in Clyde steamboat ownership. With the support of his family it might well have been thought that Captain Duncan Stewart's connection with the Clyde would continue but in the event he died at the end of 1877 and his sons withdrew from the trade two years later. Throughout the decade the Stewarts ran the *Undine* between Glasgow and Rothesay, adding the *Lorne* as a consort in 1871. With two funnels, diagonal oscillating engines and haystack boilers, this was a fast and impressive steamer, if somewhat outdated in being a flush decker when the raised quarter deck was much in use, and saloons then quite common. The *Lorne* was certainly the finest ship Duncan Stewart had owned, but she was a coal eater and her owner viewed such propensities with distaste, so much so that within a couple of seasons he was glad to dispose of his new flagship to Danish owners, replacing her with the much smaller *Elaine* from Brymner's fleet. That useful little ship maintained the Stewart connections until both she and the *Undine* were finally disposed of in 1879.

Shortly before that event, the *Elaine* was involved in an accident which nearly ended her career. The Argyllshire by-election of August 1878 was an occasion which gave rise to much excitement in the county, for it had been many years since there had been a Parliamentary contest, the sitting member having usually been returned unopposed. Now two redoubtable candidates came forward to contest the seat, Lord Colin Campbell, for the Liberals, and Colonel J. W. Malcolm, of Poltalloch, in the Conservative interest. We are accustomed in modern times to seeing voters being taken to polling stations by candidates' cars, but in 1878 the voters had to travel long distances in chartered steamers. Thus we learn that the *Chevalier* conveyed large numbers of voters from the Ballachulish and Appin districts to Oban, while at Dunoon it was recorded that 'the first extraneous element of excitement was the arrival between eight and nine of the steamer *Benmore*, with 30 of Lord Colin's Holy Loch supporters, while at Ardrishaig the steamers *Athole* and *Elaine* were timed to leave for Inveraray and Tarbert, the respective polling places, at 8 am, conveying Colonel Malcolm's supporters. His rival's followers were taken by the *Vivid* and *Benmore*. Lord Colin Campbell duly won the election by a majority of 355 votes.

The *Elaine*, returning from Ardrishaig and Skipness in the evening, was passing through the Kyles of Bute opposite Tighnabruaich when she ran on the rocks off the Bute shore,

Paddlebox of the *Edinburgh Castle*

sustaining serious damage. As the tide ebbed her stern settled on the rocks, causing the steamer to sag amidships, springing her plates and eventually causing her to sink. For a time it seemed that she would become a total loss, but with the assistance of the Greenock tug *General Williams* and a squad of men with pumps she was soon repaired and refloated, and taken up-river to be overhauled. It had been a near disaster for her owners, for the ship, in common with many of her contemporaries, was uninsured, although valued at about £5,000. But the Stewarts' luck held and they were able to retire in the following year and live comfortably on their earnings, being amongst the few Clyde owners of that period who made a financial success of the passenger steamboat trade.

CHAPTER FIVE

TOURISTS AND TEMPERANCE
(1877-1880)

CLASS distinction was a notable feature of Victorian society, in which the working classes knew their place and only the 'deserving poor' were reckoned worthy of the charity of respectable people. Social comment of a kind which appears crude and insensitive today appeared frequently in the contemporary press, as often as not couched in the sanctimonious language which the twentieth century public understandably has chosen to regard as one of the less appealing characteristics of its forebears. The Clyde steamboat trade of the sixties and seventies faithfully reflected social conditions of the time and it did not require a subtle eye to distinguish between the clientele of the best tourist steamers and the old, slow ships which conveyed *hoi polloi* to Rothesay at the Fair. The *Iona* had long enjoyed a monopoly of the tourist traffic to the Western Highlands, via Ardrishaig, and it was perhaps inevitable that a powerful challenger should eventually appear in the form of the *Lord of the Isles*, a vessel with standards so high as to erode even the Hutcheson flagship's trade. To counter the threat David MacBrayne, rising at last to a leading position in the Hutcheson firm, then ordered a steamer whose name and reputation are even now remembered with nostalgia. The *Columba* was possibly the finest Clyde steamer of any period, and she and the *Lord of the Isles* introduced a new concept of elegance and comfort into Clyde travel. Two years later came a third ship of similar standard, the *Ivanhoe*, built in response to the fervent temperance agitation of the times. These three epitomised the finest practice of the era of private ownership and established a yardstick

100

against which all subsequent vessels were measured, but few surpassed.

THE INVERARAY STATION

Tourist exploitation of Loch Fyne came relatively late in Clyde steamboat history and in the early seventies the only method of sailing to Inveraray was by means of David Hutcheson & Co's two goods vessels, the *Inveraray Castle* and *Mary Jane*. These old, slow ships sailed as consorts, alternating on the outward and inward runs and lying overnight at Glasgow or Inveraray. Passengers were carried at lower fares than by the Ardrishaig mail steamers and the service was thus very popular with Highlanders employed as servants in Glasgow, to whom the prospect of saving money on their annual trip home outweighed the advantages of half a day less on the passage. In 1875 the reconstruction and elevation of the *Mary Jane* to the status of a West Highland tourist steamer under the new name of *Glencoe* left the *Inveraray Castle* to maintain a reduced service on Loch Fyne, which continued until her ultimate withdrawal in the early nineties.

The potential of this part of Argyll as a tourist area appeared to offer good prospects to those willing to inaugurate a fast service to Inveraray. James Gilchrist, Caledonian Railway passenger agent at Greenock, seems to have played a prominent part in forming a company for the purpose, but from the first it was closely linked with the long-established Lochgoil Company whose general manager, Malcolm Turner Clark, assumed a similar position in the new concern. Operating as the Glasgow & Inveraray Steamboat Company, the owners planned boldly, ordering from D. & W. Henderson & Co, of Meadowside, a large tourist steamer designed to undertake the long return journey from Glasgow to Inveraray daily during the summer season. There was only one ship on the firth which provided an adequate yardstick—the *Iona*—and the Inveraray Company's steamer was intended to surpass her in every way. Captain William Barr, of the Lochgoil steamers, and Mr David Sutherland, who assumed catering responsibilities aboard the new ship, were very closely associated in her design and layout, planning her as a large vessel with funnels placed fore and aft of the paddleboxes, and full deck saloons.

THE CLYDE LOCK-OUT

Work on the new steamer proceeded during the early months of 1877 but an unexpected factor led to her entering service later than intended, and in an incomplete state. During March of that year shipyard workers in Partick and Govan began an agitation for a rise in wages, shipwrights asking for an increase of one penny and ship-joiners a halfpenny per hour, while riveters, fitters and caulkers demanded increments of ten per cent in respect of time and piece work. On these demands being resisted, nearly three thousand men struck work on 4 April. Their action was met by an immediate combination of owners to prevent workmen obtaining jobs in shipyards further down the Clyde and on 1 May it was agreed unanimously to lock out the shipwrights even in unaffected yards in order to hasten the end of the strike by bringing severe hardship to bear on the employees and their families. Three weeks later the lock-out became complete and 25,000 workmen were thrown idle as the employers closed ranks to resist demands for increases, retaining only apprentices to continue work on half-completed ships on the stocks.

Against this unhappy background work on the new Inveraray steamer slowed down and had to be continued by foremen and apprentices during a period of six weeks which ended with her launch on 30 May 1877. The ship was not then as complete as anticipated. The usual gathering of owners, builders and guests attended at Meadowside to watch Miss McClure, daughter of the chairman of the Inveraray Company, christen the new vessel *Lord of the Isles*, before adjourning for luncheon and the inevitable toasts, but the affair cannot have been as carefree as usual. The owners had at this stage been sufficiently alarmed by the prospect of a late completion to petition the Court to ordain the builders within forty-eight hours to arrange to complete the ship within the time stipulated in the contract or, alternatively, to allow them to provide their own workmen and do the work at Meadowside, using Hendersons' plant for the purpose. The shipbuilders denied that the contract, which was drawn up in December 1876, included a time clause, stating that correspondence between the parties clearly indicated that no guarantee as to completion had been given. Sheriff Guthrie dismissed the petition and awarded costs to the builders, and the *Lord of the Isles* was gradually finished by the depleted work force available.

Meanwhile the lock-out dragged on through the summer and into the autumn until, at last, after twenty-four weeks, it was referred to arbitration. Wages estimated to have been lost on the upper Clyde amounted to £47,240 and on the lower Clyde, where the lock-out had lasted eighteen weeks, £24,097. Strike pay distributed to the men was only £4,000. The subsequent reputation of Clydeside workers for industrial radicalism owed its origins to this lock-out and other nineteenth century experiences and the appalling crudity of the methods resorted to by the shipbuilders to coerce their workmen can arouse no sympathy nowadays. The whole affair was one of the many black clouds which made life harsh and often unbearable for the majority of working class people in Victorian Glasgow, and it cannot too often be recalled that the story of the river steamers was one of the brighter aspects of a life which for many was short, unhealthy, and poverty-stricken.

THE IONA CHALLENGED

It was the misfortune of the Inveraray proprietors that their magnificent new steamer emerged in the shade of the *Iona*, whose reputation was firmly established by 1877. Nevertheless, the new boat provided the Hutchesons with their first real challenge in years. The *Lord of the Isles* was a beautifully designed vessel, slightly shorter than her rival, but equally finely fitted out. Unfortunately, she was nearly a month late in starting the season and her owners thought it the lesser of evils to place her on the new route in a partially unfinished condition rather than lose traffic by further delay. She went down the river on 23 June to test the engines and her official trial took place a week later, when she conveyed an official party from Wemyss Bay on a cruise to Loch Long, the Kyles of Bute and Loch Fyne where, it was recorded 'at intervals all along the shore of the loch groups of inhabitants turned out to see the new steamer pass, and to give her a welcome in rounds of lusty cheers'. The party went ashore at Inveraray for an hour before returning to Wemyss Bay, Lord Colin Campbell leading the cheers of the townsfolk as the *Lord of the Isles* left the new quay, opened for traffic less than a month earlier. The owners and guests enjoyed dinner together on the run down Loch Fyne, 'handsomely served by the steward', David Sutherland, who had relinquished his post as catering superintendent of the Hutcheson fleet to join the Inveraray Company. Many toasts were drunk with great enthusiasm and it was understandably in excellent spirits that the party went ashore at Wemyss Bay later in the afternoon.

The *Glasgow Herald* thought that it was scarcely possible to conceive a more handsome or better equipped steamer and in truth the *Lord of the Isles* was undoubtedly the best finished vessel on the Clyde, even though her builders had been prevented from putting many final touches to her by their labour troubles. The main saloon on the quarter deck was 50ft long and 16ft in breadth, with the conventional form of alleyways round it, and it was described as being 'elegant in taste and luxurious in furnishing'. The dining saloon below was rather larger, being 60ft long and 22ft wide, with accommodation for one hundred passengers. There was a short saloon forward for steerage passengers, with a smokeroom

Page 105. The majestic *Columba*: David MacBrayne's flagship at full speed on the Ardrishaig mail run

Page 106. The *Ivanhoe* Route: the celebrated temperance steamer of the eighties

above it. A post office was another feature, copied from the *Iona*.

Mechanically the *Lord of the Isles* differed from her rival in being fitted with two large haystack boilers which supplied steam to a diagonal oscillating engine of unusual pattern, in which the two cylinders were placed fore and aft of the crankshaft and drove on to a single crank. The advantage of this arrangement was obscure, although it certainly permitted wider engine room alleyways than the conventional two cylinder twin crank design occupying more space athwartships.

The appearance of the new steamer was to some extent marred by her very short funnels, which were then fashionable, but when the builders took her back again in the winter of 1877-8 for proper completion these were lengthened by 3ft. They were again lengthened at a later stage in her career with a considerable improvement in her proportions; indeed, the late Andrew McQueen regarded her as one of the most beautiful steamers of her time, a judgment with which few would disagree.

The *Lord of the Isles* entered normal service on 2 July 1877, sailing daily from Greenock (Custom House Quay) at 8.15 am and returning from Inveraray at 2.15 pm. The circular tours through Hell's Glen to Lochgoilhead and via Loch Awe to join the Callander & Oban Railway at Dalmally were advertised from the outset but curiously enough the tour that was eventually to be identified above all others with the *Lord of the Isles*, the 'famed Loch Eck Tour', was not commenced until 1878 and then apparently on a suggestion by a newspaper correspondent. It met with such enthusiastic approval on the part of the Inveraray Company's directors that elaborate arrangements were put in hand to construct a small steamer to ply on Loch Eck, and to connect Loch Eck with Loch Fyne, in the north, and Dunoon, in the south, with a service of coaches.

The *Lord of the Isles*, in spite of her unfinished condition in the first season, became an instant success and the *Iona*'s

G

traffic suffered in consequence. The Hutchesons had inaugurated a route of their own in 1876, conveying passengers from Ardrishaig to Oban via Ford, sailing thence to Pass of Brander in the new steamer *Lochawe* and continuing by coach to their destination and this tourist outlet gained much popularity for a number of years. Nevertheless, for the moment the Inveraray Company was in the ascendant and the *Lord of the Isles* drew a large patronage.

The Inveraray steamer was taken out of service in early October and returned to Meadowside for alterations. Vibration had caused much complaint during her maiden season and the hull was strengthened and stiffened in a successful attempt to eradicate the nuisance. The ship was completely repainted internally and externally—it seems that she sailed in a temporary livery in 1877—and brought up to the highest standards for her second season. In her striking colour scheme of red, white, and black she was a magnificent sight and rapidly became a firm favourite.

There was nearly a disaster in September 1878 when fire broke out on board the ship at the East Harbour, Greenock, during the early morning. Fortunately the mate and second engineer of the Campbeltown Company's *Gael*, lying close by, were able to pass a hose on board and prevent the outbreak from spreading, but the fore cabin had been badly damaged and when the *Lord of the Isles* re-appeared for the 1879 season the steerage saloon had been enlarged and completely remodelled.

'THE FAMED LOCH ECK ROUTE'

The new excursion route from Dunoon to Strachur in connection with the *Lord of the Isles* was brought into use early in April 1878. Horse-drawn omnibuses and coaches were used to convey tourists from the new Strachur pier to Locheckhead at the northern end of Loch Eck, and from Inverchapel, at the southern end, to Dunoon, Kilmun and Blairmore. Traffic on the loch itself was taken up by the new gondola steamer *Fairy Queen*, built by the enterprising T. B. Seath, of Rutherglen, on the banks of the loch. Ships of this kind, for inland navigation, were a speciality of the firm, prefabricated steamers having been carried across Africa in sections for use on Lake Nyasa at an early date, as well as other small boats for a variety of different purposes in several parts of the world. The Loch Eck example was 70ft long and only 12ft broad, carrying some 150 passengers. Her launch took place on a day at the end of February 1878, with steam already up, and in spite of poor weather a large crowd gathered for the ceremony, the ship being named by Miss Gilchrist, daughter of the Caledonian agent at Greenock. After a short trip to test the machinery the little vessel was moored while the guests assembled in her small saloon, there to take wine, eat cake, and pledge 'Success to the *Fairy Queen*'.

No reference to the Loch Eck excursion would be complete without mention of the coachmen on the route, whose uniform of scarlet coats and grey top hats were much admired by travellers, but details such as these were merely incidental to a service which from the start was worked with a smartness and efficiency that attracted and retained a large traffic for the enterprising Inveraray Company. It is perhaps indicative of the quality and high standards of the facilities offered by the *Lord of the Isles* that David Sutherland, her steward, gave up the post in 1880 to become the lessee of the Great Western Hotel in Oban, then, as now, one of the foremost establishments of its kind in the Western Highlands. The ship was very much a 'society' boat and, under the successive commands of Captains Robert Young, Alexander McKinnon, and her best known skipper, Donald Downie, she achieved a reputation which extended far beyond the bounds of Scotland.

THE COLUMBA

David MacBrayne, now the principal partner of David Hutcheson & Co, viewed with concern the success of the new Inveraray venture. No expense had been spared to keep the *Iona* completely up to date and as recently as 1875 she had been virtually reconstructed by J. & G. Thomson at their new Clydebank yard near Dalmuir. New horizontal boilers were provided and the ship was practically rebuilt to keep her abreast of the times in every respect. Nevertheless, her image suffered in comparison with the even more splendid *Lord of the Isles* and David MacBrayne decided to replace her with a ship that would secure the bulk of the tourist traffic for the Hutcheson interest. Accordingly he ordered from J. & G. Thomson a new steamer which from beginning to end of a long career was generally acknowledged to be the queen of the firth—the beautiful and magnificent *Columba*. For such an important role it might have been expected that a completely modern steamer would have been designed, but the new ship was curiously old-fashioned in appearance, being generally modelled on the *Iona*, with two funnels fore and aft of the standard Hutcheson paddleboxes, a slanting bow of the type already obsolete for new ships, and a square stern long since *démodé* for Clyde steamers. She was propelled, too, by simple expansion oscillating machinery, the last example of the type ever used in a new Clyde boat.

There was sound judgment to support the apparent conservatism of builders and owners. For a tourist steamer on long runs it was essential to minimise swaying movements of the engines, a defect that could be tiresome over a long period. Oscillating engines were notably smooth in operation, and dependable, and it is not fanciful to suppose that, with the example of the complaints against the *Lord of the Isles* in 1877 fresh in mind, MacBrayne was content to specify a type of machinery which was of proved value for the *Columba*. The detailed design features could more readily be attributed to innate conservatism but in a man of sixty-five it was probably too much to look for a radical change in MacBrayne's outlook. But how impressive the new ship appeared! She was fully 300ft long, nearly 50ft longer than the *Iona*, and broader and more massive in proportion. Two new innovations were the use of steel for her construction, the first example, save for a much earlier, short-lived ship, in Clyde history, and the carrying out of saloons fore and aft to the full width of the hull. This feature alone afforded vastly improved covered accommodation in proportion to size than in any other vessel. Externally the *Columba* was a majestic example of her class, magnificent in her Hutcheson livery, invariably kept up to the highest standards of those years. Particularly in her earliest seasons, when her funnels were short and squat, she was not perhaps the most beautiful steamer that ever sailed on the firth, but she always had a rare dignity which most smaller vessels lacked, and gradually some of the less attractive features were altered so that in time her outline improved considerably. She stood head and shoulders above her contemporaries and the majority of her successors and it is not extravagant to claim that she was the most famous Clyde passenger steamer of all time.

The contemporary press waxed enthusiastic, as well it might, over the appointments of the new ship, and the description which appeared in the columns of the *Oban Times* merits reproduction as a most interesting record of the equipment of a Victorian tourist paddle steamer of the best kind:

Descending from the promenade deck—which is 220 feet long and the whole width of the vessel—two staircases lead aft to the saloon. Between these staircases is a well-lighted and comfortably furnished smoking room, from the windows of which a good view is obtainable of the engines. Further aft, and on either side of the boat, are ladies' and gentlemen's lavatories, the mountings of the wash-hand basins being silver, and everything else en suite. The saloon is a magnificent apartment nearly 80 feet long, lofty, and lighted by continuous plate-glass windows hung with crimson drapery. The ceiling both of this and of the dining saloon below is artistically stencilled in light slate-blue upon a rich ground of ribbed gold, and being panelled with boldly-mounted girders, also painted blue, has a wonderfully light and agreeable effect. The seats are placed at right angles to the windows, as in a Pullman car, and are upholstered in crimson silk velvet. From the stern windows a fine view is obtainable, and the saloon being adorned with several large mirrors, has an air of space even out of proportion with its undoubted roominess. But the dining saloon is the great feature of the *Columba*. Situated below the main saloon, and of the same dimensions, it is decorated in the most lavish and artistic manner. The panels are of polished wood—teak, maple, mahogany, and rosewood being the materials used. Some of the panels are painted to represented inlaying in pattern, and the capitals of the pillars and moulding of the cornice are heavily coated with gold. The pillars are of teak, the upper part being white, with gold flutings. Great taste has been shown in the choice of the carpets and the upholstery, the chairs being covered with a rich, old-fashioned, dark canary-coloured velvet. At the stern end of the saloon, advantage has been taken of the narrowing and shelving character of the boat above the helm to arrange a conservatory, a fine lot of rare plants being disposed in front of the mirror which closes in the view. Mr Turner, the steward, who now undertakes the purveying both of the *Iona* and *Columba*, has effected a revolution in the art of dining on board ship by the use of round instead of long, straight tables, and by serving dinners at all hours instead of at one stated time. By this means, a little party of tourists may dine at their own table without interference from others, and at any time they may choose. The steward's pantry and scullery, leading off the dining saloon, are fitted up with all the latest improvements, one of the most novel of which is a counter warmed by steam, on which there is room for ten or fifteen dishes... Of all the appointments of the dining saloon, however, the most noticeable is a series of painted glass panels each containing a motto, and a group of figures illustrative of the text. Both in treatment and in colour the style of the pictures is strictly conventional, after the medieval school, and the panels attract attention as much by the vigour and strength of the drawing as by the quaint and droll effect produced. An idea of the pictures may possibly be formed from one or two of the mottoes: 'Gude claes open a' doors'; 'A' the wit's no in ae pow', 'Fine feathers make fine birds', 'A low bush is better than nae bield', 'Marry for love and work for siller', 'Ane at a time is guid fishing', and so on. The panels are the work of Messrs W. & J. Keir, of St Vincent Street, who have also contributed a larger stained-glass window, illustrating 'The landing of St Columba on the island of Iona'... The saloon for steerage passengers is plainly though substantially furnished, and below is a refreshment bar, with semicircular counter, silver-plated rail, decanters and glasses all complete. Forward of this again is the fore-cabin very comfortably upholstered. Bath-rooms, pursers' cabins, and store-rooms are closely adjacent, and their fittings serve to show how thoroughly the demands both of passengers and officials have been anticipated.

The engines, which ran at about forty revolutions per minute to give the ship's full speed of just over eighteen knots, were supplied with steam at a pressure of 50lb per square inch by four horizontal, or Navy, boilers constructed of steel. Placed two forward and two aft of the engines, with uptakes at the outer ends, these gave the *Columba* the characteristically wide funnel spacing which distinguished her, as well as the *Iona*, in the early years. Both ships were fitted with Muir & Caldwell's patent steam steering gear, the auxiliary engine being situated beside the main machinery, but while this feature was built into the *Columba* when new, the *Iona* had only received it some years after entering service. Steam warping engines were fitted at bow and stern of the *Columba* to facilitate handling at piers, a necessary provision in a vessel of her immense length.

The new steamer went down river on 21 June 1878 to have her compasses adjusted and generally to ensure that everything was in working order. The official trip followed on 29 June, when a party of guests accompanied her as she made six trial runs over the Skelmorlie mile before sailing on a short cruise through the Kyles of Bute to Tighnabruaich. On 1 July, under the command of Captain John McGaw, she made her first sailing from Glasgow to Ardrishaig and back, leaving the Broomielaw at 7 am and calling at Custom House Quay and Prince's Pier in connection with Caledonian and Glasgow & South Western expresses from the city. A connection from Queen Street was given by the North British steamer at Dunoon, and on alternate days it was possible to change to the *Inveraray Castle* at Ardrishaig for the run to Inveraray, returning thence by the same steamer to join the *Columba* on the other days of the week. The *Iona*, far from being displaced from her old route, was put on an entirely new service involving a daily run to Ardrishaig and back via Wemyss Bay in connection with the Caledonian Railway, affording with her superb new sister-ship a lavish service to the West Highlands which effectively put a stop to the inroads being made by the *Lord of the Isles* upon the Hutcheson traffic.

THE EVILS OF DRINK

If the *Lord of the Isles* and *Columba* set new standards of comfort and quality of service, the remainder of the Clyde fleet, the Broomielaw boats in particular, showed few signs of improvement in the late seventies as far as the conduct of passengers was concerned. Examples of drunken behaviour were reported year after year in the newspapers, and while most travellers remained sober enough, nevertheless the presence of a few black sheep was usually sufficient to spoil a pleasure cruise for most of their fellow passengers. Broomielaw traffic, apart from Glasgow holiday times, tended to diminish in favour of the railway connections to the coast via Greenock, Wemyss Bay and Helensburgh; the foetid condition of the river drove many people away, but it was also a fact that the worst behaviour occurred on the up-river services. The Sunday steamers were absolutely notorious as refuges for habitual drinkers and, indeed, the public on the whole might have been content to disregard the problem had it been a one-day-a-week phenomenon. This was far from being true. Every steamer had a licence to sell spirits and the steward's department usually made a substantial contribution towards the owner's profit so that, save for extreme cases of rowdyism, he was inclined to turn a blind eye towards drunken excesses.

It occurred to several temperance advocates in the West of Scotland that a pleasure steamer run on the 'teetotal' principle might well have a good chance of success, enlisting as it would not only the support of abstainers but also the large body of people who did not care to run the risk of unpleasantness at the hands of drunken passengers. Late in 1879, therefore, a syndicate was formed to float a concern called the Frith of

Clyde Steam Packet Company, Limited. The members were Alexander Allan, of the then well known Allan line of steamers, George Smith and Captain James Brown, of the City Line, Robert Shankland, of Greenock, and James Williamson, of the 'Turkish Fleet'. The new venture gave Williamson his opportunity to strike out on his own, and from 1880 until his death in 1919 he came increasingly to dominate the Clyde coast scene, first as secretary and manager of the Frith of Clyde Company and captain of its temperance steamer, and later as the driving force in the railway-controlled Caledonian Steam Packet Company. Risking not only his personal fortunes but also his professional reputation on the success of the temperance venture, he was from the outset the major figure in the enterprise, stamping it with his enthusiasm and flair for business, and without doubt his successful conduct of the company's affairs was one of the most significant events in Clyde steamer history.

The company went to D. & W. Henderson of Meadowside, Partick, for a first class saloon steamer, which was launched on 25 February 1880, receiving the name *Ivanhoe* as she left the ways. Incongruously, in view of the temperance banner of the owners, the launching party was thereafter entertained to cake, wine and champagne! No attempt was made to produce a very large steamer, and in fact the *Ivanhoe* was 30ft shorter than the *Iona*. An effort was made rather to produce a ship of the highest standards as regards equipment and furnishings. On the same plan as the largest excursion vessels of the time, she had deck saloons fore and aft and two funnels, as in the *Columba*. Most surprisingly, in view of the popularity of the full-width saloons introduced in the MacBrayne steamer, the *Ivanhoe* reverted to the older style of narrow deck saloons with main deck alleyways round them, a feature which fell out of use for Clyde construction only a year or so later save only for the continued use of narrow fore-saloons in the North British fleet for several years afterwards. James Williamson later admitted that conservatism influenced his decision as regards the choice of the *Invanhoe*'s machinery, which was of the same diagonal oscillating type employed by the Hendersons in the *Lord of the Isles*, with two cylinders driving on to a common crank. Williamson recorded that only Rankin & Blackmore were prepared to recommend compound engines for Clyde traffic, and the virtual unanimity of professional advice supported his resolve to adopt simple expansion machinery, which he afterwards regretted.

In all other respects, however, the *Ivanhoe* was a model steamer. The first class saloon aft was beautifully furnished, as was the dining saloon under the main deck, the great feature of the latter being vines which were carefully trained across the ceiling and bore bunches of grapes which were from time to time presented to specially favoured passengers. Externally, the steamer introduced a new livery to the Clyde, her funnels being painted yacht yellow. The hull and paddle-boxes were black, with a profusion of gilt lining and ornament, while the deck saloons were painted and panelled in light colours. Discipline on board was strict, and the crew were attired in naval-type uniforms which looked very smart, James Williamson himself wearing a frock coat and braided uniform cap while in command. The ship herself was immaculately turned out, in strong contrast to the often indifferent standards aboard other vessels.

The *Ivanhoe*'s route lay from Helensburgh to Greenock, Dunoon, and Wemyss Bay to Rothesay, thence through the Kyles of Bute and down the marvellously scenic east coast of Arran to Corrie, Brodick, and Lamlash, returning to Rothesay by the Garroch Head and the east coast of Bute, thence retracing her morning path to Helensburgh. It was, and remains to this day, the finest of all Clyde cruises and, in selecting the route and affording maximum opportunity for railway connections James Williamson had gone a long way towards ensuring the commercial success of the venture. From the first it was tremendously popular, as its promoters had hoped, but to their surprise extreme temperance advocates proved in the

SAFETY AND COMFORT
ON BOARD THE
"I V A N H O E"
DURING THE
FAIR HOLIDAYS.

As this STEAMER DOES NOT SAIL TO OR FROM
GLASGOW, PASSENGERS may rely on having a
PLEASANT SAIL without the Ordinary Rabble common
on Board Clyde Steamers during the Glasgow Fair.

A R R A N

VIA HELENSBURGH, GREENOCK, WEMYSS BAY,
ROTHESAY, AND KYLES OF BUTE DAILY,
BY THE

"I V A N H O E."

Trains in connection—

From EDINBURGH at 6.15 A.M. (Waverley) to Helensburgh.
        „   „   at 8.40 A.M. (Prince's St.), Wemyss Bay.
    „   GLASGOW ....at 7.40 A.M. (Queen St.), Helensburgh.
        „   „   at 8.25 A.M. (Central),   Greenock.
        „   „   at 8.53 A.M. (St Enoch), Prince's Pier.
        „   „   at 9.55 A.M. (Bridge St.), Wemyss Bay.
Per Steamer

From CRAIGENDORAN at 9 A.M., HELENSBURGH 9.15,
GREENOCK 9.45, PRINCE'S PIER 10, KIRN 10.20,
DUNOON 10.30, INNELLAN 10.45, WEMYSS BAY
10.55, ROTHESAY 11.25, for TIGHNABRUAICH,
CORRIE, BRODICK, LAMLASH, and WHITING
BAY.

Returning from Whiting Bay at 2.15, Lamlash 2.45, Brodick
3.5, Corrie 3.25, Rothesay 4.45, Wemyss Bay 5.10, Dunoon
5.30, Kirn 5.40, for Prince's Pier, Greenock, Helensburgh,
and Craigendoran.

Connecting with Trains—

From Wemyss Bay at 5.30 P.M. for Glasgow and Edinburgh.
   „   Prince's Pier at 6.15 P.M.   „   „   „
   „   Greenock,   6.20 P.M.   „   „   „
   „   Craigendoran,   6.51 P.M.   „   „   „

RETURN FARES—

	Saloon.	Fore Saloon.
From Helensburgh or Greenock..	3s 6d	2s 6d
„ Dunoon, &c.................	3s 0d	2s 0d
„ Rothesay.................	2s 6d	1s 6d

Safety and comfort on board the *Ivanhoe*, 1882

long run more of a hindrance than a help, often demanding
preferential treatment on board the *Ivanhoe*. The real support came from ordinary excursionists who were only too glad
of an opportunity of enjoying a day's sail on the firth with
their families, free of the fear of constant embarrassment from
drinkers. To such as these, the cleanliness of the ship, the
civility of her crew, and the scenic grandeurs of 'the Ivanhoe

route' more than compensated for the absence of alcoholic refreshment and, together with total abstainers, they could well agree with the motto on the ship's drinking fountain, 'Ye may gang faur and fare waur'. For many travellers the *Ivanhoe* epitomised all that was best in Clyde steamer operation and when in the nineties she was eventually surpassed by the newer railway boats and assimilated with the Caledonian fleet as a licensed ship the change was widely regretted, even if by then the improvements which she had inaugurated had made her continued career as a 'teetotal boat' an anomaly.

Paddlebox of the *Columba*

CHAPTER SIX

NORTH BRITISH REVIVAL
(1880-1888)

EVER since the unhappy events of 1866 the North British Railway had been content to operate short distance steamboat services from Helensburgh Pier to the Gareloch, the Holy Loch and Dunoon. By 1880, its finances reconstructed, the company again prepared to mount a more ambitious programme of sailings. Helensburgh, however, spurned the railway and the North British steamer headquarters was built outside the town, at Craigendoran. The steamer fleet was built up by outside purchase and new construction and in a few years was a force to be reckoned with on the Clyde, as its fast ships attracted increasing traffic on the Rothesay route.

CRAIGENDORAN

As far as the North British Railway was concerned Helensburgh Quay had never been convenient for steamboat traffic. Situated at a distance from the company's station, it was just as inconveniently placed as the Steamboat Quay was in relation to the Caledonian Railway's terminus in Greenock. It had disadvantages of its own; seaweed and slime often covered the old-fashioned jetty and many travellers preferred alternative routes on this ground alone. But the railway part of the journey was woefully slow. The underground lines through what is now Queen Street Low Level station in Glasgow had yet to be built and Helensburgh trains commenced their journey by a long, slow cable-hauled climb out of Queen Street to Cowlairs, proceeding thence via Maryhill to Dalmuir and Bowling. Further delay was caused by single line operation

119

through the Dalreoch tunnel, west of Dumbarton, and on to Cardross, where the railway again became double. By the time travellers had walked from Helensburgh station to the quay, any advantage in speed over the river route had been largely negated and, until improvements were put in hand, the North British route posed no real threat to the Broomielaw boats save, perhaps, in its service to the Gareloch piers.

But the close of the seventies brought fresh plans for expansion of the company's Clyde steamer service, as well as improved railway connections to the coast. Ideas centred, naturally, on the construction of a new terminus in Helensburgh, on the seafront, avoiding the necessity of passengers having to walk a distance to the boats, and in due course proposals were formulated and plans submitted for a new railhead. The people of Helensburgh were appalled, and a storm of vilification and abuse broke over the railway company. The town's seaward aspect would be destroyed; the amenity would be impaired; hordes of unwanted excursionists would pour into the quiet and select watering place; these, and many other reasons, good, bad, and indifferent, were drummed up in opposition to the scheme. To be fair to the objectors, Helensburgh was in fact one of the better laid out townships on the coast and a railhead on the front would certainly have ruined its appearance, but the North British Railway was no great favourite with the public and many people were delighted when its plans were ignominiously rejected.

Little time was lost in preparing an imaginative alternative scheme. In those days, the main line to Helensburgh ran from Ardmore practically straight into the town but, under Parliamentary powers obtained as early as 1873 the company was able to plan a deviation to Craigendoran, at the east side, where a new steamboat terminal was projected. The earlier scheme had been laid aside in favour of the ill-fated Helensburgh proposals, but when these were abandoned the North British reverted to its first project. From Camiseskan, a new line swung sharply along the shore to Craigendoran, where the new railhead was to be built, and then turned as sharply inland to rejoin the existing railway at Drumfork Bridge. The company's engineers, Mr Carsewell, and Mr Miller, of Edinburgh, prepared the plans and Provost Kennedy, of Partick, secured the contract for the works. Construction began in October 1880 but severe weather in the following winter delayed operations and it was not until the spring of 1882 that the deviation was ready for use. A concrete sea wall 300ft long was a prominent feature of the eastern end of the new loop line where it crossed the sandy flats of Camiseskan Bay. The wall was made 7ft to 10ft thick, forming a barrier behind which were dumped dredgings from the pier site and other materials brought in by rail. Excavations at Drumfork revealed an outcrop of good sandstone, which was turned to good account in building the pier and station works.

The new station at Craigendoran consisted of through platforms on the Helensburgh line and a single terminal bay platform running down towards the pierhead, as well as sidings. The buildings were described as being generally of old English cast, and were constructed of varnished pitch pine. Platforms and the entrance to the booking office were protected by ornamental iron verandahs with glazed roofs, covering 450ft of the total platform length of 750ft. The pier was arranged in two long arms, allowing four steamers to berth at low tide or as many as ten at high water. The increasing size of steamers over a period of years meant that four berths were effectively available and it was common for some of the fleet to lie overnight at piers in the Holy Loch or Gareloch, thus relieving congestion at Headquarters. Over 600 greenheart timber piles were used in the construction of Craigendoran pier, pitched yellow pine being employed for the top boarding, in all some 70,000 cubic feet of timber. The new pier was built in water so shallow that it was a common sight at low water to see steamers aground. Conditions demanded light-draught vessels, and in later years the apparent conservatism of the company's successors in clinging to paddle propulsion when their Clyde competitors had taken up turbine machinery was directly attributable to the restrictions at Craigendoran.

On the afternoon of 6 January 1882 a tremendous storm burst over the West of Scotland. Heavy rainfall during the previous week and a strong wind blowing up the firth combined to produce a phenomenally high tide, 7ft above the highest mark recorded for forty years. Water flowed across the steamboat quay at Glasgow, while at Partick Wharf, which was entirely submerged, the piermaster's desk floated round his office. Down river, conditions were much worse. 'Language would fail to convey an idea of the fearful character of the storm which culminated yesterday over the West Coast,' reported the *Glasgow Herald*. 'During the night the wind freshened, and towards morning the blasts, which were accompanied by deluging rain, were somewhat alarming in their severity. By daybreak the storm had still further increased in violence, and from that time till well on in the afternoon the wind attained to hurricane force.'

Along the Renfrewshire banks of the Clyde, from Langbank to Ladyburn, there were many timber ponds, the rotting remains of which can be seen to this day. Securely penned in by stout wooden fences driven into the shallows, thousands of logs lay seasoning in the waters of the firth. Practically all the ponds were breached by the fury of the storm, and when the gale was at its height it was estimated that no less than 30,000 logs had floated away towards the opposite shore. The Helensburgh railway was subjected not only to huge waves, but also to the battering effect of hundreds of logs drifting over from the shattered timber ponds. At Bowling the high tide breached the line, destroying part of the breakwater and washing away much of the ballast, but the new deviation works at Craigendoran suffered the worst damage of all; some hundreds of yards of the new breakwater were destroyed and the railway track almost entirely washed away, while the pier itself was severely pounded for most of the day, part of the

Page 123. Two Lochside Scenes: *(above)* the North British Company's *Diana Vernon* at Mambeg, on the Gareloch; *(below)* the *Chancellor* of 1880 lying at Arrochar, after she had entered the Lochgoil Company's fleet

Captain Alexander Campbell

Captain William Buchanan

Page 124. Private Owners:

cement and brickwork being badly damaged. The line was closed for several days and passenger communication between Helensburgh and Cardross had to be maintained by a horse 'bus service worked by vehicles loaned by the Glasgow Tramway & Omnibus Company. By dint of continuous effort day and night, the damage was repaired and by 9 January a single line was reopened for traffic.

No further interruptions delayed work on the new railway, which was ready for use early in May 1882. The completion of the Craigendoran loop meant that the original section of track from Camiseskan to Drumfork could be abandoned. The last trains ran over it on Saturday 13 May and a gang of 200 men immediately began the task of slewing the track round to the new route at each end of the deviation. Working through the night and on into Sunday, the task was satisfactorily completed and the block system tested in time to allow a trial train to pass over the Craigendoran line by eight o'clock that evening. A large party of officials from North British headquarters in Edinburgh was present, and the unusual Sunday operations drew considerable crowds of interested spectators.

A NEW COAST SERVICE

As the new railway approached completion, the North British steamer fleet was augmented by the purchase of a notable vessel. In September 1881 the Wemyss Bay steamer *Sheila* was involved in a spectacular collision with MacBrayne's *Columba* at Innellan, as a result of which she sustained severe damage and had to be run ashore to avoid sinking. The unfortunate *Sheila* was repaired roughly and sent up river for a thorough overhaul. While in the hands of the shipbuilders, she was sold by Captain Campbell to the North British Steam Packet Company and consequently never again sailed for her original owners. The *Sheila* was renowned as a racer, but Mr McQueen records* that she had lost something of her original

* *Clyde River Steamers of the Last Fifty Years*

H

prowess, although only five years had passed since she entered service. Perhaps shortage of money had prevented any more than minimal upkeep; at any rate, the North British was in a position to afford thorough renovation, and the *Sheila* emerged as the speedy flagship of a growing fleet on 15 May 1882, decked in the bright red and black funnel and white paddle-boxes of the railway company's livery instead of the austere black and white colour scheme of Wemyss Bay. Lying overnight at Rothesay, the *Sheila* started the day at 7.10 am, sailing via Innellan, Dunoon, Kirn, and Kilcreggan to Craigendoran, returning on the 11.35 am down sailing in connection with the 10.40 train from Queen Street. Leaving Rothesay again at 2.25, the *Sheila* arrived at Craigendoran in time to connect with the 6.10 train from Glasgow, finishing her day at Rothesay at 8.20 pm.

Craigendoran pier was only partially completed in time for the 1882 season but as the summer advanced additional services were given not only by the company's own ships but also by two of the best-known tourist boats, the *Chancellor* and the *Ivanhoe*. The former made Craigendoran as well as Helensburgh her regular calling point from 22 May, while the *Ivanhoe* followed suit later in the month. From 1 June, the North British added more sailings, and three weeks later introduced a full summer timetable. Besides the *Sheila* on the Rothesay express service, the *Dandie Dinmont* gave a service to the Holy Loch piers, while the little *Gareloch* occupied the Gareloch route. Thus the new North British services offered a vastly extended and accelerated series of connections to many parts of the Clyde coast, to places as far away as Brodick, Ardrishaig and Arrochar. Despite difficulties of single line operation west of Dumbarton, the trains were accelerated to quite a good time of between 45 and 50 minutes from Glasgow. This had been made possible by the construction during 1879 of three very fine express tank locomotives for the coast traffic, to the designs of the company's locomotive superintendent, Dugald Drummond. Named *Helensburgh, Rose-*

neath, and *Craigendoran*, these were undeniably the most advanced locomotives in use on any Clyde coast route at that time. They were of the 4-4-0 type, with large driving wheels 6ft in diameter. Painted in the golden yellow livery then standard for North British locomotives (Stroudley's improved engine green) and elaborately lined out, they made a gay splash of colour matched, at Craigendoran, by the attractive steamer liveries of the *Sheila*, *Ivanhoe* and *Chancellor*.

Completion of Craigendoran pier in 1883 permitted further expansion of the coast service and the North British Steam Packet Company took the opportunity of advertising its presence by a change of colours. Henceforth the company's funnel became red, with a broad white band and black top, the paddleboxes were painted black instead of white, and brown panelling was introduced for saloons. It was an arresting livery, which was to be identified with the Craigendoran fleet for over sixty years. At the same time, the decision was taken to standardise on names from Sir Walter Scott's novels; the North British Railway's main line from Edinburgh to Carlisle ran close to Abbotsford, his home near Melrose, and the association with the author of the Waverley novels was made much of for publicity purposes towards the end of the century. Accordingly, the *Sheila* was given a new name, *Guy Mannering*, by which she became best known at Craigendoran.

The company placed an order for a consort, which was launched as the *Meg Merrilies* in April 1883 by Barclay, Curle & Co of Whiteinch, reviving the name of the second of the two original vessels of 1866. In this new steamer, of which so much was expected, the Clyde saw one of its few failures. The *Meg* was designed as something rather special, a 'crack' steamer, as befitted the new flagship of an important and expanding railway fleet. She was long and slim, and whereas the *Guy Mannering* was of the raised quarter deck pattern, the *Meg Merrilies* had a splendid, full width saloon for first class passengers. Steerage passengers had no such accommodation and, until a fore saloon was added at a much later date, the *Meg* looked rather unbalanced. She was propelled by simple expansion, double diagonal engines, doubtless intended as much for speed as to avoid the surging of the single engine which drove the *Guy Mannering*, and steam was supplied by two haystack boilers, placed forward of the paddleboxes. There were two funnels, which, painted in the new colours of the Steam Packet Company, gave the ship an unusually imposing appearance. She was described as:

> a very fine specimen of a river saloon passenger boat, while internally she has been luxuriously furnished with every modern requisite for securing the maximum amount of comfort for the travelling public. The saloon is very spacious, extending over the whole width of the vessel. At the entrance of the main saloon there is a smaller one for ladies. Both apartments are very nicely upholstered and decorated, and have a very handsome appearance. Behind the saloon —at the stern of the vessel—there is a space of about 10 feet which, although left open at the back and sides, is covered over, and is intended to serve the purposes of a smoking room. A dining saloon is fitted up in the fore part of the vessel.

The *Meg Merrilies* went down river for a preliminary trial on 19 May 1883 and the *Glasgow Herald* reported that while her external appearance was very attractive, she appeared to be somewhat low in the water. The official trial followed ten days later, when the steamer sailed from Craigendoran to the measured mile off Skelmorlie where she attained a speed of 17 knots despite rough weather conditions. In view of her later history, it is doubtful if the quoted figure was accurate; even after improvements, the *Meg* struggled to reach 16 knots. The truth was that she was woefully slow and all the comfort on board could not make up for that fatal defect. Under Captain John McKinlay, formerly of the *Dandie Dinmont*, she entered service as the company's flagship on the Rothesay run, where her speedy consort, the *Guy Mannering*, emphasized her shortcomings in no uncertain fashion. The *Meg Merrilies* and the other North British steamers provided an attractive new outlet to the coast, and at Glasgow Fair it was recorded that the traffic on the Helensburgh line had never been equalled, some 10,000 passengers having travelled to and from Craigendoran during the holiday.

TWO WHITEINCH STEAMERS

Perhaps too much had been expected of the *Meg Merrilies*; perhaps the Steam Packet Company asked too much of the builders. Whatever the reason, the steamer was manifestly unfit for the demands made on her and at the end of the 1883 season the owners took the almost unprecedented step of returning the vessel to Barclay, Curle & Co as not fulfilling the conditions of the building contract. It may be inferred from subsequent events that the owners' requirements had hamstrung the builders for, in ordering a replacement for the *Meg*, only leading dimensions were indicated, the company asking simply for a free-steaming, fast vessel capable of working in the shallow water around Craigendoran, and leaving the entire design otherwise to Barclay, Curle & Co.

That firm, with a reputation to retrieve, produced an absolute masterpiece. No risks were taken, and the new steamer was built along traditional lines to produce the last, and finest, example of the Clyde paddle steamer of the middle years. She was constructed partly of iron, partly of steel, an unusual combination of old and new practice; all Clyde steamers built after her were made wholly of steel. The new vessel was of the raised quarter deck type, like the *Guy Mannering*, bringing to an end this form of construction for Clyde service, and boiler and machinery were of the haystack and single diagonal types respectively, a combination not only familiar but of proved reliability. The *Meg* had a distressing habit of running short of steam, but the large boiler of her successor gave no grounds for concern in that respect, and her large, fifty-inch cylinder with a stroke of seventy-two inches was of the same size as that of the *Guy Mannering*. The old Wemyss Bay boat had met her match at last; her new sister, named *Jeanie Deans*, was unquestionably her superior and could outrun any other ship on the Clyde, the great *Columba* not excepted. It was done, of course, at the expense of the strong, rhythmic fore and aft surge inescapable with a single engine, caused by the large, heavy piston moving back and forth in the cylinder as the vessel was sailing. But the speed of the new boat more than outweighed her faults. What mattered was that the North British now owned two very fast steamers with which the company was in a strong position to compete effectively for the Rothesay traffic.

The *Jeanie Deans* was a beautiful vessel, slender and graceful where the unfortunate *Meg Merrilies* was cumbersome and gawky. Her accommodation was in no sense inferior, according to a contemporary report:

> In designing the ship the owners and builders had two objects in view—namely, comfort and speed. To make the vessel comfortable and attractive to the coast visitors great attention has been bestowed on the fittings and furnishings, which are altogether of a very elegant character. The ladies' cabin is fitted up in a novel and certainly an improved fashion, which cannot fail to be appreciated by those for whom it is intended. The main saloon presents a chaste appearance, being upholstered in gold velvet, the colour of which is in harmony with the handsome tapestry panellings.

Thus equipped, besides being speedy and good looking, the *Jeanie Deans* became an instant favourite, drawing much of the coast traffic to the Craigendoran route. Her unhappy predecessor, thrown back on the builders' hands, was modified and left the Clyde late in May 1884 on charter to a Mr Wilson, of Belfast, for passenger service on Belfast Lough.

The Craigendoran route quickly became popular, but occasionally the patience of the North British clientele was sorely tried by failure to adhere to the printed timetables. 'As a daily traveller from the coast to the city,' complained one correspondent, 'I would speak a word for the Helensburgh route as regards cleanliness, civility, and comfort, but these advantages are counterbalanced by the irregularities of the service. One generally arrives a little late at his destination, but the way

to obviate this is hardly to make the steamer start three minutes before its time, as it did this morning from Kirn.'

The *Jeanie Deans* was naturally much in the limelight in
her early years, and in demand for excursions; on the Queen's
Birthday holiday in 1885, for example, she sailed to Brodrick,
a rarely visited place for the North British fleet of those years.
But she was best known on the Rothesay route, where her
speed and handiness made her the ideal instrument for her
master, Captain McKinlay. One morning in June 1885 she
left Rothesay at her usual departure time of 8.35, five minutes
later than the *Viceroy*, sailing in connection with the Glasgow
& South Western Railway at Prince's Pier. The latter was held
for some minutes at Innellan, allowing the *Jeanie* to close the
gap between them, and the North British boat, having lost the
main body of passengers to her rival, was under way again in
a few moments. She was after the *Viceroy* like a hare, and
overtook her near Dunoon. The *Jeanie Deans*, arriving there
five minutes early, awaited her normal departure time and, as
the pier was then a single berth structure, prevented the *Viceroy* from calling until she herself had left. The same proce-
dure was repeated at Kirn and Hunter's Quay, where the
Jeanie sailed off with most of the passengers, leaving the *Viceroy* to arrive late at Greenock, probably having missed the
connection with the up morning express to St Enoch. Such
incidents were widely deplored, but the unwritten rule of the
game was that the first boat took the passengers and in these
circumstances racing was no uncommon practice.

Another new steamer joined the Craigendoran fleet in 1885.
Barclay, Curle & Co, restored to favour after their success with
the *Jeanie Deans*, turned out a neat little saloon steamer
called *Diana Vernon*, which was launched on 2 June by Mrs
Robert Darling, wife of the popular general manager of the
North British Steam Packet Company. The new boat was not
intended for the fastest services, but rather for the short distance pier-to-pier work around the Holy Loch. Fitted with the
usual combination of steel haystack boiler and single diagonal

engine, she was in respect of design the archetypal Craigendoran steamer of the next fifteen years, having saloons fore and aft. These were rather short, and the decking over the fore saloon was originally railed off so that it did not form part of the promenade deck. This was found to be necessary, as the ship was 'tender', but when normally loaded she steered beautifully, being one of the handiest Clyde ships of her time. Her advent allowed an expansion of the North British services to the Gareloch and the Holy Loch, where the *Diana Vernon's* consorts were the *Gareloch* and the ageing *Dandie Dinmont*. The *Guy Mannering* was a steamer which led something of a dangerous existence during her early years. Her desperate encounter with the *Columba* at Innellan in 1881 might easily have brought to a premature conclusion a career which had been exciting enough in the racing days of the late seventies. Under North British ownership, and with a change of name, reliability and maturity appeared to have settled upon the bright young thing from Wemyss Bay in her new role as a senior member of an important railway fleet—until, on an afternoon in the middle of September 1886, she engaged in combat with the new *Diana Vernon* at Kilcreggan and, for the second time in five years, had to be run on to the beach to avoid foundering.

The *Guy Mannering*, fifteen minutes late on her up run from Rothesay, approached Kilcreggan pier at the same time as the *Diana Vernon* arrived from Craigendoran in close pursuit of the new Kilmun steamer *Madge Wildfire*. Smoke from that vessel as she left the pier seems to have obscured the view of both North British skippers, but the funnels of their own craft also formed pretty effective barriers. Each captain appears to have taken a preliminary glance at the other steamer before concentrating on navigating his own ship into the pier. Each appears to have assumed that the other would give way. Neither did so. The *Guy Mannering* arrived first, got her ropes ashore, and was almost immediately sliced into by the sharp stem of the *Diana Vernon* which cut her down to the keel, leaving an eight-foot wide gash in the hull. With water pouring into her, the *Guy Mannering* at once discharged her passengers and Captain Dewar ran his vessel aground in a re-enactment of the accident of five years earlier. The unfortun-ate steamer was cobbled up temporarily on the following day and proceeded under her own steam to Barclay, Curle & Co for proper repairs, but the *Diana Vernon*, practically un-scathed, required nothing more than a quick examination for possible damage. The incident was a classic example of the kind of misunderstanding which could have had the most serious consequences, and amply reinforced the increasing demand for the kind of system of pier signalling which came into general use a few years later.

THE GLASGOW UNDERGROUND

Until 1886 Craigendoran trains ran from Glasgow Queen Street via Maryhill, but in the early summer of that year a new railway was opened to traffic, cutting across Glasgow from east to west, and running underneath the Queen Street ter-minus where a low level station was built. This line, the Glasgow City & District Railway, provided an important link between the North British Railway's eastern terminus at Col-lege and the then purely goods branch from Maryhill to Stob-cross, near the city's western boundary with the burgh of Partick. Completion of the new route, driven entirely through tunnels and cuttings, allowed the bulk of the coast traffic to be diverted from the main terminus at Queen Street. Several advantages accrued; the route to the coast was shortened, the tedious, time-consuming ascent to Cowlairs was avoided, and further traffic was tapped at new stations in the predomin-antly built-up districts through which Helensburgh trains now passed—Charing Cross, Partick, and Great Western Road (now Anniesland). From a junction immediately west of the last-named, another short section of new line cut below the Forth and Clyde Canal at Temple, and climbed steeply through rock cuttings to join the original Helensburgh route about half a mile east of Milngavie Junction. At a stroke the coast train service was notably improved, but there yet remained the operating problem of the single line section from Dumbarton through the single bore tunnel at Dalreoch, a nuisance remedied only at the close of the century.

THE LOVELY LUCY

The *Dandie Dinmont* was past her best in the middle eighties. She was certainly a comfortable ship, but her speed was quite inadequate and the Steam Packet Company began to cast around for a prospective purchaser. The *Dandie* became spare in 1886, running as required in the capacity of odd job vessel; clearly, her days were numbered. In 1887 it was reported that a sale had been arranged to the Turkish government but apparently some difficulty arose that prevented it being carried through and the old ship stayed on at Craigendoran. Robert Darling needed a new boat to maintain his fleet's expanding trade to the Holy Loch and in due course invited tenders for a steamer to be ready for the 1888 season. Hutson & Corbett, the marine engineering firm at Kelvinhaugh, Glasgow, secured the order, but sub-contracted the building of the hull to T. B. Seath & Co of Rutherglen. The new steamer was launched on 24 May 1888 by Miss Darling and taken in due course to Kelvinhaugh to have her boiler and engine fitted. The name chosen for the vessel was *Lucy Ashton*, after the tragic heroine of Sir Walter Scott's novel, *The Bride of Lammermoor*. Little could her builders and owners have foreseen that this latest addition was to outlast all her contemporaries and finish her career of over sixty years as one of the best known and popular Clyde steamers of all time.

Indeed, they could have been forgiven for looking upon the *Lucy Ashton* as a very ordinary member of the Clyde family. Only 190 feet long, propelled by the standard combination of single diagonal engine and haystack boiler, she was really quite a straightforward river steamer. None could deny that her appearance was attractive; in fact, she was one of the smartest boats on the firth in her original condition. Nevertheless, she was no racer, merely a solidly built ship for summer and winter work out of Craigendoran, but on these duties she continued to perform reliably year in, year out, until she became something of an institution. In her early days, however, there was nothing remarkable about the *Lucy*.

Deck saloons were provided fore and aft, the promenade deck being carried right forward over the fore saloon, which had the usual alleyways. The paddleboxes were fairly large, with radial vents; at the centre there was a carved head of Lucy Ashton in gilt. The ornamental pillar above the centrepiece and the curved nameboard were also gilded. The vessel was steered from a platform placed between the paddleboxes, in accordance with the common practice of the period, and above the wheel was a narrow bridge carrying engine room telegraphs at each side. The first class saloon aft, while being described as upholstered and painted in an exceedingly elaborate style, was nevertheless unlikely to have been as well furnished as those of the best excursion steamers, for the *Lucy Ashton* was essentially a short distance craft for ferry service. Under command of Captain Duncan MacNeill, formerly of the *Diana Vernon*, she replaced the *Dandie Dinmont* on the Holy Loch service, usually lying overnight at Ardenadam to take the first up run of the day to Craigendoran.

The decade closed with the North British Railway's coast traffic through Craigendoran well consolidated. Operating a fleet of soundly designed steamers on profitable routes, wasting no money on unnecessary frills, the railway company provided a reliable, economical service and in many respects it was most unfortunate that the rivalry of its south bank competitors, the Caledonian and Glasgow & South Western Railways, during the nineties deprived the North British of the rewards of its sensible policy and inevitably involved the company in retaliatory measures which could only be ruinous in the long run. But at the close of the eighties the North British line had risen from the long years of retrenchment following the debacle of 1866 to being probably the best rail and steamer service on the Clyde coast, and certainly enjoyed the status of being one of the smartest fleets on the whole firth.

Paddlebox of the *Jeanie Deans*

CHAPTER SEVEN

INDIAN SUMMER
(1880-1888)

B Y 1880 it was plain that the future of Clyde services lay with railway routes to the coast. The foul condition of the river above Greenock and a tendency for the up-river boats to fall short of mounting public demands for comfort drew trade away from the Broomielaw to the railheads of the lower firth. It was a vicious circle, as some proprietors found to their cost—less comfort, fewer passengers; fewer passengers, falling receipts; and with less money available, the chance of building new ships receded. Captain Bob Campbell's partnership with Hugh Keith was an early casualty, although his personal popularity and ability won for him financial support and a second chance. By the middle of the decade, private ownership was clearly in decline, and over the firth loomed the certainty of changes far greater than the Clyde had ever known. Westwards from Greenock, through cuttings and long tunnels, the new Gourock extension of the Caledonian Railway gradually took shape, together with the largest pier on the Clyde, heralding the battle of the railways which, during the ensuing quarter of a century, swept away most of the private steamboat owners and made Clyde passenger services second to none in European waters.

THE LOCH LONG ROUTE

Perhaps the Lochgoil Company's fine new *Edinburgh Castle* emphasised the fact that by 1879 the *Chancellor*, maintaining Arrochar connections from Helensburgh for the Lochlong & Lochlomond Steamboat Company, was well behind the times.

At any rate, the decision of that company's directors to invite tenders for a new steamer towards the end of the same year might not have been without significance. Matthew Paul & Co, of Dumbarton, received the contract for a first class saloon steel paddle steamer, to be built for the sum of £7,900 to plans and specifications submitted. While constructing the new vessel's machinery, they sub-contracted building of the ship herself to Robert Chambers, another Dumbarton firm. The builders and engineers, whose association with Clyde passenger services began and ended with this vessel, turned out a splendid little excursion steamer. The close similarity between the design of the 1864 *Chancellor* and contemporary Loch Lomond steamers has already been noted, but in 1880 the new steamer for the Clyde section turned out to be the prototype of the Loch steamers for the next thirty years. Given the name *Chancellor* at her launch on 21 April 1880, the new boat allowed the company to dispose of her predecessor, which was advertised for sale early in the same month, being sold within a few days to Hugh Keith for £2,000, sailing either on the Gareloch or Holy Loch services thereafter under the name of *Shandon*.

Her successor was built with deck saloons fore and aft, and was the last example for Clyde service to have alleyways round the after saloon, although *The Queen*, built for Loch Lomond three years later, was similar. Designed for the prestige service up Loch Long, the new *Chancellor* was furnished in an unusually resplendent manner, and much attention was again directed to the elimination of machinery vibration. While oscillating engines were still widely employed their disadvantages ruled them out for new construction and simple expansion twin crank diagonal engines were chosen for the new steamer. Although costly to build compared with the single engines in vogue at that period, they gave a vastly superior performance in service, eliminating most of the surging motion which was so tiresome with the simpler form of machinery. Steam was supplied from a single haystack boiler of conventional type. It was noted that when the *Chancellor* ran her trials on 28 May the absence of oscillation was remarkable— 'in fact, the disagreeable sensation was only suggested to the steamer's passengers by its absence.' She went down the firth on a day of heavy swell and strong breeze, but attained a speed of 16.9 knots on the run from the Cloch to Cumbrae, proceeding thereafter to Arrochar while lunch was served in the elegant dining saloon to a party of official guests.

Under command of Captain Neilson, who had transferred from her predecessor, the *Chancellor* took up service on 1 June 1880, lying overnight at Arrochar and sailing at 6.40 each morning to Blairmore, Cove, and Helensburgh to connect with the 8.55 up train to Glasgow. Leaving again at 10.35, she conveyed passengers who had left Dundas Street* station by the 9.15 train, and returned to Arrochar, calling at Greenock, Dunoon, Kirn, Hunter's Quay and Blairmore. She left Arrochar again at 2.30 pm, calling at all these piers on her run to Helensburgh, and gave a connection from the 4.50 train from Dundas Street to Kilcraggan, Cove and Blairmore, returning finally to Arrochar for the night.

The long-standing connection between the Lochlomond Steamboat Company and the Clyde service to Arrochar was broken in March 1885 when the *Chancellor*, together with the goodwill of the Arrochar trade, was disposed of for £8,500 to the Lochgoil & Lochlong Steamboat Company. The sale was conditional on maintenance of connections with the steamers on Loch Lomond and in practice the change of ownership meant little to the public, the *Chancellor* continuing to ply as before in connection with the North British Railway at Craigendoran and the Glasgow & South Western at Prince's Pier. She thenceforward carried the attractive funnel colours of the Lochgoil Company but retained white paddleboxes. She was thoroughly overhauled by her new owners before entering their service, the saloons being completely

*ie Queen Street

refurnished. On trial over the measured mile she achieved the satisfactory speed of twenty statute miles per hour, thereafter entering service under the command of Captain Archibald Muir, formerly ot the *Windsor Castle*.

PERSONALITIES AND EVENTS

Sandy McLean was perhaps the most popular steamboat owner on the Clyde. Many years of sailing up and down the river, first on the *Vulcan*, and later aboard the *Marquis of Bute* and the *Athole*, had made him a kenspeckle figure and possibly even he himself hardly realised, being a modest man, how much he had endeared himself to the citizens of Clyde resorts. A serious illness, from which he had happily recovered by the early months of 1880, gave his many friends an opportunity of showing their affection in a tangible way. The Glasgow Cowal Society arranged a cruise on board the *Marquis of Bute*, then renovated with a new boiler and sailing faster than ever, and took on board parties of guests at several piers before the steamer headed for Auchenlochan pier, in the western Kyles of Bute. There she was moored while the large company enjoyed dinner and proceeded afterwards to the business of the day. Some indication of the importance attached to the occasion can be had from the presence in the chair of Mr Thomas Russell, Member of Parliament for Buteshire, who, in proposing 'The Health of Captain McLean', referred to that gentleman's long connection with the Glasgow and Rothesay trade:

As they all knew, Captain McLean had a touch of roughness in his external appearance, but within he was a genial-hearted man. (Applause). In all the positions of life Captain McLean had fulfilled his duty... This social influence was, however, he believed, the chord which struck most hearts. The longer they knew Captain McLean the more they esteemed him. (Applause). The service of plate which he, as chairman, was about to present to their friend was contributed to by a very large number, including many people who were not asked, but who were anxious to show their appreciation of one who had

Glasgow Fair: the Broomielaw on Fair Saturday, 1885, showing (left to right) the *Meg Merrilies* in Bob Campbell's colours; the *Benmore*, running in opposition under Buchanan's ownership, but still in Campbell livery; the *Eagle* and *Vivid*, both in Buchanan colours; and the *Chancellor*, in her first season in Lochgoil Company ownership

Page 142. The Kintyre Route: an unusual view on board the Campbeltown Company's *Davaar*, showing the spartan passenger facilities of the eighties

befriended them in other days. (Applause). The chairman concluded by presenting Captain McLean with a handsome silver dinner service, comprising a set of dish covers, entree dishes, and soup tureen, richly chased, showing the signs of the zodiac, &c, and a handsome three arm epergne for fruit stands, with figures on the base representing the seasons, along with a gold collarette and locket for Mrs McLean. The epergne bore the following inscription: 'Presented by members of the Glasgow Cowal Society, and friends in the Island of Bute and Glasgow, to Captain Alexander McLean, steamboat-owner, Magistrate of the Burgh of Rothesay, J.P. of the County of Bute, with a dinner service, and necklace and locket for Mrs McLean, as a mark of respect, 18th May, 1880.'

The happy occasion of Captain McLean's testimonial was followed within a week by the premature death of James Gilchrist, the energetic and competent Caledonian Railway superintendent at Greenock. His influence on the steamboat trade had been considerable for it lay with him to arrange railway connections to and from the coast and to control, to an extent not known again until the nineties, the interchange traffic between rail and river. Privately, he was more directly involved as a director of the Lochgoil Company, and it had been due in great measure to his drive and initiative that the Glasgow & Inveraray Company had been formed and the *Lord of the Isles* built for the passenger trade to Loch Fyne. The rehabilitation of the demoralised Wemyss Bay Railway in 1866 had also been due to him. Like Captain McLean, Gilchrist was widely respected and only the regulations of the Caledonian Railway had prevented him personally from accepting a well-subscribed testimonial some years earlier, although the funds were placed in trust for his family. His death, at the early age of fifty-five, left a gap which was not adequately filled until Captain James Williamson, of the *Ivanhoe*, entered the Caledonian service at the close of the decade.

The great storm which broke over the Firth of Clyde on 6 January 1882 caused widespread havoc. The *Chevalier*, under command of Captain McGaw, essayed the Ardrishaig mail

J

run from Greenock, but no other steamer dared venture down firth. She succeeded in rounding Ardlamont Point and headed towards Tarbert, but the captain eventually realised that it would be too dangerous to proceed further. 'The sea in Lochfyne was something fearful to encounter,' reported the *Glasgow Herald*, 'wave after wave dashing on board with terrible force, and the spindrift blinded every one exposed to it.' The *Chevalier* attempted to call at Rothesay on her way back, only to find that the quay was wholly submerged, as were the piers at Innellan and Dunoon, and the steamer had to continue direct to Greenock.

Destruction was general round the entire estuary. When the timber ponds between Greenock and Port Glasgow broke up, thousands of logs floated all over the river, causing damage to the *Vivid* and the *Athole*, both of which fouled timber on their way down to Greenock. Many piers were badly mauled; the wooden screen and waiting room at Helensburgh were washed away, Row pier was reported to be a mass of debris, and the pier house undermined, Dumbarton pier 'suffered greatly' as floating logs pounded it, and Cove pier was stated to have been utterly wrecked. Largs, Wemyss Bay, Millport and Kilcreggan were also seriously damaged. The main problem, of course, was to recover the timber from the wrecked ponds and gangs of men were swiftly recruited to assist in its recovery. They immediately demanded evtra pay for Sunday work—time and a half, and one shilling each for food. 'The advance had to be conceded,' noted the *Glasgow Herald* wryly.

Such weather on the Clyde was happily rare although the Glasgow Fair, which fell annually in mid-July, acquired an evil reputation for heavy rainfall. But it was not always bad, and the steamers frequently benefited from brilliant weather at this and other holiday times. In 1883 Fair Saturday was exceptionally fine and traffic from the Broomielaw very heavy. The *Sultan* left for Rothesay as early as twenty minutes past six, and no less than nineteen other steamers followed in succession until the departure of the *Sultana* at noon. All the boats were fully loaded, it being estimated that the average complement lay between 700 and 800 people. The departure of the *Columba*, with 1,500 passengers, and the *Lord of the Isles*, with about 1,000, after seven o'clock, marked the peak of the morning's activity, which was typical of the Broomielaw at the zenith of its popularity.

Most travellers from Glasgow were on pleasure bound, but now and again there were exceptions. When the *Hero* sailed down river one morning in June 1883 she carried many who were destined never to see Scotland again—four hundred and twenty emigrants, 'single men, single women, and families, for embarkation on board the iron clipper "Hannah Landles", bound for Port Mackay (Queensland)... The vessel is under contract with the Queensland Government, and the passengers have been carefully selected, principally from the agricultural districts of Scotland...' The last sentence possibly concealed the fact that many of the emigrants had been cleared from their homes by 'improving' landlords and had little alternative but to seek a living away from their native country.

A long-standing cause of complaint to passengers between Cathcart Street Station, Greenock, and the Steamboat Quay was the noisome East Quay Lane. This narrow thoroughfare in one of the poorest areas of the town had been a disgrace to the district and had undoubtedly lost a good deal of traffic to the Caledonian Railway, for many passengers avoided the route if at all possible. Early plans for improvement envisaged the purchase of the neighbouring properties by the railway company and extension of its line down to the Steamboat Quay but the scheme was found to be impracticable and had to be abandoned. Eventually the Greenock Improvement Trust, with powers under the Artizans Dwellings Act, took action to demolish all the properties between East Quay Lane and Highland Close, and form a wide, new road. The cost, including compensation to existing proprietors, was nearly £60,000 but by Whitsunday, 1884 the work had been completed. In recognition of his part in these long-overdue measures, Bailie Graham Brymner was posthumously honoured by the corporation in its unanimous decision to name the new road 'Brymner Street'.

BOB CAMPBELL'S ECLIPSE

The partnership of Hugh Keith and Robert Campbell controlled a fleet of seven steamers during the early eighties, operating principally on the Holy Loch, Loch Goil, and Gareloch routes from Glasgow. Towards the close of 1884 the firm was in dire financial straits. It may be inferred that trade had been none too good, and at the end of the year bankruptcy was all but inevitable. At this point, Captain Buchanan approached the partners and arranged with them to buy the steamers and the goodwill of the business. Campbell and Keith really had no option but to accept his offer; the alternative was sequestration of their estates, and Buchanan had saved them from the hard fate of bankrupts in Victorian Scotland. Hugh Keith seems to have been content to accept the situation and his association with the Clyde services ended in January 1885, but Bob Campbell evidently felt that he had had a raw deal. He made it plain to Captain Buchanan that he intended to resume services in opposition to him at the earliest opportunity and Buchanan, perhaps to avoid humiliating an old colleague, failed to insist upon protecting clauses forbidding this in their agreement. It was an oversight which cost him dearly, and led to bitterness between the two owners, for almost immediately Campbell got substantial financial backing from friends and within a few months was planning to resume a service from Glasgow to Kilmun.

Early in March 1885 he purchased none other than the *Meg Merrilies*, the unlucky vessel which the North British Steam Packet Company had returned to her builders at the close of the 1883 season. Barclay, Curle & Co had carried out alterattions, including the removal of the promenade deck extension over the stern, modifications to the underbody, and adjustments to the paddle wheels. Thus improved, the *Meg* was despatched to Belfast for a season to retrieve her fortunes. There is no doubt that Campbell got quite a bargain in this nearly new steamer for, if still painfully slow, she was no worse than in her first summer and the requirements of the Holy Loch trade demanded nothing unusual in the way of speed. On the credit side, she now offered regular travellers on that route all the comfort of a modern, first class deck saloon, and the smoothness of her double diagonal engines. The regulars were suitably impressed. Bob Campbell was a great favourite, his misfortunes rallied widespread support and sympathy, and when the *Meg Merrilies*, majestic in her attractive new Campbell colours, swept down river for the first time on 19 March the presence of her owner on the paddlebox was 'hailed by large numbers at the various quays with evident satisfaction.'

It was the turn of Captain Buchanan to feel aggrieved, and with considerable justification. Had he not acquired the whole fleet and goodwill of the Kilmun connection? Now the man whom he had rescued from a desperate position was to all intents and purposes repudiating an agreement entered into in good faith, albeit with little alternative. Captain Buchanan was deeply offended, and obviously thought that Bob Campbell had acted dishonourably. He accordingly published an advertisement in the *Glasgow Herald* of 23 May, drawing attention to the fact that he, and he only, was entitled to conduct the Kilmun trade. Nothing daunted, Campbell published his version of the matter and an exchange of advertisements continued until the end of the month. It is fairly clear from these that Buchanan underestimated the financial support available to Campbell and failed to protect his position by methods which a more ruthless purchaser would have employed. The outcome of the affair was that both owners competed for the Kilmun traffic during the 1885 season in a quite uneconomical way. Buchanan used Campbell's old flagship, the *Benmore*, still in the Campbell colours, almost certainly to underline his moral right to the Holy Loch connection. Bob Campbell used his fine new steamer, wisely abandoning his early intention of renaming her *Blairmore*. So the *Meg Merrilies* and the *Benmore* sailed in opposition through the summer, but Buchanan was fighting a losing battle from the start. He was the incomer, Campbell the local man, and even a reduction of the *Benmore's* fares below those of the *Meg* failed to win the traffic. Buchanan bowed to the inevitable, and withdrew the costly *Benmore* from the Kilmun route at the close of the season, maintaining a less ambitious service thereafter with the old steamer *Vesta*.

The *Meg Merrilies* was a good enough vessel for the trade but with the money now at his command Bob Campbell wanted something larger and faster. He therefore ordered a second steamer, which was launched as the *Waverley* from McIntyre's Paisley yard on 19 May 1885, being thereafter towed to Glasgow to have her powerful diagonal engine and haystack boiler fitted by Hutson & Corbett. She got away from Paisley just in time; a few days later her builders suspended payment, and had to sell out to Fleming & Ferguson, whose shipbuilding activities in Paisley ceased as recently as the nineteen sixties.

The *Waverley* took up the Walter Scott theme of nomenclature which became identified with the reviving fortunes of the Campbell family. She was a well built steamer, similar to the *Meg* in having a full deck saloon aft, but vastly superior in performance. It is probable that she would have given the *Jeanie Deans* a good run for her money but unfortunately there is no record of a contest between the two. She joined the *Meg Merrilies* in June on an expanded service to Kilmun which finally sounded the knell of Buchanan's opposition service; the *Waverley* and the *Benmore* left Glasgow at the same hour, noon, and once clear of the upper river the new Campbell boat would have left her rival far astern.

CAMPBELL FINALE

Captain Campbell's financial affairs had recovered sufficiently by the end of 1885 to allow him to consider expansion into fresh fields. The *Waverley* was too large for economical employment between the Broomielaw and Kilmun, and an order was therefore placed with S. McKnight & Co, of Ayr, for a smaller paddle steamer more in keeping with the requirements of the trade. Construction of the new boat was rapid, and her launch took place on 17 June 1886, only twelve weeks after the contract was signed, the name *Madge Wildfire* being given her as she left the slipway. She was virtually complete save for upholstery and painting and, of course, the fitting of machinery. In general style the *Madge* was a smaller version of the *Waverley*, having a saloon aft, a single engine and the inevitable haystack boiler, just about the cheapest form of Clyde steamer that could be built at the time but, nevertheless, a robust and seaworthy boat built to the Board of Trade's highest class standards for a river steamer. The *Madge*, as she came to be known affectionately during her Clyde career, had distinctive paddleboxes with an unusually large number of radial vents, by which she was instantly recognisable.

The *Waverley*, released for the kind of work for which she was eminently suited, was placed on a new route from Custom House Quay to Rothesay, Millport, Ardrossan and Ayr, reviving for the last time on a regular basis the service popularised by the successive *Bonnie Doons*. Drags and waggonettes were provided at Ayr to convey passengers to the Burns Monument at Alloway, the steamer trip being advertised as 'The Land o' Burns Popular Excursion Route'. But 1886 was the year of the Edinburgh International Exhibition of Science, Industry and Art, and Clyde excursion traffic was adversely affected. 'In no previous summer for many years past were there so many unlet houses at the various coast resorts,' reported the *Glasgow Herald*. 'Rents, also, were substantially reduced in almost every locality.' It was hardly surprising that the Ayr venture was less than successful and early in 1887 the *Waverley* was despatched, no doubt thankfully, to the Bristol Channel on charter in command of Captain Alexander Campbell. Her success in those waters was considerable and when the charter arrangement ended the Campbells decided to run the steamer on their own account in 1888. The decision was probably that of Alex and Peter Campbell, for their father was in bad health. At any rate, the *Waverley* remained at Bristol as the pioneer of one of the most successful fleets ever to be operated in British coastal waters, and the *Meg Merrilies* and the *Madge Wildfire* remained on the Clyde.

Bob Campbell was not an old man—he was not sixty—but he had had a strenuous life and the financial worries of the early eighties must have taken their toll. In the spring of 1888 he was dying, consoled no doubt in his last days by the improvement in his fortunes and the good prospects of his sons' Bristol venture. He passed away at his Glasgow home on 10 April and the occasion of his death was the signal, perhaps, of the end of an era in Clyde steamer history. The funeral was one of the most impressive ever known on the Clyde as Bob Campbell's coffin, draped in a Union Jack, was taken to Kilmun on board the *Madge Wildfire* and carried to the grave by eight of the steamer's crew. The mourners numbered several hundreds, but Bob Campbell had always been a favourite, as the *Herald* obituary noted: 'His popularity on the Kilmun station was very great, and, being of a warm, impulsive temperament, he was personally a general favourite of all classes. While his manner might occasionally be considered brusque by strangers, deceased was known to possess a kind and generous heart, and during his busy life many excellent traits of unselfish generosity were displayed by him.'

BUCHANAN'S ZENITH

Withdrawal of the Stewart family from the Clyde in 1879 left a gap in the Rothesay service. Captain Buchanan's affairs were improving steadily at the time and, possibly seeing an opportunity of taking advantage of their retirement, he ordered a new steamer from H. McIntyre & Co, of Paisley, who had turned out the *Brodick Castle* two years before. That firm produced for him a steamer of similar dimensions and style, but with important differences. The haystack boilers of the new ship reverted to the commoner positions fore and aft of the engines, giving a better balanced profile. The machinery was the most surprising feature, being of the steeple type, the last example to be built for Clyde coastal service. Since the appearance of the *Dunoon Castle*, thirteen years earlier, this form of engine had fallen into disuse and its revival, even in a unique two-cylinder form in the new Buchanan boat, was quite unexpected. Freedom from surging was probably the principal reason for its adoption as late as 1880. The new steamer was named *Scotia*, and entered the Broomielaw — Rothesay service on the Queen's Birthday holiday, 20 May, being placed on the ten o'clock down run, returning at 2.30 pm, under command of the veteran Captain Alex Gillies.

Externally, the *Scotia* resembled the *Brodick Castle* in having a deck saloon aft, although in the newer ship it extended the full width of the hull. The paddleboxes of both steamers were large, those of the *Scotia* being of particularly striking design. Unlike her older sister she was not built with a forecastle, the quieter waters of the upper firth making such an addition unnecessary, but she was robustly built and had a channel certificate permitting her to sail with a complement of some 200 passengers to any port in the British Isles. A contemporary report stated that 'internally, her arrangements are of the most complete description, the main saloon and dining saloon being fitted up in a very attractive manner'. There was a handsomely furnished ladies' cabin and a gentlemen's smoking room, while the open quarter deck aft of the saloon was also 'given up to the devotees of the fragrant weed'. The cabins were decorated with panel paintings based on incidents in Scott's poem *The Lady of the Lake*. Captain Buchanan entertained a party of 200 guests when the *Scotia* ran a maiden cruise to Brodick on 15 May, the vessel attaining a speed of 17 statute miles per hour over the Arran measured mile, no great speed, but the hull was reported to be foul.

The acquisition of Keith and Campbell's steamers gave Captain Buchanan numerically the largest fleet on the Clyde in 1885, consisting in all of eleven vessels, mainly concentrated on the upper part of the firth. After 1885 the *Benmore* was transferred to the Rothesay route, sailing as consort to the *Eagle* and *Guinevere*. For a short period she appeared as a two-funnelled steamer after reboiling but her trim was adversely affected and the *Benmore* soon reverted to her better known condition. In her altered state she resembled the *Eagle*, as built, and the *Brodick Castle* in having both funnels forward of the paddleboxes in the style that became general for latter day paddle steamers, but Captain Buchanan was one of the few Victorian owners who appeared to favour this arrangement.

Meanwhile, the Buchanan fleet suffered the loss of the *Vesta*, the oldest of Campbell's Kilmun steamers taken over in 1885. One day at the end of March of that year the *Vesta* approached Greenock Steamboat Quay on her afternoon up run and, while canting in Cartsdyke Bay, a little further up stream, was run into by one of the Clyde Navigation Trust's hopper barges and so severely damaged that she had to be run on to the sandbank opposite Steamboat Quay to avoid sinking in deep water. Her passengers were taken off by the *Meg Merrilies*, which arrived just as the accident occurred. The *Vesta* lay half submerged at high water and eventually had to be given heavy repairs before returning to service. It might have been thought that the old steamer had had enough adventures but, only a few months later, at the beginning of March 1886, she was utterly (and appropriately for a ship of her name) destroyed by fire while lying overnight at Ardenadam pier in the Holy Loch. Her age and condition made her loss no real disaster to Captain Buchanan and she might well have been disposed of at an early date in any case. The *Hero* was sold to the River Tay Steamboat Company, Limited, in May 1886 and on the disposal of the *Brodick Castle* early in the next year the fleet was reduced to eight ships.

THE ROYAL ROUTE

The addition of even such a well fitted boat as the *Scotia* to the river fleet in 1880 was, however, more than counterbalanced by the withdrawal of the *Iona*, which David MacBrayne despatched to Oban in June to maintain the Loch Linnhe section of the Royal Mail route between Oban and Corpach. Her transfer to the West Highlands was no doubt a matter of policy, for the last section of the Callander & Oban Railway was opened in July, affording for the first time through railway communication between London and Oban via the London & North Western and Caledonian Railways. Probably MacBrayne realised that the inevitable competition demanded a substantial improvement in standards in order to retain traffic but in the event there was plenty of room for the Royal Route as well as the new railway.

The *Iona* continued to appear on the Clyde in spring and autumn each year but did not return for summer service until 1886. Despite her replacement as flagship of the fleet by the *Columba* there was no question of the *Iona*'s standards falling off; rather did she improve from year to year as her owner kept the ship in the best of condition. A fine description of the *Iona* at this stage of her career appeared in the *Oban Times*:

Captain McGaw, as of yore, is still in command, and Malcolm Blair acts as chief officer, while trusty Donald Leitch, who has stood at the helm of the *Iona* or *Ionas* for the last eighteen or nineteen years, is still 'the man at the wheel'. Mr Alex Paterson, the courteous and obliging purser, is assisted by Mr Wm. McDonald, and Mr Devlin, chief engineer, who has served the company faithfully a long series of years, has once more resumed his old position at the engines. Last, but not least, the creature comforts are attended to by that eminent *chef de cuisine*, Mr Turner, who has given such satisfaction in former years. During the winter months the *Iona* has undergone a thorough overhaul, and Messrs Hobbs & Samuel, Hydepark Street, Glasgow, who were entrusted with the repainting, gilding, and decorating, have not only effectually effaced the wear and tear of the previous season, but have if possible made her look more charming and beautiful than ever. Nothing could be more inviting than the saloon with its white and gold decorations, its warm red curtains, and luxurious lounges, while the dining cabin with its rich furnishings and bouquets of fresh cut flowers, is equally attractive. The post office arrangements, which gave such general satisfaction last year, are still being continued; but the feature of the season will be the introduction of gas, or at least its equivalent in the shape of Miller's Alpha gas-making apparatus, which has been brought into notice by Mr Joshua Horton, gas engineer. The gas is produced by a combination of compressed air and oil, or what is understood by gasoline. The apparatus consists of four main parts, performing separate and distinct duties. In the first is produced a constant uniform current of air of the required pressure and volume by means of a self-acting apparatus. The second contains a chamber known as the carburettor, in which this current becomes equally carburetted. The third is an elevator for furnishing the latter with a proper supply of hydrocarbon to replace that consumed in the course of manufacture; and the fourth is a governor for regulating the quantity and pressure of gas in the several pipes. The inventors claim that by this system of gaslighting neither furnaces, retorts, coolers, purifiers, nor meters are required; the burners yield products of combustion as harmless as those evolved from the purest wax, and in the process not a particle of coke, tar, dirt, or residue of any kind is produced. It is not contended that this gas will take the place of ordinary coal gas where a gas-work already exists, nor of electric lighting where the amount of light required is sufficient to justify the outlay and cost of upkeep, but in ships it is expected to supply an important desideratum. It is produced about the same price as coal gas in country towns, and is said to be free from all deleterious, sulphurous, and ammoniacal effects.

David MacBrayne took delivery of a new paddle steamer in May 1885, designed for the Oban and Gairloch tourist route in summer and the Ardrishaig mail run in winter. The new ship was named *Grenadier* and was built by J. & G. Thomson at their Clydebank yard. She was destined to be the last vessel of her type turned out by these builders for the West Highland service, ending a long and successful association of over thirty years. Their last venture was a classic; the hull of the *Grenadier* was beautifully designed, being modelled on that of the Atlantic liner *America*. She had a fiddle bow, which suited her long, slim hull to perfection; short deck saloons fore and aft, to the full width of the hull, were provided, with large observation windows; and neat paddleboxes of traditional pattern completed the ensemble, which was attractively set off by the *Grenadier*'s two red and black funnels, placed rather closely together fore and aft of the paddles. The last feature was due to the provision of Navy boilers, as in the *Iona* and *Columba*. Aesthetically, this was the only flaw, remedied when the ship was reboilered in 1903 with new funnels spaced further apart, but she was undeniably a beauty even in her early years. Lavishly furnished, as befitted a tourist vessel, she was regarded as second only to the *Columba* in this respect.

The compound paddle engine made its first Clyde appearance in the *Grenadier*, although in a form which was never repeated. J. & G. Thomson stuck to their well-tried oscillating machinery, which was an anachronism in 1885 even allowing for the smooth-running qualities of that type of engine. The compound principle was possibly adopted for reasons of fuel economy, allowing the ship a longer range on her Hebridean routes. She worked at a boiler pressure of 95lb per sq in, and on trial maintained a steady $18\frac{1}{2}$ miles per hour for a long period under easy steam, a perfectly satisfactory speed for summer cruising and the winter mail run. It was in the latter duties that the Clyde knew her best, most of the *Grenadier*'s sailings on the firth taking place in the off season. Nevertheless, her first service was a short interval of three weeks on the Ardrishaig route before proceeding to Oban in early June 1885. Her addition to the fleet eventually allowed the *Iona*, released from the north, to revert exclusively to Clyde service in the summer of 1886, supplementing the *Columba*'s Ardrishaig runs. Lying overnight at the latter pier, the *Iona* sailed for the Broomielaw at 6.30 in the morning, returning from the city at 1.30 and reaching Ardrishaig again at half past seven in the evening.

THE CRARAE QUARRY DISASTER

The Glasgow & Inveraray Steamboat Company recognised the value of publicity as a stimulus to traffic carried by the *Lord of the Isles*, and the tourist of the eighties had a wide choice of excursions and tours available to him under the auspices of the company. One of the most popular attractions to day-trippers was an arrangement with the owners of the Crarae quarries, on the western shore of Loch Fyne, by which the steamer arrived in time to allow passengers to watch large rock blasts before continuing on her journey to Inveraray. Late in 1886, a particularly impressive blast was planned to take place and special arrangements were duly advertised. The date chosen, 25 September, was the jubilee of the Statute Labour Committee of Glasgow Corporation, which had a close association with the quarry proprietors, who had for many years provided stone for paving the city's streets. No less than seven tons of gunpowder were to be used in what the steamer people called 'a monster blast', and after it had taken place the opportunity was offered passengers of going ashore at Crarae, visiting the quarry, and rejoining the steamer on her return sailing to Greenock.

Over a thousand people were on board the *Lord of the Isles* as she sailed down the firth on a day of dull, overcast weather. By the time she reached Rothesay a steady drizzle had set in and dark, heavy clouds hung low on the hills as she forged her way through the Kyles of Bute and rounded Ardlamont. The sense of occasion was emphasized by the presence of several Glasgow councillors, while Malcolm T. Clark, the Inveraray Company's manager, also accompanied the party.

A 60ft passage had been driven into the quarry face, with

two 20ft branches each containing 7,000lb of gunpowder, and it was calculated that some 52,000 tons of the rock—porphyry, a reddish-coloured, igneous stone—would be displaced by the explosion. The *Lord of the Isles* arrived off Crarae at one o' clock and gave the prearranged signal, a blast from her siren; the great explosion followed, impressive enough in its way, but perhaps a trifle disappointing, and when it was all over the steamer made her way to Crarae pier and put ashore nearly 300 passengers, who walked the short distance to the quarry as the *Lord of the Isles* sailed north to Inveraray. Some of the ladies in the party preferred to remain on board, as

EPTEMBER 18, 1886.

ANOTHER MONSTER BLAST.
(7 TONS GUNPOWDER),
AT CRARAE QUARRIES, LOCHFYNE,
SATURDAY, 25TH SEPTEMBER.

It has been specially arranged that the Explosion take place on arrival of, and on a given signal from, "LORD OF THE ISLES" opposite the Quarries. It has also been arranged for those desirous of inspecting the Quarry after the Blast, that they be landed at Crarae Pier, and taken up again on the return of Steamer from Inveraray.

Passengers can leave the undernoted Ports and join "LORD OF THE ISLES," as under :—

Helensburgh at	8.45 A.M., join at Prince's Pier.
Blairmore Cove, &c.,	7.45 A.M., join at Prince's Pier.
Gareloch Ports, &c.,	7.45 A.M., join at Dunoon.
Craigendorran,	8.45 A.M., join at Dunoon.
Millport and Largs,	8.20 A.M., join at Rothesay.
Wemyss Bay,	9.15 A.M., join at Rothesay.

INVERARAY AND OBAN,
And the FAMED LOCH ECK COACH ROUTE.

"LORD OF THE ISLES"

Daily from Greenock at 9.0 A.M., Prince's Pier 9.20 (Trains—Central, 8.5; St Enoch, 8.30; Queen St., 8.0), for Inveraray and Oban, calling at Intermediate Ports; Returning from Oban at 10 A.M. and Inveraray at 2.15 P.M.

RETURN FARES :—

To Kirn or Dunoon .. 1/ 1/0 | To Kyles of Bute.... 3/0 2/0
„ Rothesay........... 1/9 1/3 | „ Inveraray........ 5/6 3/0
For the Loch Eck Round (Steamer and Coach), 10s.
M. T. CLARK, 5 Oswald Street.

The ill-fated *Lord of the Isles* excursion of 1886

much on account of the weather as a lack of interest in what was probably regarded as a masculine preserve. Amongst them was Mrs Shaw, who waved goodbye to her husband, Bailie Shaw, and her son as the steamer left the pier. She had no idea that she would never see the boy alive again.

In high good humour, the steamboat party arrived at the quarry and went inside to gape at the huge mass of stone which had been displaced. It was undoubtedly an impressive sight, and many of the group were naturally awe-struck. Not so one of the Glasgow councillors, who jokingly wondered how many streets could be paved with the rock.

Suddenly, the boy Shaw reeled and collapsed and hardly had his companions had time to grasp the situation before a dog belonging to one of the ladies who had come ashore fell dead at her feet. Its owner immediately collapsed and all at once people began to fall to the ground as they were overcome by poisonous fumes released by the explosion. Some were fortunate and escaped the worst effects by running from the quarry; many collapsed outside and were revived by the fresh air. One victim fell on the main road, coughing blood. Those outside the quarry helped to drag the victims clear, but they were too late to save the lives of seven people, one of whom died later in the day. Two Glasgow councillors, John Young and Thomas Duncan, succumbed to the fumes and a number of other passengers were seriously affected. A terrible scene was enacted as the victims were laid on the road and frantic attempts made to resuscitate them, many of the quarry workers and their families helping in the work.

The *Lord of the Isles* returned to an appalling sight, as the dead and injured were brought on to Crarae pier. There were moments of sheer horror as the passengers who had remained aboard discovered what had happened. Bailie Shaw had much difficulty in finding his wife, to break the news of their son's death in the disaster. The corpses were laid out in the steamer's fore cabin and the survivors left on deck to recover in the sea air as the *Lord of the Isles* set off down the loch. It was an

Page 159. Railway Favourites: *(above)* the gaily dressed *Victoria* sets off on her official trials in 1886; *(below)* the *Guy Mannering* in her halcyon days on the Craigendoran route

Page 160. Brodick Fair: the *Eagle*, in her final Clyde condition, landing passengers

awful journey. Rain began to fall heavily and in the early darkness the oil-lit saloons were uncomfortably overcrowded as the chastened passengers huddled inside. Telegrams were collected and put ashore at Tighnabruaich, and as the news reached Greenock and Glasgow there was wild excitement. 'The return voyage was, as may well be imagined, exceedingly wearisome,' reported the *Glasgow Herald*, 'and everyone was glad when Prince's Pier was reached.' A huge crowd had gathered to see the steamer's arrival, and watched with ghoulish interest the removal of the dead and injured. It was the end of one of the unhappiest days in Clyde history and the *Lord of the Isles*, one of the finest vessels on the firth, was always thereafter associated in the public mind with the tragic outcome of her owners' well-publicised excursion.

THE GOUROCK RAILWAY

During the later eighties signs of activity disturbed the peace of the attractive village of Gourock as engineering contractors drove ahead with the largest project which the Clyde coast had known for years. The Caledonian Railway had long planned to extend its Greenock line westwards but absence of competition in earlier years induced the directors to allow their Parliamentary powers to lapse. Nevertheless, large tracts of ground at Cardwell Bay, Gourock, were purchased against a future emergency. It was a wise step. The opening of the Glasgow & South Western route to Greenock in 1869 began a long, slow decline in Caledonian traffic via Cathcart Street and Custom House Quay and by the end of the seventies it was clear that no amount of improvement of existing facilities could retrieve a lost cause. If the traffic were to be recaptured there was no alternative to a boldly planned extension to Gourock, by-passing Prince's Pier and providing a new railhead well down river from that terminus.

The necessary powers were granted after a battle in Parliament, and work began on the great task of driving the new

K

railway through cuttings and tunnels below Greenock, emerging at last at Fort Matilda, about a mile to the east of the old steamboat pier at Gourock. From this point, some height above the little township, the new Caledonian line descended on a sweeping curve to its magnificent terminus on the great new pier that dominated Cardwell Bay. At the end of 1888 the works were fast approaching completion and the directors invited several private owners to tender for the steamboat connections required when the railway opened in the following summer. So discouraging was the response that the railway company took the momentous decision to make its own arrangements. The *Madge Wildfire* and *Meg Merrilies* were purchased, together with the Kilmun connection, from Bob Campbell's sons, and the familiar white funnels passed for ever from the firth. Much else was to disappear into the limbo of things forgotten during the ensuing decade as the Scottish railways carried their competition into the Clyde arena, raised the standards of steamer services far beyond the means of the smaller shipowners and swept most of their kind off the firth. The opening of the Gourock route therefore marked perhaps the most important watershed in the history of Clyde steamers and effectively divided the old, easy-going days of the mid-Victorian period from the era of railway control, colour, and rivalry so well known to later generations.

Paddlebox of the *Madge Wildfire*

CHAPTER EIGHT

THE LOWER FIRTH
(1880-1888)

IN contrast to the often fiercely competitive conditions of
steamboat traffic on the upper firth, the outer reaches
around Arran and Kintyre presented a scene of relative
calm, for the sparse traffic offered little incentive to the more
enterprising owners. Trade was therefore monopolised by
established firms giving an adequate, if unexciting, service to
remoter communities. The citizens of Millport discovered
that monopolies had their disadvantages when the Wemyss
Bay steamers were abruptly withdrawn for several weeks in
1882, although the opening of Fairlie Pier later in the year
gave an alternative rail and steamer route to the Cumbrae.
The eighties could be seen afterwards as a decade of steady
but unspectacular improvement of services on the lower firth,
relieved every so often by the dramatic or humorous incidents
which enlivened the steamboat scene of those years.

Sheila IN TROUBLE

Newspapers printed a report at the beginning of September
1881 to the effect that the Wemyss Bay flagship *Sheila* had
been bought for service on the Thames and would shortly
leave the Clyde. If true, one is led to wonder why her owners
found it necessary to dispose of a steamer which was the newest and best in their fleet. Certainly she was reputed to have
lost something of the speed which had made her such a redoubtable opponent for Williamson's *Sultana* but she was no
sluggard by the standards of her day. Possibly her coal bills
were extravagant, and indeed a defect of that nature far more

than a loss of speed would damn her in the eyes of her careful owners. It may well be conjectured that any falling away from her earlier records might have had more to do with instructions that the *Sheila* should not be driven at ruinous cost than to inherent mechanical defects in the vessel herself.

Captain Duncan Bell had been master of the *Sheila* since she entered the Wemyss Bay fleet. He was well known as a competent, hard driving skipper and an incorrigible racer. On 9 September 1881, carrying passengers by the 2.15 pm train from Bridge Street, he took his steamer out of Wemyss Bay and headed for Innellan as the *Columba* rounded Toward Point on her inward sailing from Ardrishaig. Bell determined to reach Innellan before his rival, and the *Sheila* was driven full out across the firth. Captain John McGaw, on the *Columba*, was equally determined that no lesser vessel would delay the flagship of the Royal Mail fleet. He gave a long blast on the whistle, which Duncan Bell affected not to notice. There was apparently little love lost between him and the MacBrayne skipper—'The captain of the *Columba* had a fashion of threatening everybody by whistling to them to keep out of his way', he said later. Both ships, pressed to their full speed, closed rapidly. Normally the *Sheila* was brought into Innellan in a wide sweep from the north, ready to sail on to Toward, but Bell knew that the manoeuvre would cost him the race on this occasion and he sailed straight on, nearly at right angles to the pier. The *Sheila* just beat her rival, getting her bow to the south face of the pier and a line ashore, as the *Columba* bore down. John McGaw, realising the danger, rang full astern, but it was too late. His steamer, sailing at full speed, could not be stopped in time. The *Sheila* was trapped against Innellan pier as the *Columba*'s stem cut through her plates to a depth of nearly 2ft below the water line, and the MacBrayne steamer drew astern leaving the *Sheila* settling by the bow.

Captain Bell acted with commendable promptitude and immediately landed all his passengers before running the

Sheila ashore beside the pier. Happily, no injuries had resulted from the collision but passengers on both ships were naturally much alarmed. The *Columba* was scarcely marked and was able to continue her journey to Glasgow soon after the incident. It was fortunate for the *Sheila* that the *Columba* had the old-fashioned slanting bow, for she might otherwise have been sliced in two. Captain McLean, of the *Marquis of Bute*, now came to the rescue, conveying Wemyss Bay passengers to Rothesay and returning later in the afternoon with a gang of carpenters who patched up the poor *Sheila* with boards and sheepskins, making her sufficiently seaworthy to proceed to Greenock aided by a tug, the water in her hold being kept at bay with pumps. She immediately went on to the slip for a thorough repair but in the event she was never to sail again as a member of the Wemyss Bay fleet. Captain Alexander Campbell took the opportunity of disposing of her to the North British Steam Packet Company while she was being overhauled, and it was as flagship of the railway fleet that the *Sheila* resumed Clyde service in 1882. Her place at Wemyss Bay was taken by the *Bonnie Doon* of 1878 which had spent two years on the Thames after the abandonment of Glasgow-Ayr sailings by Seath & Steele in 1880. She was slightly longer than the *Sheila*, and probably a good deal more economical to run.

The contest of September 1881 was re-fought in the Court of Session in Edinburgh nine months later, when Alexander Campbell brought an action for damages against David Mac-Brayne for the sum of £532. The case lasted for several days and many witnesses were examined. It was plain that they fell into two groups. Those sailing on board the two steamers were uniformly of the opinion that their own vessel was nearer the pier than the other. Lord McLaren dismissed their evidence as being of little value, because of the genuine difficulty of judging distances from different standpoints, but was inclined to accept the evidence of the other group of witnesses ashore who agreed that the *Sheila* had been nearer the pier than the *Columba*. Clearly, however, she had not approached Innellan in the normal way and had brought the accident upon herself. His Lordship felt unable to find for the pursuer, apportioning blame for the collision equally to both masters; and on that reasonable basis the action was settled.

A WEMYSS BAY QUARREL

The Court action over the *Sheila's* collision ended a bad patch in the affairs of Captain Campbell's Wemyss Bay fleet. Spectacular though it was, however, that accident was not as serious as the dispute between Campbell and the Wemyss Bay Railway directors during the winter of 1881-2, which caused a complete withdrawal of the steamer services for over ten weeks. The root of the trouble lay in the division of through fares between Glasgow and the coast resorts served by Campbell's steamers. The Caledonian Railway, the Wemyss Bay Company and the steamboat proprietors all took an agreed percentage, but conditions had changed since Gillies and Campbell assumed responsibility for the steamers in 1869. Traffic had increased substantially and the Wemyss Bay directors felt that the steamboat owners were making a good profit at their expense. Negotiations for new rates came to nothing and Campbell withdrew all his steamers on 31 December 1881. Public opinion was largely in his favour; it was recorded that as the last Wemyss Bay boat left Largs 'three cheers for Campbell were called for and heartily given.'

Millport, being situated on an island, was worst affected. Rothesay, Toward and Innellan were all adequately served by other owners and suffered little inconvenience; neither did Largs, which was on the mainland, with good road connections to Wemyss Bay. Captain Buchanan came to the islanders' assistance by arranging to run the *Brodick Castle* from Millport to Ardrossan in the early morning, there to connect with the Glasgow & South Western Railway's train to St Enoch, and a return service was offered in the middle of the afternoon, but it was a bare minimum and the inhabitants were indignant at being penalised in a quarrel which was none of their making. Public meetings were held, protests sent to the railway companies and the Board of Trade, and attempts made to float a company to run steamers independently. It was tantalising that the Glasgow & South Western's new railhead and pier at Fairlie, almost within sight of Millport, were not quite complete. At the end of February the Town Clerk of Rothesay was instructed to write to the secretaries of the two railway companies to urge them to come to an amicable settlement. The Caledonian secretary replied briefly, stating simply that responsibility lay with the Wemyss Bay Railway, but the secretary of that concern took the chance of presenting his board's case in some detail:

The Wemyss Bay Railway Company are prepared as hitherto to convey any number of passengers to and from Wemyss Bay at the fares now in force. These fares are amongst the lowest in the world, and less than one-third of the statutory rates which we are empowered to levy. But we have no Act of Parliament empowering us to own or work steamers, and we have no power or authority over the independent steamers on the river. Consequently it is to the owners of these steamers ... that your remonstrances ought to have been addressed. You are probably aware that of late years the Caledonian Company and the Wemyss Bay Company have given a very considerable subvention to the steamboat company which worked the traffic from Wemyss Bay to Rothesay and Millport, but this traffic has lately attained to such immense and such lucrative proportions that my directors are of opinion that it can now stand on its own legs, and they are determined not to be parties to a continuance of such subvention. At the same time, my directors will cheerfully afford every facility to owners of any steamer or steamers who may be disposed to work the traffic from Wemyss Bay to Rothesay, or another part of the coast, but my directors fail to see why they should be expected to convey Rothesay or Millport passengers at a lower rate than those going to Wemyss Bay or Skelmorlie; or, to put the case more strongly, why they should carry a passenger who is going to Largs by steamer cheaper than one who takes the omnibus or walks. The stoppage of this subvention would appear to be the cause of the unseasonable outcry which prevails against the Wemyss Bay Railway ...

The quarrel between rail and steamboat interests dragged on into March, but by then the Caledonian Railway, fearing permanent loss of traffic, intervened and both sides eventually agreed to resume services. As usual in such cases the dispute caused a good deal of inconvenience to innocent third parties and cost the Wemyss Bay route the support of a section of the public. Captain William Buchanan, too, was a loser in the affair. The *Brodick Castle,* which had maintained a skeleton service to Millport for several weeks, was replaced temporarily by the almost new *Scotia* while she went into the shipbuilders' hands for renovation prior to the opening of the summer season and, while backing out of Millport on the evening of 21 March the *Scotia* came to grief. The weather was stormy and rather than remain in harbour the master decided to ride at anchor out in the firth. Unhappily, and probably due to unfamiliarity with this part of the Clyde, he ran the *Scotia* round the wrong side of a buoy. The vessel struck a submerged rock known as Fairlie Patch, tore her hull open, and rapidly sank, fortunately in shallow water, so that her crew got ashore without trouble. The *Scotia* was badly holed, and heavy seas caused additional damage, so that for a time it seemed that she might become a total loss. Happily, the weather improved before worse happened, and the steamer was raised and towed on 31 March to Glasgow for repairs.

THE FAIRLIE ROUTE

While these events were taking place the new Glasgow & South Western railhead at Fairlie was rapidly approaching completion, forming the terminus of a branch which ran north from Ardrossan. In its open view across the lower firth to Arran it was perhaps the most scenic railway to the coast but the route from Glasgow was circuitous and, apart from traffic to Millport and Kilchattan Bay, never competed on terms of equality with the Wemyss Bay line. Nevertheless, a final extension northwards to Largs secured the bulk of the traffic to that popular resort after 1885 by affording travellers an all-rail route to Glasgow.

Fairlie Pier station was opened for traffic on 10 June 1882 and the Glasgow & South Western Railway arranged with a private firm, Hill & Co, to maintain a passenger service to Millport and Kilchattan Bay. These owners purchased from Duncan Dewar, the Sunday steamer proprietor, his vessel, *Marquis of Lorne*, formerly Stewart's old boat, the *Victory*. Now rescued from her sinful ways, the old ship was re-christened *Cumbrae* and became a reformed character in the sober service of the Messrs Hill. While she was adequate for the short crossing to Millport, it is difficult to understand why a better vessel was not immediately placed on the station on the opening of the new route. The railway company really failed to make as much of its opportunity as it might have done, and the half-hearted effort at Fairlie was emphasized by the vigorous expansion of the North British Railway at Craigendoran in the same year.

The service was augmented by Hill & Co in the following year when they acquired a second 'Sunday breaker', the vessel on this occasion being Henry Sharp's *Dunoon Castle*. She was reboilered and given a thorough overhaul, re-appearing in single-funnelled condition after a spell of several years with two, and, under the new name of *Arran*, returned to the path of virtue and sobriety. In her case the conversion must have given more than usual satisfaction to the God-fearing, for the *Dunoon Castle* had been in her time one of the most notorious steamers on the river.

THE CAMPBELTOWN TRADE

Regular travellers to Campbeltown heard with pleasure that a new steamer had been ordered for the company's fleet, to take up service in the summer of 1885, replacing the *Gael*. That favourite of earlier years had been disposed of early in 1884, leaving the *Kintyre* and *Kinloch* to maintain a reduced service for a season. Her successor was launched on 18 May 1885 by the London & Glasgow Shipbuilding and Engineering Company, Limited, at its Govan yard, receiving the name *Davaar* as she entered the water. She was another screw steamer, a larger and more powerful version of the *Kinloch,* and her clipper bow and beautiful lines revealed the master hand of Duncan Robertson. The new boat was driven by a two-cylinder compound vertical engine, a form of machinery which now became standard in the Campbeltown fleet, for the *Kintyre* had been converted to compound three years earlier. The *Davaar* was fitted out with two cylindrical steel boilers, with uptakes into two thin funnels, placed closely together, a not unattractive arrangement which gave the ship a more imposing presence than her smaller sisters.

Built to class A1 at Lloyds for channel purposes, the *Davaar* was specially fitted for cargo as well as passenger traffic. She went on a trial trip to Campbeltown on 22 June and attained a speed of $14\frac{1}{2}$ knots, slightly in excess of contract requirements, despite a heavy sea and a north-westerly gale. The appearance and accommodation of the new steamer delighted a large crowd of the inhabitants of Campbeltown who welcomed the *Davaar* on her arrival under the command of Captain Kerr, senior master of the company's fleet. The ship was open for inspection and her visitors greatly admired the internal arrangements. 'She is fitted up with all the latest novelties for the comfort and safety of the passengers,' reported a contemporary newspaper. 'Aft on the main deck is a beautifully furnished saloon, with a state-room and ladies' cabin. Under these is a capacious dining saloon. Forward is ample accommodation for steerage passengers and the officers' quarters.'

Provision of such a splendid new steamer as the *Davaar* came at an opportune moment for her owners, their monopoly being challenged from the beginning of June 1885 by a new concern, the Argyll Steamship Company, Limited, the managing owners of which were James Little & Co, of Glasgow and Greenock. They operated primarily a goods service from Kingston Dock, Glasgow, with the steamer *Norseman*, outwards on Mondays, Wednesdays and Fridays, returning on the alternate weekdays, calling at the same piers and ferries in Kilbrannan Sound as the Campbeltown Company's ships. In the following year, however, the Argyll Company took delivery of a new ship from Robert Duncan & Co. Named *Argyll*, this vessel had room for 250 passengers, including dining saloon for sixty people, and was better able to compete with the *Davaar* and her sisters. She ran trials on 28 May 1886, attaining a speed of over 12 knots in rough weather. The *Argyll* maintained the timetable of the previous years but added Fairlie to her ports of call in each direction, affording a useful rail connection to Glasgow by way of the Glasgow & South Western route. By 1888 the service had been extended from Campbeltown to Stranraer on Fridays, returning directly to Glasgow on Saturdays, easily the longest sailing on the Firth of Clyde.

WEMYSS BAY EXPANSION

We have already noted the disposal of the speedy *Sheila* by Captain Alexander Campbell in 1882 and her replacement by the *Bonnie Doon*. The latter was a conventional Clyde steamer, but an unfortunate series of mechanical mishaps gave her something of a reputation on the river. Local wits lost little time in attaching to her the nickname 'Bonnie Breakdoon', which hung like an albatross round her until she went south in later years, but no doubt the tales of her misfortunes lost nothing in the telling. Nevertheless, she was in the public eye on two occasions in July 1883. On the 17th, while leaving Ardrossan Harbour on her return sailing from Ayr, a paddle float came loose and the vessel hove to while repairs were carried out. A heavy sea running at the time caused the *Bonnie Doon* to drift on to the rocks before she was able to move again, causing slight damage to the hull, and preventing her from returning to Glasgow. The passengers were sent back by train, while the steamer herself was patched up and sent to McKnight of Ayr for proper repairs.

Back in service again a few days later, this time on a cruise to Tarbert Fair, there occurred on board a rare example of a Clyde mutiny. Three firemen came to the engineer as the steamer left Tarbert, demanding money or refreshments, and on these being refused they struck work and defied all orders. Deck hands took their places and fired the steamer on her homeward trip, the recalcitrant firemen meanwhile being placed in irons and handed over to the Rothesay police when the *Bonnie Doon* reached that port.

The Wemyss Bay fleet was augmented in 1884 by the purchase from Hill & Co of the *Arran*. Although reboilered and improved only a year earlier, this was a distinctly old-fashioned steamer by the standards of the middle eighties, a fact emphasized by the position of her funnel abaft the paddleboxes. Nevertheless, fortunately for her owners' financial position, she was economical to run and it was generally admitted that she and the other vessels in the Wemyss Bay service were 'models of cleanliness and general comfort'. But the main improvement of that year was the appearance of a new train for the Wemyss Bay summer traffic from the Caledonian Railway workshops at St Rollox, Glasgow. On 20 May, a train of twelve vehicles—four first class, six seconds, and two brake thirds—was run to Glasgow Central station to be exhibited before taking up the Wemyss Bay service. It was the first complete 'set' train owned by the company, and every item used in its manufacture had been made at St Rollox. Finished in the then standard brown livery, elaborately lined out, the carriages were 'elegantly upholstered' and fitted with Westinghouse brakes and Pintsch gas lighting. It was the first in a series of splendid trains which the Caledonian Railway introduced specially for Clyde coast traffic up to the outbreak of the first world war and went far towards consolidating the already marked preference of many travellers for the Wemyss Bay route. The high proportion of first and second class vehicles was noteworthy, reflecting the clientele who travelled daily to Glasgow from their temporary summer homes at Wemyss Bay, Skelmorlie, Innellan, Toward and Craigmore.

On 17 February 1886 Captain Alexander Campbell signed a contract with Blackwood & Gordon for the construction of a new excursion steamer intended as a replacement for the *Bonnie Doon*. From contemporary descriptions it is evident that the new boat was intended to be something rather special and it is not unreasonable to suppose that the railway companies had brought pressure to bear on Captain Campbell to provide a steamer more in keeping with the increasing importance of the route than his older ships. Whatever the reasons leading to her appearance, there was no doubt that the new steamer outclassed all her consorts and came well up to the highest standards of speed and comfort in rival fleets. She was launched on 26 May by Miss Campbell, daughter of the owner, who named the vessel *Victoria*, in honour of the Queen. Installation of boilers and machinery was completed rapidly and the new flagship was ready for delivery on the contracted date, 29 June 1886.

The *Victoria* was handsome, with two well-raked funnels fore and aft of the paddleboxes, and large, airy deck saloons for first class and steerage passengers. The engines were of two cylinder, simple diagonal type, the last example to be installed in a Clyde steamer although it persisted in use in new craft for Loch Lomond until the turn of the century. Presumably first cost deterred her owner from stipulating compound machinery for the *Victoria*, but in 1886 the pros and cons must have been very finely balanced. However, a surface condenser was fitted instead of the outmoded jet type, and in all other respects the ship was thoroughly up to date; Brown's patent steam starting gear, Bow & McLachlan's patent noiseless steam steering gear, and Thomas Reid & Sons' steam windlasses and capstan were all features of her accessory equipment. The *Glasgow Herald*, in describing the *Victoria*, noted a fresh novelty:

The steamer is fitted throughout with electric lighting by Messrs Bennet & Co, Glasgow, and, as this is the first of the river fleet fitted with this luxury, it is sure to be a great attraction for evening trips. The upholstery work is by Messrs A. Stewart & Co, Union Street, and is of the most pleasing and complete description. The principal saloon is all finished in solid hardwood, polished walnut, and plane tree, richly done with blue velvet. The fore saloon, while affording ample shelter in wet or stormy weather, can be used as a smoking room for first and second class passengers. The internal arrangements of the vessel are of the most complete description, and in every respect the *Victoria* will fully maintain the high standard of beauty and comfort of a Clyde passenger steamer.

Under command of Captain Duncan Bell the new beauty entered service in July and proved all that her owner could desire—fast, comfortable, and popular. She was in immediate demand for charter work and within her first fortnight in the fleet was used as club steamer by the Royal Northern Yacht Club during the annual regatta. Such work was profitable and Captain Campbell found it preferable to employ the *Victoria* as much as possible on excursion traffic from which, of course, he drew all the revenue, as distinct from railway connections which yielded him only a percentage of through fares. There were inevitable recriminations; the railways naturally wanted the fine new *Victoria* to connect with their trains, and protested in vigorous terms to Captain Campbell. Equally naturally, that gentleman sought the maximum return from what was to him a large investment. For a time the opposing views were partially reconciled, but gradually the *Victoria* found herself delegated more and more to charter work. She repeated her regatta duties in 1888 and in August of that year, amongst other cruises, sailed from Ayr to Arrochar with an excursion party, while in September she went to Carradale, the fares on the latter occasion being donated by her owner to the Glasgow Cumbrae Benevolent Society, of which he was president. Such conduct led to increasing estrangement between railway and steamer interests and eventually to a final rupture shortly after the end of the period. There can be little doubt that it was difficult to make ends meet on the Wemyss Bay route and few would condemn an owner who looked for the best possible returns. Alexander Campbell was a reliable proprietor who gave a good service for over twenty years, and deserves more credit than has usually been accorded him.

THE ISLAND OF ARRAN

The Isle of Arran was probably the most unspoiled part of the whole firth in 1880 owing to the policy of its proprietor, the Duke of Hamilton, of discouraging excursion traffic. No feuing of land was permitted and in consequence Arran knew nothing of the mushroom development which, further up the estuary, had produced communities such as Innellan, Craigmore, and Hunter's Quay and led to the expansion of existing towns, of which Dunoon and Rothesay were the most notable. Prior to the opening in 1872 of the first steamboat pier, at Brodick, passengers had been wholly dependent upon ferries between shore and steamer, and in 1880 the position was little better although at high water steamers were able to disembark travellers at a stone jetty at Lamlash.

When competition between the *Guinevere* and *Glen Rosa* for the Glasgow and Arran trade ended in an arrangement for sharing traffic and cutting costs from June 1880 onwards, the two ships sailed to Lamlash on alternate days, turn about, proceeding on the remaining days of the week to Rothesay and thence via the Kyles of Bute to Skipness and Lochranza. Passengers were interchanged by a coach service from Lochranza to Corrie, by means of which a circular tour of the north end of the island was made available to tourists. It was an attractive excursion, but the use of ferries at Corrie and Lochranza, and the superior accommodation aboard the *Ivanhoe* probably combined to draw traffic to the temperance steamer. The Skipness and Lochranza sailings were unsuccessful and the Shearers ended a brief connection with the Clyde passenger trade by disposing of the *Glen Rosa* to London owners in 1881.

Following that event Hugh Keith continued his Arran service with the *Guinevere*, under command of her popular master, Captain John Reid. The *Ivanhoe* was undoubtedly a powerful rival but for a certain class of passenger her lack of licensed facilities more than offset smartness and comfort and the *Guinevere*, otherwise a much inferior steamer, continued to pick up sufficient trade to justify her existence. Both vessels lay at Lamlash for a time before returning to the upper firth and Mr J. G. Moir, a passenger on the *Guinevere* one day in August 1881, found himself much inconvenienced by the lack of a proper pier at that pleasant resort. Having gone ashore for a walk round the village, he returned to the jetty five minutes before the steamer was due to leave, only to find that she was anchored out in the bay, it then being low tide. Mr Moir discovered that his fellow passengers had gone aboard but produced his return ticket and asked to be ferried out to the *Guinevere*, confident that the boat which was pointed out to him had been provided for the purpose by the steamboat owner. He was astonished and offended on discovering that such was not the case, and wrote to Hugh Keith demanding that he be recompensed for his unexpected outlay. Mr Moir was even more deeply offended when no reply was forthcoming and duly published his side of the correspondence in the columns of the *Glasgow Herald*:

> I stepped into the boat fully in the belief that it was provided by you for the conveyance of passengers, but the boatman began to give some hints that this was not the case, and after endeavouring to discover how much he was likely to get out of me, he ultimately told me that I would have to pay him 6d for his services, for which I afterwards learned the usual charge was 2d... As I would not submit to his extortionate terms the boatman then shoved off and brought me ashore again. For his services I gave him 3d, and paid another 2d for being ferried to the *Ivanhoe* and 1s 6d for my return passage to Rothesay by that steamer. This outlay of 1s 11d, which I was obliged to make through the fault of your people, I now ask you to refund me... Should I not have a satisfactory reply from you, however, I will feel it my duty to bring you before the bar of public opinion by sending a copy of this letter to the newspapers, and allowing your

supporters and the public in general to judge whether you have done the just and gentlemanly thing.

Unfortunately, there remains no record of whether Hugh Keith's sense of honour impelled him to meet the just demands of the incensed and articulate Mr Moir.

The *Scotia*, built in 1880, replaced the *Guinevere* on the Broomielaw to Arran route via Kilchattan Bay in 1885. This was a logical step on the part of Captain Buchanan as the latter vessel was past her best and by all accounts had not been well maintained in Keith's ownership, almost certainly due to lack of money. The newer and faster *Scotia* was better able to compete with the *Ivanhoe* on the popular Arran tourist run, but remained on her new route for only two seasons.

Early in 1887 Captain Buchanan sold the Ardrossan–Arran steamer *Brodick Castle* to English owners and her place was filled by the *Scotia*, which became identified with these sailings until the early nineties. In view of the rough conditions encountered from time to time on the lower firth, she was given a short forecastle which did nothing to improve her outline. The *Eagle* in turn took over the *Scotia*'s old run from the Broomielaw to Arran daily during the summer months. That steamer suffered yet another major alteration to fit her for her new duties, a narrow deck saloon with alleyways being built on top of her raised quarter deck. The almost invariable practice on conversion of a steamer to the saloon class was to cut away the raised deck and the *Eagle* was the solitary example of a vessel retaining the old cabin. Her appearance was bizarre after reconstruction but stability was unaffected and the ship's passenger accommodation naturally much improved.

Her rival, the *Ivanhoe*, continued to sail as a teetotal vessel but there were rumours of falling receipts. 'While in the past the course adopted by the directors in this respect may have had some advantages,' ran a *Herald* report, 'it has, we believe, been pecuniarily demonstrated that the principle does not earn dividends of a satisfactory kind.' It was darkly hinted that the ship would shortly be licensed for the sale of 'spirit-

L

uous liquors', a rumour that was indignantly denied. 'One Who Knows,' however, wrote that the tale was substantially true, and that Captain James Williamson's request to his co-owners that wines and spirits be sold on board had been withdrawn only in deference to the views of two or three ardent abstainers amongst the leading directors. Their wishes obviously continued to prevail, and it was not until the *Ivanhoe* passed into railway control as late as 1897 that her passengers were at last able to enjoy 'a wee refreshment'. Whatever the true state of the Frith of Clyde Company's finances, there can be no denying that but for the ingenuity and enthusiasm of James Williamson the whole venture might have collapsed. Prominent amongst the excursions by the *Ivanhoe* were the immensely popular evening cruises, while special fireworks cruises were also well supported, and there were excursions in conjunction with unusual attractions, of which a performance of Handel's *Messiah* on the Braes of Coulport on a summer evening in 1886 was one of the most memorable. These and many other examples of his untiring attention to detail and flair for publicity made James Williamson the obvious choice as manager of the Caledonian Railway steamers when that company through its subsidiary broke into the Clyde services at the beginning of 1889.

Paddlebox of the *Scotia*

CHAPTER NINE

A COAST MISCELLANY

THE proximity of Glasgow to the beautiful estuary which was so largely responsible for the growth of the city's trade and influence during the nineteenth century led to rapid development of parts of the firth as dormitory areas, encouraged by and in turn providing traffic for the swiftly expanding steamboat services. By 1864 the 'coasting season' was a recognised feature of life in the West of Scotland. Few could afford to travel daily from coast to city throughout the year, but it was common for the well-to-do to take a house for the summer, transferring family and servants to one of the many watering places for several weeks. Others preferred simply to spend a summer holiday on the firth, while the majority had to be satisfied with day trips. Thus there developed a pattern of basic services all the year round with a huge expansion from April to October to accommodate the annual surge of summer trade. Coast housing was usually at a premium, and although feuing in certain areas resulted in much speculative building there were other parts, notably Arran, where it was the policy of the landowners to resist indiscriminate exploitation of the district. Nevertheless, piers were constructed all round the firth, while ferries served clachans where the traffic justified nothing more elaborate. The main traffic route was unquestionably that from Glasgow to Rothesay and here, together with the Gareloch and the Holy Loch areas, were found the majority of the coastal communities and the most profitable services. Competition between steamboat proprietors for the lucrative seasonal traffic resulted in outright racing which, although exciting, led to many a dangerous incident and occasionally a serious accident. Public concern led in the final years of the period to the introduction of a proper system of pier signalling, and the worst excesses were thus curbed, but the steamboat scene during the middle years of Queen Victoria's reign was never free from excitement and colour, reaching an annual peak in the Fair Holiday exodus from Glasgow.

THE UNCLEAN CLYDE

In 1864 the Caledonian Railway had virtually smothered steamboat opposition between Greenock and Glasgow, and only the poorest classes preferred the river route on the grounds of economy. The railway became the main channel for traffic from the lower firth, which transferred from the steamboats at Greenock. Most of them included calls at the Steamboat Quay on their passage up or down river, and the bulk of the passengers tended to favour the railway rather than the river route. There were two reasons, the first being speed, and the second the nauseating condition of the Clyde itself. The truth was that the river was simply an open sewer, receiving the untreated discharge, domestic and industrial, of Glasgow, Govan, Partick, Rutherglen and other towns.

Visitors to Glasgow were universally appalled, even allowing for the lax standards then generally prevailing. 'An Englishman' felt impelled to voice his disgust in a letter to the *Glasgow Herald*:

> Permit me, through the colums of your valuable daily newspaper, to call the attention of the authorities of Glasgow to the deplorable state of the river Clyde. It is nothing better than the foulest sewer of any large town in England; and it is only astonishing to me that effluvia constantly emitted has (sic) not been the cause of some serious epidemic... You have a city of palaces, magnificent streets, well paved and kept thoroughly clean, but your main artery, which should be as pure as possible, is a continuous stream of reeking filth and noxious vapours...

Despite this and many other protests, however, the Clyde remained grossly polluted until the end of the century, the

effect on the steamboats being ultimately to destroy the bulk
of up-river trade. Passengers were only too thankful to travel
home from Greenock by train to avoid the ordeal of sailing
up to the Broomielaw.

THE COASTING SEASON

Dunoon, Rothesay, Largs and Millport were the largest coast
resorts, attracting most of the year-round traffic to and from
Glasgow, but perhaps the most popular area of the coast was
the complex of lochs and inlets around the Tail of the Bank,
the great anchorage off Greenock. To the north ran the quiet
and then unspoiled Gareloch, and the wilder Loch Long,
while the Holy Loch, striking westwards into the Cowal
shore, was a much sought after retreat. Small villages, each
with its pier, studded the shores and from them all came
steamers every morning, carrying Glasgow merchants and
traders to their businesses in the city, creating a maritime
traffic jam round the Steamboat Quay at Greenock.

In the early years new housing was concentrated on existing towns, but feuing by landowners—the Scottish feudal
system of granting ground in perpetuity—led in due course
to the appearance of newer communities. The southern tip of
the Cowal peninsula became popular, and Innellan was always a favourite resort not only on account of its own attractive position but also because of its proximity to Wemyss Bay.
Enterprising landowners often built piers at their own expense and feued the ground in the expectation of a surge of
speculative building. Mr Lamont, of Knockdow, advertised
the farm of Toward in this way in 1870, but for some reason
development was sluggish on that site, never equalling the
building at nearby Innellan. Nor did the construction of a
new pier and feuing of fourteen acres of ground at Carrick
Castle in 1878 lead to massive exploitation of that sequestered
and charming hamlet at the mouth of Loch Goil. Communication was manifestly of considerable importance to prospec-

tive residents and the tendency was for new building to concentrate on or near existing resorts. One of the finest of such developments was near Rothesay, where the pier at Craigmore served a well laid out group of handsome stone villas which survives to this day in practically unaltered condition.

The island of Arran, however, remained largely undisturbed by all these developments. An observer wrote in 1881:

This paradise is a half-forbidden garden to our toiling thousands. If there is not a flaming sword to guard the entrance, there are sufficient restrictions to prevent the multitude from finding even a very temporary home here... The Duke is absolute lord... He is a king whose word is undisputed, and is absolutely undisputable... Every tenant here, with the very rarest exceptions, is a tenant at will. He has his holding at the cheapest rental—in fact, as a rule, at a nominal rent... Practically every tenant and every holder of a house and a garden is at the mercy of the landlord. The house, which has been built at the occupier's expense, and the garden which he has cultivated, may at any moment be taken from him without explanation, and without compensation, except as a civility from the Ducal factor... Are the people in a dreadfully crushed and rebellious condition? Nothing of the kind. I do not believe there are a more contented peasantry and tenantry in Europe, and I would add, upon the whole, a more prosperous. The Duke... is the least exacting of landowners... (allowing) his tenants liberty to do otherwise pretty much as they choose, and to let their houses and cabins to visitors. Of course, he will only admit a limited number. If you go to Arran you must, as a rule, submit to live in a very poor house, and to pay a very high rental for it. You have any number of social inconveniences, but the air, the scenery, the freedom, make up for these in a way... The Duke will offer no facilities for the introduction of comforts to the visitors who would throng to Arran if these were provided. He will give no portion of his estate off for villas with feu charters...

In view of this policy it was understandable that steamboat services to the island were late in developing, while piers also were built at a relatively late stage to replace ferries at places such as Whiting Bay, Lamlash and Lochranza. Indeed, throughout the Victorian period Arran had more in common with the Highland areas of the west coast than the Clyde estuary, a view supported by the fact that the census of 1881 revealed that of a total population of over 4,700 persons, no fewer than 2,880 spoke Gaelic.

PIERS AND FERRIES

What of the coast piers themselves? Unlike many English coastal resorts, the Clyde towns and villages regarded their wharves principally or exclusively as landing stages for steamboat passengers. At no time was there a Clyde counterpart of Southend or Bournemouth piers although at Dumbarton, the longest Clyde pier before Whiting Bay was built in 1899, there were some brave attempts to popularise musical promenades for a few seasons. Rothesay, one of the largest and certainly the most important quay during the nineteenth century, was a natural rendezvous for holidaymakers, providing a grandstand for viewing the comings and goings of the river fleet. The pier at this popular resort formed part of a small harbour, and extensions were made as traffic increased. In its final form three steamers could berth simultaneously across the front of the pier, with provision for others at the ends or inside. In response to complaints about the poor standard of accommodation provided by the waiting rooms, proposals were advanced during the mid-seventies for replacing them by extensive new buildings, and a competition was arranged for submission of the best design. It was won by James Hamilton, a Glasgow architect, but the plans were shelved for another eight years while the authorities vacillated. By the early part of the following decade increasing trade made extensions imperative and Hamilton's new buildings were put in hand, being completed in June 1884. They were in Scottish baronial style, with a central clock tower, then and for many years afterwards, one of the features of Rothesay. Glass-covered verandahs sheltered the front of the buildings in which were found offices as well as waiting rooms, a refreshment room 'elegantly fitted up and having coffee room attached,' and a bookstall. The building was constructed in white brick, and cost £1,407; the four-dial clock, by Edward & Sons, of Glasgow, cost an additional £55.

Rothesay was more fortunate in its facilities than Glasgow, where the condition of the Bridge Wharf was notoriously inadequate and, faced with a downward trend in traffic, the steamboat proprietors submitted a petition to the Clyde Navigation Trustees in January 1882 condemning the out of date accommodation and requesting that improvements be made:

> It has become apparent that the traffic from Glasgow is slowly but surely falling off, the greater number of passengers preferring to travel via Greenock, Helensburgh, and Wemyss Bay. To what may we attribute this decrease in the passenger traffic? Undoubtedly the most important factor is—setting aside the impure condition of the river—the insufficient accommodation provided for passengers and steamers at the Bridge Wharf. In proof of the truth of this statement, it is not necessary to do more than call attention to the structure which has done duty as a shed for nearly 40 years, inviting comparison with the goods shed on the immediately opposite side of the harbour, which has been rebuilt three times within the same period...

The Trustees, however, declined to rebuild the shed, attributing the falling traffic to 'the keen competition of the railways,' and reminding the owners that very little use had been made of new waiting rooms built at the Broomielaw only a year or so earlier. Beyond arranging improvements in the methods of coaling steamers, a cause of considerable grievance, the steamboat proprietors and their passengers had to rest content with a wharf which grew steadily more dilapidated as the years went by.

A recurrent cause of complaint was the vexed question of pier dues. The usual practice on the Clyde was to charge steamer passengers for the use of the pier at which they landed or embarked. One penny was a quite usual sum, but more was exacted at a few piers, and considerably more by ferrymen who, on the other hand, provided a more obvious service. It became customary to 'let out' the pier dues annually by public auction; some indication of the growing importance of Helensburgh may be gauged from the fact that the price accepted for the tolls in the year to 15 May 1865 was £535, but by 1879 it had risen to £1,230. Blairmore, typical of the smaller piers on the upper firth, was let out for £200 in 1865 but at the neighbouring Kilmun and Strone, both owned by David Napier, tolls were abolished in August of that year, the charges for maintenance thereafter being levied on steamers calling at these piers, 'a practice', observed the *Glasgow Herald*, 'which we trust that other quay proprietors will be induced to follow.'

Despite the example of Mr Napier, pier dues remained in force, for routine upkeep had to be met from some source. In a number of cases limited companies were formed to build piers. One of these, the Kilchattan Bay Pier Company, heard this report at its annual meeting in 1882:

> ...that the whole accounts and claims in connection with the erection of the pier had been paid up, that the total cost of the pier did not exceed £2,000, the original estimate, but on account of some expenses connected with the formation of a road it was put down as a little above that sum. After deducting expenses of management there was this year a net profit of £150, and a dividend of 4s 2d per share was proposed to be paid, which would be as nearly as possible 6 per cent on paid-up capital. The directors also recommended that the pier be let this year from 1st March to Mr John Cumming at a rent of £160, being £18 less than last year...

Proprietors of the Craigmore pier, in Bute, were less fortunate. Opened in 1877, its affairs failed to prosper and by 1888 accumulated debt amounted to £1,680 while it was estimated that an additional sum of £400 would be required to put the structure into good order. The promoters in this case obviously overestimated potential traffic.

Arran had a reputation for high pier dues, the charges being widely regarded as grossly excessive. Writing in the summer of 1888, a Brodick resident noted that the return fare from Brodick to Lamlash, a distance of some three miles, cost 1s 8d, of which pier dues accounted for 8d, and drew attention to the hardship imposed on inhabitants and other persons resident in the island, suggesting that for pier-to-pier journeys in Arran itself, exemption from pier dues should be granted. 'Clachan,' writing in support of his arguments, from Lochranza, observed sourly that 'if he could only come round our length he would find that instead of 2d to get off the pier, the large sum of 4d is extracted. It is simply preposterous...' Another writer, 'Meallmohr,' agreed, observing that for years before the pier was built the ferry landing fee was 4d, being only reduced to 3d when the steamboat owners threatened to land passengers in their own boats. 'I think the attention of the Duke should be drawn to the shameless extortion going on at Lochranza, but would suggest to your Brodick correspondent that he should let well alone, or he may some day by mulcted in 4d every time he lands like us unfortunate Lochranza people, or in 6d like the more-to-be-pitied Pirnmill people.'

Now and again heavy dues at certain piers led to more than protests. At Dunoon, in 1865, local discontent brought about proposals for the construction of a new pier. The existing jetty had been built by a private company formed in 1835, but dues on goods and passengers were regarded as being not only the cause of annoyance and complaint, but also detrimental to the prosperity and development of Dunoon. It was widely believed that the shareholders were taking unfair advantage of a monopoly to enrich themselves at the expense of the community at large, a view supported by the fact that three directors who had suggested a reduction in dues had been expelled from the board. A public meeting was held in Dunoon to arrange for a new company to be formed, and the sum of £1,500 was speedily raised; a provisional order under the General Pier and Harbour Act, 1861, having been obtained, a bill was brought before Parliament seeking powers to construct a new pier. It was opposed by the existing company and referred to a Committee of the House, which unanimously threw out the bill on the grounds that the new pier would affect the passage of steamboats to and from the existing pier. No more came of this determined attempt to break the monopoly at Dunoon but evidently the matter was taken to heart by the owners, who built new waiting rooms and offices and greatly extended the pier, completing the work by 1870.

Not every new Clyde pier was greeted with unalloyed enthusiasm by local inhabitants. The estate of Barremman, on the western shores of the Gareloch, just north of Clynder, was purchased by Mr Robert Thom for £20,500 in 1871. Within a short time the new proprietor feued part of the ground for villas and in 1877 brought out a proposal to erect a new pier only 600 yards away from the existing one at Clynder. Much sympathy was felt for Mr Chalmers, the owner of Clynder, who derived his living from it and a public meeting expressed strong disapproval of Mr Thom's action. It was to no avail, for the necessary Parliamentary powers were obtained and Barremman pier opened to traffic at a formal ceremony on 8 June 1878. Traffic at Clynder was adversely affected, and the older pier closed to steamboat traffic as early as 1892. The new structure at Barremman, typical of many smaller coast piers, was built of wood throughout, greenheart piles being used, these having proved immune to attack by sea worm. The pier was 100yd long, the gangway 14ft broad, and the pierhead 80ft long and 24ft wide. Waiting rooms were provided for passengers and there were facilities for dealing with horses and cattle, goods loading being assisted by a large crane. The average draught of water at low tide was 12ft, increasing to 22ft at high water. Barremman was opened with little ceremony, but when the new pier at Dumbarton was completed in 1875 the occasion was regarded as important enough to justify a general holiday in the town. Dumbarton Old Quay, situated some distance up the River Leven, had fallen largely out of use since the withdrawal of the Dumbarton and Glasgow steamers and it was thought desirable to construct a new pier to tap the main stream of the Clyde traffic. Accordingly, there was built by the Burgh a new wharf, running from below the castle rock out across sandbanks to the main Clyde channel. It was no less than 640ft long, with a pierhead 90ft long and 25ft wide. Constructed entirely of American pitch pine, the structure cost £8,000 to build, but it is sad to recall that it was never really a success. The distance from the town centre made it less useful than it might have been, and passengers preferred to travel to Craigendoran by train to join the North British steamers rather than rely on an indifferent service by the poorer up-river boats, for the best tourist steamers seldom called at Dumbarton.

ACCIDENTS AND MISHAPS

No passenger service of the intensity and frequency seen on the Clyde in Victorian days could have been conducted without an occasional accident, and when the relatively primitive nature of the ships themselves, the embryonic state of safety regulations, and the reckless attitude of many skippers are all taken into consideration, the mystery is that no large-scale disaster ever occurred on the firth. Indeed, the only two ships lost in ordinary service during the period were the *Lady Gertrude* and the *Vesta*, whose destruction was attributable in each case to quite different causes, amounting to sheer misfortune. Nevertheless, several alarming accidents took place, any one of which might well have led to heavy loss of life.

The ugly possibilities attending a panic on board a crowded steamer were seen on the *Athole* on a summer evening in 1866. Her complement had been augmented at Glasgow by passengers from the *Rothesay Castle* which had been unable to leave the Broomielaw on her usual afternoon down run owing to a mechanical failure. On the way down river, the *Athole*'s bearings began to overheat and jets of water were played on them, generating in the process clouds of steam and causing some alarm amongst the passengers, who were unaware of the reason. Off Fort Matilda, several of the paddle floats suddenly broke loose, damaging the paddlebox and making what was described as 'a frightful noise'. Many women began to scream, and a surge of passengers to the ship's side caused her to list dangerously, allowing water to pour through one or two of the cabin windows which happened to be open. There ensued a panic, 'ladies convulsively seizing hold of the gentlemen within reach, and praying for help'. The disorder was quelled with some difficulty, but had the steamer been in any real danger of foundering the consequences would have been appalling. The Campbell steamer *Vesper*, coming down river astern of the *Athole*, came alongside and took on board many of the passengers before towing the disabled steamer to Gourock quay and completing her own run.

Rare cases of fatalities on board Clyde steamers were usually due to accidents which could as well have happened ashore, a common occurrence being a victim falling down a stair, but an unusually sad incident resulted in the death of a child on board the *Vivid* in July 1866. On leaving Govan, a drunken steerage passenger threw the coiled casting line attached to one of the mooring ropes into the water, where it instantly became caught in the paddle wheel, drawing the mooring rope with it. A little girl was standing on the rope coil and, before Captain Campbell had time to stop the engine, her foot was trapped and literally torn off. The child was taken ashore at Renfrew Wharf and removed to the Royal Infirmary, where she died a few hours later. 'The value of the rope,' ended the newspaper account of the tragedy, 'is stated to be about £15.'

Suicides accounted for most of the other shipboard deaths of those years. An account of such an incident on 9 September 1865 related that, as the steamer *Leven* was passing Dalmuir, a man between thirty and forty years of age 'committed self-destruction by leaping into the river... Shortly before...a gentleman observed him tying the fingers of both hands. He left a shilling piece on the paddle-box, which, it is supposed, he intended for payment of his fare.' A man named Daniel O'Donnell was reported to have committed suicide in similar fashion from the *Herald* during the following year. He had been drinking freely during the voyage from Campbeltown, so that eventually the steward refused to supply him with any more liquor. O'Donnell, however, prevailed upon other passengers to buy it for him and gradually became boisterous and abusive. Off Whiteinch he suddenly ran to the paddlebox, exlaimed 'Here goes; success to Dannie!' jumped overboard, and was seen to swim downstream. Boats were lowered and a search made for half an hour, but the unfortunate man was never seen again.

RACING AND STRIVING

Overcrowding of steamers and drunken behaviour were so obviously against the public interest that they drew general condemnation but another malpractice, steamboat racing, was freely indulged throughout the Victorian heyday. Many accidents resulted from over-precipitate approaches to piers by rival steamers, and denunciations of racing were regularly thundered forth by the local press. Glasgow River Bailie Court was in a position to impose stronger sanctions on erring skippers, and an annual procession of captains who had been summonsed for reckless navigation testified to the prevalence of the 'sport', for it was in that light that racing was regarded by most of the travelling public. Several captains were admired for their prowess in competition and indeed the financial rewards accruing to a ship which arrived first at a crowded pier and bore away the majority of the passengers were enough to explain, if not to excuse, some of the risks which were taken. Provided racing took place in the open firth, few could reasonably object to a good contest, but the increasing number of collisions due to recklessness at piers led to mounting public concern and ultimately the introduction of a satisfactory system of signalling in the late eighties.

Several steamers were widely acclaimed as greyhounds. The *Glen Rosa*, sister of the *Sheila*, was just as speedy as that vessel but her usual run to Arran took her out of the public eye to some extent and her reputation as a racer was never the same. Nevertheless she appears to have shown her heels to the splendid *Ivanhoe* on many occasions. But steamers did not need to be unduly fast to indulge in racing. The *Guinevere* was a reliable ship, but no record breaker; however, on 21 July 1877 she left Lamlash ahead of the *Glen Rosa*, which pursued her slower rival to the Garroch Head, where the two vessels closed and sailed neck and neck, eventually colliding and damaging their paddleboxes. The escapade led to John Reid, master of the *Guinevere*, and Peter McDermid, captain of the *Glen Rosa*, appearing together at the River Bailie Court on a charge of 'culpably and recklessly managing their respective vessels and striving and racing with each other.' As often happened, a good deal of conflicting evidence was led, but Captain Reid was found guilty of having failed to give away to the faster steamer and fined £5, with the alternative of sixty days' imprisonment, the charge against McDermid being found not proven.

The opening of the Wemyss Bay Company's service to Arran in 1865 led to fierce competition between the *Largs* and McKellar's *Venus*, both of which were timed to leave the island at the same hour on the morning up run. 'A regular race takes place,' reported the *Glasgow Herald*, 'both vessels being pushed to their utmost speed in order to outrun the other... Yesterday morning the *Largs* and the *Venus* came into collision near Corrie Ferry which, of course, caused great alarm amongst the passengers. The *Venus* had her bulwarks injured, but the *Largs* escaped without injury. We trust that, for the safety of the travelling public, some arrangement will be come to... whereby further mishap from the same cause may be prevented.'

But such exhortations usually fell on deaf ears.

It often happened that two steamers became regular rivals

through running on the same route at similar times and of these the *Columba* and *Lord of the Isles* became probably the most celebrated. Serving the same piers from Glasgow to the Kyles of Bute, these two splendid ships raced often, and the description of one of their encounters which appeared in the *Glasgow Herald* in September 1888 recalls the intense excitement which was aroused:

Yesterday a fair trial of speed took place between these crack river steamers on the stretch from Rothesay Bay to Colintraive, Kyles of Bute. Both steamers left Rothesay Pier at the same time, the *Lord of the Isles* having, if anything, the advantage of about her own length of a lead. It was evident to the crowd on the pier, as well as the passengers on both steamers, that a trial of speed was about to be made. As Ardbeg Point was reached, the *Columba*, on the outside berth, forged ahead and crept up on the stern of the *Lord of*

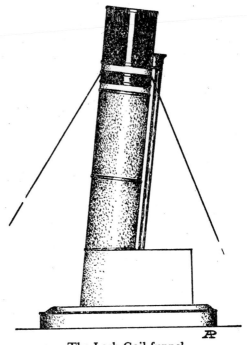

The Loch Goil funnel

the Isles, the clouds of smoke emitted from the funnels gradually changed to flame and showing that steam was well upon both steamers. At the entrance to the Kyles it was evident to those on board both vessels that the *Columba* was slowly but surely making way, and when fairly into the Kyles she passed the *Lord of the Isles*, winning, so to speak, a stern race by two boat lenths. Approaching Colintraive, the *Columba* slowed in order to take the pier, and the *Lord of the Isles* passed on, her crew and passengers maintaining a suggestive silence, whilst the *Columba's* passengers cheered vociferously.

M

CHAPTER TEN

LIFE AFLOAT

THOSE familiar with the railway steamers of later years would find little in common between those well-run ships and the majority of the Clyde passenger steamers of mid-Victorian times. The period covered in this book saw the culmination of a rougher and cruder age in which the rumbustious social background of the sixties gradually resolved itself into a stifling respectability now widely regarded as the hallmark of the entire Victorian era. The history of the river steamers shows a comparable trend towards elimination of abuses such as indiscriminate racing, reckless navigation, overcrowding of vessels and overloading of ferries which occurred all too frequently in the sixties and seventies and led on more than one occasion to the verge of disaster. The late Andrew McQueen, writing of those years, remarked upon the freedom from serious accident which had characterised the Clyde services, but from the evidence available it can be seen that this was largely due to sheer good fortune; some of the collisions that took place were hair-raising, and the conduct of many skippers indicated a sublime disregard for the safety of the passengers in the reckless scramble to take piers. Gradually, however, public opinion forced an improvement and regulations were introduced and enforced which had the desired effect of eliminating the more disgraceful features of life afloat. The trend was hastened by the undoubted success of such well run steamers as the *Lord of the Isles*, *Ivanhoe* and *Columba*, which showed that higher profits and standards went together, and paved the way for the sweeping improvements which followed after 1888.

OVERCROWDING OF STEAMERS

To Clyde skippers whose livelihood depended upon successful trading, the temptation to fill their steamers beyond safe limits was well nigh irresistible, particularly when Glasgow public holidays brought thousands to and from the coast and the chance of a good load to offset several poor trips was not lightly to be disregarded. Board of Trade control was not then as effective as in later years and throughout the period instances of gross overloading occurred. In the spring of 1865 a correspondent of the *Glasgow Herald* drew attention to the dangers and made a number of suggestions for dealing with the problem in a memorandum to the Board of Trade, but that body contented itself with issuing a proclamation calling upon all to respect the law, trusting that steamboat proprietors would of their own accord adopt the writer's plan for issuing control tickets. This appears to have been no more than a pious hope, despite the printing of a formal warning in the papers later in May.

The abuses continued. An anonymous writer in the *Herald* of July 1878 asked:

> Is there no Board of Supervision or authority to prevent the overcrowding of the river steamers on holiday occasions, or on trip days? Yesterday I came up with a steamer from Arran, and at Rothesay it took in a crowd of people in all conditions of intemperance. On they crowded till the decks were packed like a cattle steamer. We took in a few more at Innellan, Dunoon, and Kirn; where they found room was a mystery. We staggered across to Greenock under our load; it was quite calm fortunately, and so we rolled but little. I don't know how many people were on board, but packed as we were, there would have been little chance for anyone . . . it will be a wonder if some accident does not happen one of these days. . .

Slowly, the authorities began to take a grip of the situation, and a number of prosecutions were brought against offending owners. In June 1886 the Board of Trade communicated with local authorities on the coast, calling attention to the matter and requesting prompt action to deal with overcrowding, in particular, of late steamers from Rothesay and Dunoon on Saturday nights, and the *Glasgow Herald* hoped that 'as the authorities are thus early bestirring themselves, the evil is likely to be minimised this season, and the comfort and safety of the public will be thus greatly assured.' But the overcrowding problem was never wholly solved during the period, and as late as April 1887 Mr William Wilson could report to the Clyde Trustees that he 'was credibly informed that at last holiday there were steamers so terribly crowded that the people were shrieking in danger and anxious to get ashore, and hundreds preferred to sleep in the open air at the coast rather than come home with these overcrowded steamers. . .'

Along with overcrowding of steamboats went frequent overloading of many of the coast ferries. 'A Coast Residenter' wrote of his experience at Ardentinny in 1881:

> On the arrival of the steamer *Chancellor* over 60 full-grown persons, besides the two boatmen, were taken off in one ferryboat. This number was called by the steamer's ticket collector and his men, and was witnessed by the captain. Once in the boat it was impossible to get out of it as it became packed, and it is quite miraculous that the passengers were landed in safety, as the gunwale of the boat was within two inches of the water. There was another ferryboat lying on the shore, but it was allowed to lie unused while this overcrowding was taking place. There was no satisfaction to be got from the officers of the steamer, nor from the ferryman, whose only anxiety was about his '2d each' on landing. Is this dangerous practice of overcrowding to be permitted until we have another sad accident reported?

Such were a few of the incidents which ultimately brought about effective public protest and a long-overdue tightening of regulations. The Clyde was immensely fortunate in being spared a major disaster but the conduct of operations in earlier years positively invited misfortune. Given overcrowding of the kind then prevalent, and a collision and sinking, the appalling death roll of the *Princess Alice* disaster on the Thames in 1878 could as easily have been repeated on the Clyde; that nothing remotely as awful ever occurred was as much a matter of luck as of good judgment and skilful navigation.

THE DEMON DRINK

Beyond a doubt, the most consistently deplorable feature of life afloat was the prevalence of drinking, a problem equally well known ashore but one which could be not only offensive but also positively dangerous on board the small ships then in service. This great social evil stemmed from widespread poverty in the rapidly growing industrial complex which was nineteenth century Glasgow and its neighbouring burghs; to the city came thousands of immigrant Irish during the famine years in the forties, and large numbers of Highlanders cleared from their ancestral lands by 'improving' landlords, two Celtic streams which joined to give Glasgow its special character. The Celt, unlike his southern cousin, tended to drink spirits rather than beer, and cheap whisky, often illicitly distilled, offered him a certain, if temporary escape from the grey misery of overwork in poor conditions, of slum housing, and illness which all too often undermined his health, killed his children, and shortened his own life. Thus, it is not surprising to learn that in the year 1868 there were upwards of 1,780 public houses in Glasgow alone, not counting the adjacent communities of Partick and Govan. With a 'dram' in him, a man might forget his troubles, if only during a day's sail 'doon the watter,' but in the company of his fellows conviviality too often became license, the bounds of propriety were overstepped, and the excursionist awoke to hard reality in the bleak surroundings of a police cell in one of the coast towns.

Social reformers, such as William Booth of the Salvation Army, who understood the causes of the problem, were few in those years and the conventional attitude, crystallised in the correspondence columns and leading articles of the newspapers, was to deplore drunkenness and condemn the perpetrators of the often outrageous incidents on board steamers and amongst excursionist crowds at the coast. It is fair to add that these were usually grossly offensive to the majority of passengers on board the river steamboats. The *Glasgow Herald*, no doubt with reluctance, published a long letter from 'an Edinburgh man' in 1865 which drew attention to the excesses of parties of excursionists at Dunoon; his description was echoed time and again during the ensuing quarter of a century by others who had every reason to be sickened by the behaviour of Glasgow's citizens in their cups.

> No visitor to the Clyde can fail to remark the excursion trips which sail from Glasgow down the river; and few can fail to see in them much that is to be deplored and ought to be reformed. A happy company they are not, but a dissipated and reckless. The presiding demon is drink, and almost all the men, and not a few of the women, prove too sadly his baneful influence...
>
> It was only last Saturday that three trips came to Dunoon... The scene, Sir, was such as to startle the most practised nerves. I have been in many countries, and seen many nations, but never did I see a gathering of such low, drunken, blasphemous mortals... It was sufficient to call down the wrath of Heaven upon men, much less to make the angels weep over fallen and degraded humanity. Here, one man drunk and foaming, was roaring a song whose words he could not pronounce, and whose air was rather a prolonged yell than melody. There, another was fighting, swearing, and blaspheming. There, a boy, drunk and corpse-like, was being rescued from a watery grave, having reeled into the water from the pier. Here, a young woman was leaning, in a state of drunkenness, against a wall. There, a young man was being forced off the steamer by his comrades, regardless of his struggling and his cries for drink. Drink, drink, drink, was written on the haggard faces of all—was invoking these songs—was causing that degradation...

The *Herald's* correspondent referred to privately-organised excursions, but conduct on the ordinary service runs was every bit as disgraceful. Saturday evening steamers to Glasgow were more than ordinarily infested with drunken passengers and it was a common sight for the police to come aboard at Custom House Quay, Greenock, to remove the offenders. On a June evening in 1877, for example, it was recorded that a general fight broke out during the course of which Captain Orr, the Greenock police chief, was person-

ally assaulted and several constables 'came in for a considerable amount of abuse' before two passengers were arrested.

But if the average steamboat owner turned a blind eye to
all but the most flagrant excesses on board his vessel, comfort-
ing himself with the thought that his receipts were improved
in the cabin bar, none went to the lengths of the Sunday
traders, Henry Sharp and Duncan Dewar, in their whole-
hearted exploitation of loopholes in the drink laws. By
common consent, the service offered by those enterprising
entrepreneurs reached the absolute nadir, at least in so far
as the respectable inhabitant of the city was concerned. Not
only did they offend general public opinion by sailing their
steamers on the Sabbath, but they did so in the interests of
drink. The so-called Forbes-Mackenzie Act—the Licensing
(Scotland) Act, 1853 (16 & 17 Vict c 67)—was an early example of social legislation designed to eliminate some of the
worst evils of drink and it provided for a certificate to be
issued to a publican authorising him to sell liquors (spirits
and wine) provided 'he do not open his House for the sale of
any liquors, or sell or give out the same, on Sunday, except
for the accommodation of lodgers and bona fide travellers...'
The Act, however, did not extend to the river steamers and
Sharp, who owned licensed premises in the Gallowgate, soon
found it profitable to buy an old steamer and run it on Sun-
days. Bankruptcy in 1866 proved but a temporary obstacle
to his nefarious activities and he was soon back in the trade.
Duncan Dewar followed the same course and in time their
ships became absolutely notorious. In the words of Andrew
McQueen:

> ... there is no doubt that the clientele of the Sunday boats and the
> condition of things on board amply sufficed of themselves to justify
> their evil reputation... Travellers by these boats were almost en-
> tirely 'drouths', out to secure the alcoholic refreshment denied them
> ashore. The boats were simply floating 'pubs'... Their routes and
> destinations were matters of little moment; and it is probable that,
> when they arrived home, a large proportion of the passengers had
> no very definite idea as to where they had been.

Sharp and Dewar operated a succession of second hand boats, including the *Petrel*, *Kingstown* (a double-bowed, ex-Irish ferry), *Cardiff Castle*, *Dunoon Castle* and *Marquis of Lorne*, many of which had been good steamers in their day, but in the hands of their unscrupulous proprietors they entirely lost their reputation. 'The Sunday boat,' declared the *Graphic*, 'is the only boat on the river looked upon with disfavour by the "respectables" of Glasgow. She is supposed to be the refuge of the destitute convivialists, who are deprived of their "mornin'" glass of "mountain dew" by the Act of Forbes Mackenzie for Sunday closing, and so are driven to join the army of "Boney Feedy" travellers. A young man seen landing from the Sunday boat is considered to have forfeited all claim to further respect.'

On 28 July 1878 the *Dunoon Castle*, of which Henry Sharp was a joint owner, was the scene of a particularly disgraceful riot. She had carried a larger complement than usual in the morning, her numbers being swelled by Glaswegians anxious to hear the great preacher Charles Spurgeon at Rothesay, but the exhortations of that eminent divine seemed to have had little immediate effect for it was recorded that by the time the *Dunoon Castle* reached Gourock on her return journey the effects of a plentiful supply of drink were becoming apparent amongst the passengers. From Greenock, and all the way up river, there was a general melée, in which drunken passengers fought with each other, using foul language and assaulting anybody who attempted to restore order. Hats were knocked overboard, an elderly man was attacked, and no passenger was safe from assault. The skipper, Charlie Brown, fulminated in vain from the paddlebox and slackened speed several times, but to no avail; the riot continued for over two hours, the vessel being in an uproar as the supply of drink continued unabated. When the *Dunoon Castle* eventually arrived at the Broomielaw at eight o'clock, she was met by Sergeant Donald McDonald with a strong detachment of police from the Marine Division, who had their work cut out to arrest the ringleaders and clear the ship. He found two men 'fighting like cannibals' and peaceful passengers on the bridge and climbing up about the funnel to get out of their reach. When the passengers disembarked, the streets got into such a state of commotion that it was nearly an hour before they were cleared. Sergeant McNeil told of bringing reinforcements to the aid of his colleague and explained during the subsequent Court proceedings that it was quite usual for detachments of police to be at the quayside to avaid the arrival of Sunday steamers—'a good deal of liquor is used on board, and we expect disturbances.'

Considerable public protest was aroused by this incident and the *Glasgow Herald* devoted a leading article to the subject of intemperance, which brought a letter from another disgusted traveller complaining not only of drunkenness but also of other unedifying features of river sailing then too well known to the general public, namely, the filthy condition of the river itself, and obscene language amongst passengers. In advocating the running of a steamer on temperance principles, the writer suggested that more people would travel by a vessel of that type if they could be assured of

a good day's sail without being compelled to witness the continuous ... profane and obscene language that is so freely bandied about, and so familiar to the ears of the natives of the 'Second City'. It is too bad that strangers who come here to enjoy a few weeks' holiday ... should have their pleasures marred by the senseless, ignorant conduct of a number of vulgar Glasgow rowdies. I have been on board of Sunday steamers, not only in this country, but elsewhere, and I am free to confess that I have never seen on any river in Europe or America such disgraceful scenes as I have witnessed on board the beautiful boats which daily run on the bosom of our sweet-smelling, pellucid river*... A week or two ago the writer went with a party of strangers who were most anxious to see the beauties of the romantic scenery of our Highland lochs, of which they have heard so much. The weather was splendid, the boat was comfortably full at both ends, and everything looked as if we were going to have a good time of it without anything happening to distract our atten-

*Sic!!

tion. We had just got as far down as Govan, the river was low, the water was as black as ink, and the smell was—well, such as no one who had a nose would ever think of asking his lady love or anyone else to hasten with him to Kelvin Grove to inhale the perfume, certainly not of 'Araby the blest.' We had not yet got clear of the sweet-smelling Kelvin ere many of our female passengers began to overhaul their bags and baskets in search of the irrepressible black bottle, which having found, they pulled out the cork using their teeth for a screw, then applying the neck of the bottle to their mouths, they took a long hearty pull of the contents, handed it to their neighbour, who followed suit, which is a necessary precaution, they say, to correct any evil consequences which might arise from inhaling the gas of the Kelvin. The above process continued all the way down, and by the time we reached Greenock the horse play was in full swing—dancing and singing, swearing and tumbling about, screaming of women and children, who could not get out of the way quickly enough, was truly pitiful to witness... We left the boat at Greenock, and came home by train, glad to escape...

The prevalence of such scenes eventually led to steps being taken to prevent abuse of the Forbes-Mackenzie Act and during the eighties legislation was introduced which stopped the sale of alcoholic drink on board steamers returning to port on the same evening. Thus effectively were the operations of Sharp and Dewar curbed, and both withdrew from the river whose steamer services they had done nothing to improve. They are remembered only as two of the most discreditable exploiters of the Victorian working classes of Glasgow, and the wonder is that their activities should not have been ended at a much earlier stage.

CRIME ON BOARD

Drink and its consequences were only the most obvious perils facing passengers of those days. More subtle dangers presented themselves in the shape of nefarious individuals who carried on the lucrative practices of pocket-picking and card-sharping. Time and again one reads of passengers having been robbed of wallets or purses by pickpockets, working alone or in gangs. At the end of May 1865 a lady arrived by the *Mountaineer* at Greenock, only to discover that a pocket had been cut from her dress and the sum of £14 stolen, apparently by one of a group of 'ladies and gentlemen who continued to show her much attention during the day, and were continually in the vicinity of her person, pointing out objects of interest...and making themselves very agreeable. 'Passengers,' said the *Herald*, 'would do well to be on their guard while travelling at this season, as the authorities inform us that day after day perfect shoals of these social pests, some well dressed, and others in more humble attire, are infesting the river-boats at present.'

Cardsharpers were more difficult to deal with, for the nature of their activities often left their victims unwilling to complain of being swindled, thus revealing their own stupidity. Times without number the papers fulminated on the gullibility of travellers who allowed themselves to be drawn into card games with complete strangers. Often the sharpers relieved their victims of valuable belongings as well as cash. The loss of gold watch and chain was often reported, and those foolish enough to join in games were as often as not left penniless. Onlookers who tried to intervene were usually threatened with volence, and received no thanks. The legal position was obscure, and there was little that the police could do. The remedy, of course, was never to become involved, but it was a lesson which many learned only by bitter experience. A particularly impudent swindle was reported on board the *Nelson* in May 1866, which at least had the saving grace of humour. A young man was induced to play with a gang of sharpers on the trip between Glasgow and Bowling and was speedily relieved of £6. The story continued:

After the simpleton had lost his money, one of the 'gentlemanly-looking men' who previously played with the fellow with the cards, and always won, took him down to the steward's cabin, and treated him to a bottle of London porter. While partaking of the beverage, the confederate began to upbraid the dupe for having been inveigled into playing, and remarked that this would be a lesson to him, which he trusted he would not forget. Ultimately the card-sharpers returned . . . 5s to assist him home.

EVENING CRUISE
AND
GRAND OPEN - AIR CONCERT
(Weather Favourable),
ON THE
BRAES OF COULPORT (LOCHLONG),
On FRIDAY, 2D JULY.

The Programme will consist of Selections from
THE "MESSIAH,"
BY THE
WEST OF SCOTLAND CHORAL UNION
(150 VOICES),
AND
COLE'S ORCHESTRA.
Conductor.....................Mr H. A. LAMBETH.
Leader of Orchestra.......... ....Mr W. H. COLE.
SOLO VOCALISTS—
MISS AGNES B. STEWART, Soprano.
MR WALTER BRUCE, Bass.
Concert to Commence at 8 P.M., and will conclude at 9 P.M.,
Steamers returning immediately thereafter.
Steamer "ADELA,"
From Millport at 6.30 P.M.; Largs, 6.50; Wemyss Bay, 7.15.
New Steamer "VICTORIA,"
From Rothesay at 7 P.M.; Craigmore, 7.5; Toward, 7.15;
Innellan, 7.25.
Steamer "MARQUIS OF BUTE,"
From Dunoon, 7.15; Kirn, 7.30; Hunter's Quay, 7.35.
Steamer "WAVERLEY,"
From Ardenadam at 6.50 P.M.; Kilmun, 6.55; Strone, 7.0;
Kilcreggan, 7.20; Cove, 7.30; Blairmore, 7.40.
Steamer "IVANHOE."
From Helensburgh at 7.0 P.M., Prince's Pier, 7.15.
Fare, including Pier Dues at Coulport, 1s.
Steamers will leave Coulport on Return Journey in the
following order, viz. :—1st, "Adela;" 2d, "Victoria;" 3d,
"Marquis of Bute;" 4th, "Waverley;" and 5th, "Ivanhoe."
N.B.—Should the weather prove unfavourable the above
arrangements will be carried through on Friday the 9th July.

Handel's 'Messiah', *Ivanhoe* style, 1886

EXCURSIONS

One of the great features of life in those days was the steam-boat excursion. Factory excursions, Sunday School trips, charitable outings and Volunteer charters were arranged summer after summer to every part of the firth. People rose at unearthly hours of the morning to trek on foot to the

Broomielaw and sail long distances. Excursions were major events in the lives of working people of the time, whose annual holidays amounted in all to perhaps ten days or a fortnight, who worked daily for hours incredible to modern minds, and whose existence was constantly threatened by ill health and poverty. Many a Glasgow child looked forward with unbelievably eager anticipation to his Sunday School 'trip', and remembered it for years afterwards as one of his all-too-few red-letter days. His parents welcomed the annual factory outing with scarcely less pleasure, tempered only by the thought of the drunken excesses which too often disgraced these occasions. The best outings were strictly supervised by employers, and if they were men of wisdom as well as compassion, they ensured that their workpeople and families spent the day happily at some remote pier innocent of the temptations of Rothesay, Dunoon, or Largs. One reads, for example, of the employees of Thos Edington & Sons sailing on board the *Aquilla* to Lochgoilhead in May 1865, leaving Glasgow at 6.30 a.m. accompanied by the Phoenix Flute Band and two fiddlers, who provided music for dancing and 'amateur sentimental singing and recitation.' This happy occasion was typical of many, but one wonders what caused the employees of the Coatbridge Phoenix Iron Works to publish an advertisement in the *Glasgow Herald* on 4 August 1865 recording that they were 'highly dissatisfied with the treatment they received from the agents and captain of the splendid new steamer *Rothesay Castle*, and treated them on disembarkation with three hearty groans!'

One of the events of the year was the annual carters' excursion which, in 1870, presented something of a spectacle:

The excursionists, to the number of about 800, mustered at the County Buildings about six o'clock, and having formed in procession, they marched to the Broomielaw. Having then embarked on board the Rothesay Castle, they proceeded to Lochgoilhead, where they spent a very pleasant day, returning again in the evening between 8 and 9 o'clock. The procession through the city was headed by a Rifle Volunteer Band, which occupied a large waggon drawn by eight fine horses. The office-bearers of the association, who each wore a bright-coloured sash, and a broad Kilmarnock bonnet, followed on horseback; and as a number of the members were also mounted, the excursionists attracted a considerable amount of attention both on the occasion of their departure and arrival, the streets through which they passed—in the evening especially—being crowded with spectators.

Undoubtedly the most welcome excursions were those arranged annually for poor children in Glasgow by Mr Walter Wilson, owner of the Colosseum, a well-known department store in the city. With a flair for publicity, Wilson prospered and in his day he was one of the best known men in Glasgow. He had a genuine concern for the poor and his annual outings to the Clyde coast gave many a poor child a precious day's trip which would otherwise have been denied him. Wilson did things in style, usually chartering three or four steamers to carry several hundred children to Rothesay, there to spend a happy day of sporting activities before returning to Glasgow in the evening. But the occasion of Queen Victoria's Golden Jubilee on 21 June 1887 provided the opportunity for the largest Clyde steamer excursion of all time, the description of which duly appeared in the *Glasgow Herald*:

> Yesterday Mr Walter Wilson, of the Colosseum Warehouse, treated about 15,000 of the poor children of Glasgow to a trip to Rothesay. The tickets were distributed by clergymen and city missionaries, the superintendents of Sabbath schools, and the officials of kindred organisations, and the class for whom the treat was intended—the deserving and well conducted—were thus reached without difficulty. For so large a number extensive preparations had to be made. Five river boats were chartered exclusively for the children, and arrangements were made whereby certain numbers of them might travel by the ordinary steamers. For their refreshment during the journey and on their arrival at their destination, 16,000 packages of buns, biscuits, and scones, about 30 cases oranges, 361 cases of sweets, each containing about 640 packages, 8 cart-loads of milk, and 8 cartloads of aerated waters were provided. The weather was excellent, although a little sultry. The vessels were timed to leave Glasgow between seven and nine o'clock; but as early as half-past six the Broomielaw swarmed with children, ticket in hand, from all parts

of the city. Their embarkation was a work of some difficulty, and resembled nothing more than the shipment of a huge flock of sheep. About a thousand monitors, who had voluntarily undertaken the duty, were assisted by the police, and the greater number of the little excursionists had been despatched by eleven o'clock. The *Athole*, which had on board about 1250, was the first to leave. She was followed in quick succession by the *Eagle*, the *Lancelot*, the *Shandon*, the *Guinevere*, the *Elaine*, the *Vivid*, and the *Benmore*. Detachments were sent by the *Columba* and the *Lord of the Isles*, and those for whom no room could be found in the steamers at Glasgow were despatched by railway to Wemyss Bay, Greenock, and Craigendoran, to be conveyed to Rothesay by the regular steamers running between these places and Bute. Arrived at Rothesay, the various detachments, headed by brass bands which had accompanied them from Glasgow, were formed into procession and marched to the public park, granted for the occasion by the Provost and Magistrates. When the main body of the children had arrived the National Anthem was sung, and a short address was delivered by the Rev J. Watson Reid, of Christ Church, Glasgow, at the conclusion of which he proposed that a vote of thanks should be given to Mr Wilson. Mr Wilson responded, and in turn proposed a similar compliment to the Provost and Magistrates for granting the use of the park. The Provost briefly replied, bidding them all welcome to Rothesay, and shortly afterwards luncheon was served. In distributing the meal the monitors had to contend with very great difficulties. They were scarcely so numerous as was necessary for so large a body of children, and as the cakes and milk were somewhat slow in coming round the children became impatient, and finally ignoring all order, swarmed about the barricade from which the refreshments were being given out. Those who had received supplies and those who had not became indistinguishable, and, naturally, the weak and the very young were the sufferers. The distribution occupied so long, and the heat had become so intense, that only a portion of the programme of sports arranged to take place in the afternoon could be gone through. For these prizes had been presented by H.R.H. the Duke of Cambridge, the Hon. the Lord Provost, the Earl of Rosebery, Mr Provand, M.P., Mr M. H. Shaw-Stewart, M.P., Mr C. Hozier, M.P., Mr Cunninghame-Graham, M.P., and others. The majority of the competitions were postponed until some suitable date when they will take place in Glasgow. The reassembling and shipment of the children for Glasgow was also a matter of difficulty, but was accomplished without incident. The first detachment left by the *Columba* shortly after three o'clock. The remainder were got on board the various steamers provided for them an hour or two later. At the Broomielaw an immense crowd of parents and friends awaited the arrival of the children, and joined in their cheering as the boats brought them alongside the quays...

Whence, no doubt, they went home 'tired, but happy.'

The *Columba's* paddlebox thistle

CHAPTER ELEVEN

ENGINES AND BOILERS

JUST as the basic hull of the typical Clyde steamer had been refined into something far in advance of the primitive vessels of pioneering days by the early sixties, so also had boilers and machinery evolved into much more elaborate systems of propulsion than those installed in older ships. Thus, side lever engines and other variants of stationary machinery ashore gradually gave place to engines designed specifically for marine use; these, by 1864, were basically of three main types, the steeple engine, the oscillating engine, and the diagonal engine.

STEEPLES AND OSCILLATORS

The oldest of these in principle was the so-called 'steeple' type, invented by the well known Scottish engineer David Napier in 1832. It derived its name from a fancied resemblance of the engine frame to a church steeple. The cylinder was placed to drive upwards at a sharp angle on to the crosshead which slid up and down in vertical slidebars, and immediately underneath it was placed the crank. The steeple engine was for long a favourite with private owners and survived until 1902 in the *Vivid*, the last Clyde steamer in normal service to be propelled by an engine of this type. The advantages of the steeple included economy of space in the engine room, and the absence of fore and aft surging associated with single cylinder engines of the diagonal pattern, but it was not well adapted to enlargement and modification for use in the larger and more powerful ships of the seventies and eighties and it fell speedily out of use in our period—indeed, its de-

N

cline can be stated to have been well in progress by 1864. The final application in the *Scotia* in 1880 was indicative at once of the desire of her owner to secure its advantage of smooth propulsion for a large ship while also, by designing a double version of the type in this rare example, admitting its lack of power in the single form.

The oscillating engine enjoyed a considerable vogue during the earlier part of the period. It derived its name from the action of the cylinders, which oscillated to and fro on trunnions. Slide bars and crossheads were unnecessary, for the piston rods were integral with connecting rods driving directly on to the cranks. It was a simple and compact engine which enjoyed much favour for a long period. This form of machinery was perhaps most identified in later years with the MacBrayne fleet, in which it survived well into the present century. J. & G. Thomson of Govan and Clydebank specialised in oscillating engines but Henderson of Renfrew also fitted them into several steamers. In this form of engine, too, there was found notable smoothness in working for there were invariably two cylinders, allowing partial balance of moving parts, and the cylinders were in any case usually placed under the crankshaft so that, as in the steeple engine, the thrusts were vertical rather than horizontal. It was possibly for this substantial practical benefit that David MacBrayne had the *Columba* and *Grenadier* fitted with oscillating engines long after they had been given up in other fleets, for these tourist vessels sailed long distances every day and it was essential to avoid the tiresome swaying of the diagonal engine of the period which, over several hours, could be unpleasant. Fuel costs in the seventies and eighties were unbelievably low and questions of thermal efficiency matters of merely academic interest, so that the large quantities of coal burned daily by the excursion steamers did not form an unduly large item in the ships' expenditures. The social conscience of later generations recognises that all this was done at the expense of appalling conditions in the Scottish coal mines, coupled with quite inadequate wages for pit workers, but without denigrating David MacBrayne and other owners it is fair to suggest that such matters beyond their own personal control probably seldom occurred to them other than as general social and political issues. So the famous ships of the Victorian heyday were propelled by inefficient engines, but at a cost in fuel which only in much later days began to be a matter of concern to the owners.

The oscillating engine had a substantial disadvantage which eventually proved to be its undoing. Greater power was required for larger, faster steamers and generally this demanded higher steam pressures for which the oscillating cylinders were ill adapted. Steam tightness was a grave problem requiring constant attention, whereas with fixed cylinder machinery there was little trouble. When compounding was introduced in the *Grenadier* it was the only example of an oscillating engine of this type, for the higher pressure aggravated the problem. Reference has already been made to the cheapness of coal in those years, and it is at least possible that the increased thermal efficiency and corresponding reduction in fuel consumption compared with those of a simple oscillating engine were factors in allowing the *Grenadier's* sailing range to be extended for, it will be recalled, her summer station was originally the Oban and Gareloch route, and later the Staffa and Iona run from Oban round the Isle of Mull, quite a substantial daily mileage without opportunities of intermediate re-coaling.

Two variants of the basic oscillating engine were incorporated in a few Clyde vessels of the period, both being described as diagonal oscillating machinery. Both versions had oscillating cylinders driving upwards at an angle on to the crankshaft instead of vertically, as in the classic oscillating engine. The two large steamers built for the North British company in 1866, the *Meg Merrilies* and *Dandie Dinmont*, were built with two cylinder twin crank machinery approximately similar in layout to the double diagonal and compound diagonal engines of later years save that the cylinders oscillated, but this form never gained popularity. The second variation, applied to the *Lord of the Isles* and *Ivanhoe*, was a D. & W. Henderson patent involving two cylinders driving from fore and aft of the crankshaft on to a common crank. This unusual arrangement, which avoided the complication and cost of twin cranks, allowed more space athwartships than a conventional oscillating engine, but its use did not extend to more than a few ships, possibly due to patent problems.

DIAGONAL ENGINES

Unquestionably the favourite engine for new construction during the quarter of a century of our period was the diagonal, either single or double. The diagonal engine took its name from the position of the cylinder placed on its bedplate, inclined diagonally upwards towards the crankshaft. It was an elementally simple form of machinery, robust, and free from complication, for the slide, or flat, valve admitting steam to the cylinder was operated by a slip eccentric arrangement. Single diagonal engines developed into massively constructed affairs with heavy, cast-iron entablatures bolted to the cylinder block to form a solid unit incorporating the slide bars. The reliability and relative cheapness of the type soon caused it to oust earlier forms of machinery and for several years in the seventies and early eighties it could be fairly described as the standard pattern of Clyde steamer engine. Like the other types alreay described, however, it also had its disavantages, mainly associated with the single form of the diagonal type. When only one cylinder was employed, it will readily be appreciated that there was an unbalanced force, caused by the sliding to and fro of the heavy piston. It was *not* caused by the crank, or the alternate fore-and-aft thrusts of the steam, which were self-balancing. Smaller steamers with correspondingly smaller pistons did not suffer to quite the same degree as larger vessels from the always tedious and—to some people

—occasionally nauseating surge of this form of engine, but in later ships, such as the *Sheila* and *Jeanie Deans*, it was very pronounced.

The second disadvantage of a single engine was the occasional tendency to stop in dead centre—that is, with the piston at the end of its stroke, so that steam could not enter the cylinder to initiate the return stroke. Pinch bars in the earlier ships allowed the engineers to bring the crank over the awkward position but not until the introduction of auxiliary starting machinery at a later stage was this particular defect cured. It may be mentioned in passing that it may well have been responsible for the loss of the *Lady Gertrude* in 1877, as well as a number of other incidents when steamers were involved in collisions through failure of the machinery to respond at critical moments.

The need for increased power eventually caused the introduction of the logical development of the single diagonal engine, namely the double version with two cylinders and twin cranks placed at ninety degrees to each other. At one stroke the disadvantages of the single engine were overcome. Two cylinders meant a substantial degree of balance between the pistons although, as both were moving in the same direction for a short time at the end of each stroke, there was still a slight surging, but the main problem was virtually eliminated. 'Dead centre' on either of the two cranks was no trouble, for the other was at right angles to it where its piston could exert maximum force to start the whole engine. The substantial benefits of the double diagonal were responsible for its being chosen for ships such as the *Eagle*, *Meg Merrilies* and *Victoria*, and its use might have been widely extended but for certain factors. In the first instance capital costs were higher than those of a single engine, discouraging private owners from adopting the double type; secondly, increasing coal costs towards the end of the period eventually forced the logical step forward to the compound version of the same engine which came to dominate the Clyde scene in the nineties and in the first decade of the twentieth century. The simple expansion, double diagonal engine therefore remained a rarity except on Loch Lomond, where it remained popular for many years under private and railway ownership alike.

The only other form of machinery employed by Clyde owners was the vertical two cylinder type in the single screw steamers of the Campbeltown Company. The *Kintyre* was at first fitted with simple expansion machinery of this pattern but the *Kinloch* and *Davaar* were compound from the outset and the older ship was in due course converted. Driving directly on to a propeller shaft with only one screw, these relatively fast-moving engines were rather smaller than those of their paddle contemporaries, and therefore correspondingly less impressive in appearance.

The reluctance of owners to incur unnecessary expense in providing their ships with more complicated types of machinery has been noted. Along with this went a tendency to avoid disposing of a set of engines if they could be used again, and during the period there were several instances of machinery doing service in more than one steamer. Sometimes this arose from misfortune, as in the case of the loss of the *Lady Gertrude*, the engine of which was salved from her wreck and placed in the new hull of the *Adela* in 1877. In the case of the *Alma*, a steamer of indifferent reputation, her steeple engine was used again after she ended her short career, thereafter propelling the much more useful *Victory*, and in this instance it was evident that the *Alma's* hull had not been well designed. This was not so in the case of the *Eagle*, whose reliability and economy improved notably after the replacement of her original double diagonal machinery by a single engine in 1877.

BOILERS AND CONDENSERS

Despite the examples cited above, it was rare for a steamer to go through more than one set of machinery, but the replacement of boilers was virtually a routine matter with the majority of ships, for these were subjected to heavy wear and tear and were often abused, particularly in the earlier years, through such malpractices as over-rapid steam raising and inconsistent firing, leading in turn to fatigues and stresses which shortened the life of tubes and combustion chambers. The classic boiler of the quarter of a century covered in this review was the haystack, so called by its exterior appearance. This elementary form of water tube boiler gained wide popularity and, in conjunction with a single diagonal engine, formed the most common power unit of Clyde passenger steamers for the whole of the period. The haystack boiler normally incorporated four ashpans separated by water-filled partitions supporting a 'dish' above the furnaces. From the dish rose a nest of water tubes to the steam drum forming the dome of the boiler. The drum was constructed with a circular flue in the centre leading to the funnel. Hot gases from the furnaces rose through the nest of water tubes and into the uptake, controlled from the engine room by a simple butterfly valve in the inner funnel. The haystack was a complicated boiler to construct but its advantages were considerable. It was lightly built, well suited to the fairly flimsy hulls of most ships of the time, in which shallow draught was necessary in sailing to such piers as Helensburgh, Craigendoran, and other places where shallow conditions obtained. The main advantage, however, lay in its ability to raise steam rapidly, and under natural draught conditions to maintain a good steam supply to the engine.

The fire tube boiler referred to variously as the locomotive, horizontal, or navy type, enjoyed some vogue during the period, but latterly lapsed from popularity, not to be revived again until the later eighties and thereafter. The MacBrayne steamers *Iona*, *Columba*, and *Grenadier* were all built with boilers of this type, and originally had their funnels spaced widely apart, as in the first two vessels, or very close together, as in the last, due to the funnel uptakes being placed at the ends of the boilers. The navy boiler, to give the most gener-

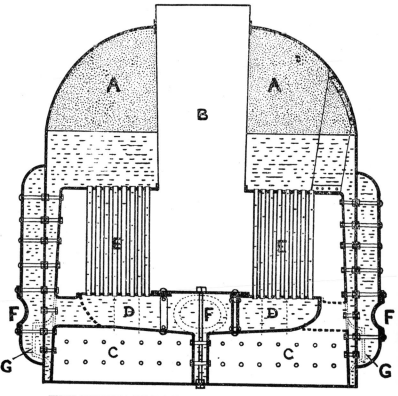

THE HAYSTACK BOILER OF THE P.S. 'IVANHOE'

A Steam dome
B Uptake to funnel
C Furnaces
D Water-filled pan
E Water tubes
F Manholes for inspection and cleaning
G Fire doors

ally accepted title, was in principle similar to that of a railway locomotive, being cylindrical, with the combustion chamber joined to the uptakes by a nest of fire tubes. This was a heavier type of boiler than the haystack and generally less successful in that it steamed less reliably in conditions of natural draught. The lengthening of the rather stubby funnels originally fittted to the *Iona* and *Columba* may well have had as an objective the improvement of steaming. Certainly the original type of boiler was regarded as being less than ideal, for these ships and the *Grenadier* eventually were all refitted with haystacks. The secret of success with navy boilers was forced draught in a closed stokehold, conditions which did not generally obtain until the introduction of the more modern railway steamers from 1889 onwards. There had been the noteworthy exception of the *Meg Merrilies* in 1887 when forced draught was employed to improve a notoriously indifferent steamer but natural draught was all but universal during the whole of the period.

Engines of the sixties, seventies, and eighties were robustly made. Cast iron was generally employed for entablatures and cylinders, and wrought iron for moving parts, including crankshafts. The solid-forged steel crankshaft was a thing of the future, and common practice was to build up shafts with webs shrunk on to them. Paddle wheels were of wrought iron, generally with eight floats of feathering type, but several older steamers survived well into the period with the old fashioned, non-feathering floats. In contrast to those of later years, paddle wheels tended to be of large diameter and narrow in width, but practice gradually moved towards wider floats on wheels of smaller diameter, contributing in no small measure to the aesthetic improvement of Clyde steamers in general, culminating in the beautiful vessels of the nineties. Most steamers before 1890 were fitted with wooden floats, usually of elm planking, which could be speedily replaced in the event of being smashed by floating objects.

Clyde steamers of the sixties were provided with jet condensers to receive and condense exhaust steam from the engine. The effect of this was slightly to improve the thermal efficiency of the machinery, mainly by heating feed water to the boiler. The principle was to pass exhaust steam into the condenser chamber, at the same time pumping a jet of cold sea water through by means of pump rods worked off the crosshead or some other convenient moving part. While admirably simple, the trouble with this form of condenser was that sea water caused pitting in the boiler, shortening its life. Gradually, therefore, towards the end of the eighties, it began to be ousted by the surface condenser, a more complicated device in which exhaust steam passed through a nest of tubes round which fresh sea water was constantly pumped, allowing the condensate to remain free of impurities and so avoiding boiler damage. In the early years steam from the safety valves was allowed to blow away to waste in the atmosphere, and there are many references to the nuisance caused by noise, and hot water falling across decks when steamers 'blew off.' The *Iona* was built with a discharge pipe leading under water, avoiding these problems, but it became general in later days to pass surplus steam into the condenser to prevent waste.

Auxiliary machinery was generally limited to the larger ships, and in the case of the mighty *Columba* it included warping sheaves at bow and stern to assist in handling the ship at piers. She and many others were equipped with steam steering gear when new, but a number of the older vessels were given this improvement later in their careers, the *Iona*, for example, being so fitted during overhaul in 1873. The heavy wooden wheels associated with manual steering were replaced by light, brass wheels when steam steering was substituted.

COAL AND COSTS

One of the main drawbacks of the Victorian steamboat was its propensity for emitting dense volumes of black smoke, accompanied by showers of smuts and cinders. Passengers found the latter nuisance unbearable, for clothing was often damaged by hot embers, and the pleasures of a day's sail could be effectively marred by a speck of coal in the eye. The evil persisted throughout the period, for no legislation was introduced to enforce owners to seek improvement, except while their vessels were stationary at piers. The masters of the *Athole* and *Vesta* were convicted in June 1869 of having failed to ensure that the furnaces were properly fired so as to prevent emission of smoke at Greenock Steamboat Quay. They were the first offenders under newly introduced regulations and were admonished, but a constant stream of cases was recorded over the years, apparently with little impression. Once a steamer was sailing, nothing could be done to stop careless firing, and with due attention it was a simple matter to conform to the minimum requirements of the law at piers. Consequently, the use of cheap coal in primitive boilers continued as the rule, rather than the exception, until the advent of the modern, railway-owned ships in the nineties. There were some attempts at amelioration of the problem, it is true, confined, as might have been expected, to excursion steamers whose owners had most to gain from smoke elimination, but on the whole these came later in the period and did not become general in the Clyde fleet. Thus, the *Ivanhoe*'s boilers were equipped in 1888 with Bonthorne's furnace doors, designed to prevent heavy smoke emission, apparently with some success. Another venture of the same year involved the *Edinburgh Castle* which, in February, was experimentally fired with Brode's patent coal briquettes from Westrigg Colliery on her regular return sailing from the Broomielaw to Lochgoilhead. Results were promising; steam was raised quickly and maintained easily, there was no smoke nuisance and a complete absence of sparks and soot from the funnel. But nothing eventuated from the trial and it is reasonable to conclude that patent royalties may well have raised the cost of briquettes above the level which owners found economic.

The root of the problem lay in finance. Clyde steamer fares were amazingly low in proportion to the facilities provided and mileages involved, a tradition which has continued into modern times. The natural corollary was that profits were insufficient to encourage private owners to experiment with newer forms of machinery and boilers, and understandably the cheapest designs held sway. The greater resources of the railway companies permitted the introduction of expensive compound and triple expansion engines, and navy boilers, from the late eighties, but such novelties were subsidised by profits from more lucrative traffics than the Clyde was able to offer. Clyde steamers of the mid-Victorian period, in the main, catered to a large, poorly paid, industrial population whose good fortune it was to have the firth at its doorstep as a holiday area. It was unrealistic to expect that these people would pay high fares, and the inevitable result was that standards rose slowly. The steamer proprietors should not be too readily condemned for they, too, were victims of the economic circumstances of the time, and with a few exceptions they provided over a long period a service which was widely acknowledged as the best of its kind in the world.

APPENDICES

STEAMBOAT LIVERIES

A modern traveller, if he could be transported back to the middle years of the Victorian period, would certainly look upon the majority of Clyde steamers of that time as rather drab ships. On reflection, it would occur to him that the rarity of deck saloons, and the absence of topside plating, were responsible, for these were invariably painted in light colours in modern vessels, brightening the whole appearance of Clyde steamers. In the sixties, seventies and eighties, hulls were almost uniformly black, usually with pale pink or flesh-coloured underbody, and deckhouses and sponson housings were either black or varnished wood. Those vessels equipped with deck saloons looked much brighter and more attractive, since these items of equipment were painted in a variety of light shades, and were frequently panelled in other colours. Funnels, of course, were richly varied, but it was strange that combinations of black and white were widely employed, although it is acknowledged that many of these had long tradition behind them. The virtual absence of yellow or buff, those widely used colours of a later era, is noteworthy, but red, a shade that has died out in latter years on the Clyde, was very commonly used, giving a welcome splash of colour to many an otherwise dull colour scheme.

Paddlebox design was richly varied and if the steamers of the earlier decades did not quite match the superb designs of the railway steamers of the years immediately before the first world war, nevertheless some very attractive paddleboxes could be seen. Generally, in proportion to the size of ships, paddle wheels were of greater diameter in the middle years of the century than was afterwards fashionable and some steamers, most notably the *Edinburgh Castle*, were distinctly 'humpbacked' in appearance. These large paddleboxes were usually painted black, the white colours of Duncan Stewart's fleet and the North British Steam Packet Company up to 1883 being exceptional, but other boats were so painted from time to time. One and all were decorated with an appropriate panel or device, and with a greater or lesser amount of ornamental gilding. The vessel's name often appeared on a scroll following the curve of the paddlebox but sometimes the words *Royal Mail* appeared instead in the case of ships engaged in mail contract work.

Radial vents were popular for paddlebox designs, the *Undine* and *Lorne* being the last steamers to be built with the kind of exuberant pattern characteristic of the fifties and early sixties. The *Scotia* was also noteworthy for her unusual paddlebox design. Horizontal slots formed a more practical design, and many steamers combined them with elaborate centre panels as, for example, the *Athole*. Later North British steamers had a prominent gilt vertical column above the central panel, dividing the paddlebox into two sections. Designs for panels varied widely, from rising sun motifs on some of the Wemyss Bay boats to representations of Edinburgh Castle on the Lochgoil Company's flagship and a bust of the Queen on the *Victoria*. No two ships were alike, and the continuous variety of detail on Clyde boats of the period was a constant delight.

Uniform for crews owed little to nautical influence during the early part of the mid-Victorian years. Most skippers wore bowler hats, and on more formal occasions a frock coat and 'tile' hat were often worn. Few achieved a reputation to equal that of Captain Robert Young, one of the most competent skippers of the period, nicknamed 'Captain Kid' on account of the gloves which he usually wore. It was related of him that he had been known to ascend to the bridge in three successive suits on the voyage from Glasgow to Millport. James Williamson referred to him with obvious affection, but thought him over-refined; this was apt, and 'Sandy' McLean and Bob Campbell were more typical of the older Clyde skippers, competent men all, but not noted perhaps for social graces. Robert Young eventually retired early from the river boats, devoting himself thereafter to teaching music, in which he had some ability, and he died in the late eighties. James Williamson was himself an exception to the general run of captains. Placing great importance on smartness, his *Ivanhoe* crew wore sailor suits and he himself habitually wore a frock coat. The senior MacBrayne men also wore smart uniform caps, and indeed the standard of turn-out on excursion vessels was much superior to that of the smaller up-river steamers. This was inevitable, for the rich patrons of the *Lord of the Isles* and *Columba* would not have tolerated the casual attitude with which the poorer people of Glasgow had perforce to be content while sailing 'doon the watter'.

The following detailed notes on some of the better known fleets should be read with the understanding that they relate to owners' general practices, from which they often deviated in matters of detail from one season to another.

David Hutcheson & Co and David MacBrayne

Change of ownership in 1879 led to no alterations in the livery of this fleet, whose ships' hulls were painted black, probably with Indian red underbody. Elaborate gilded scrollwork at bow and stern was a particularly prominent feature of the firm's steamers, that of the *Iona* being very fine, and gilt lines were carried round the hull and sponsons from stem to stern below mainrail level. The paddleboxes, of standard pattern with five or seven radial vents, were also richly gilded. Saloons were 'stone colour', and deckhouses varnished teak. Lifeboats were plain varnished wood in earlier years, but latterly were painted white.

Funnels were bright red, with thin black hoops and black tops. Readers are referred to *West Highland Steamers* (Duckworth & Langmuir) for a discussion of the relationship between the Cunard Company, the Burns' steamers and the Hutcheson/MacBrayne fleet, and the origins of these colours which were common to all these concerns at one period.

North British Steam Packet Company

Until 1883 these railway vessels sported red funnels with black tops and white paddleboxes. Hulls were painted black, and saloons cream. On the completion of Craigendoran in its final form, the company's funnel had a broad white band added below the black top. The stay ring dividing the red and white sections of the funnel was always painted black. Paddleboxes became black, and these were of radial vent pattern until the close of the company's existence, eight vents being ultimately standardised. The *Sheila*, however, despite a change of name, retained her Wemyss Bay type of paddlebox throughout North British ownership. The ship's underbody was painted pale pink, carried well above the waterline, a feature applied throughout the eighties, but later practice was to use dark red paint with a thin white line separating the red from black at water level. Saloons after 1883 were panelled in brown and cream, and so in time were the sponson houses, but photographic evidence indicates that these features on the *Meg Merrilies*, *Jeanie Deans* and *Guy Mannering* were black at first. Double gilt lines round hull and sponsons were latterly standard, but the *Jeanie Deans* had a single line originally and this feature might well have been the original intention for all steamers in the fleet.

The Buchanan, Williamson and Stewart Fleets

The steamers owned by Captain Buchanan, Captain Alexander

Williamson and Captain Duncan Stewart shared a common livery of black hull and black funnel with a white band, the latter possibly a connection with the Castle Company of much earlier times. Stewart's vessels had white paddleboxes, but those of the other two owners were black, with the customary gilding and ornament.

The circumstances under which the former Campbell steamer *Benmore* sailed for Captain Buchanan in her original owner's colours in 1885 have been explained in the chapter entitled 'Indian Summer'.

Lochgoil & Lochlong Steamboat Company and Glasgow & Inveraray Steamboat Company

These steamers had black hulls and paddleboxes, with the usual gilt ornamentation at bow and stern and on paddleboxes. The *Chancellor* of 1880, however, retained white paddleboxes after passing into Lochgoil ownership in 1885. The Lochgoil Company's funnel was red, with two thin white bands divided by a thin black band, and a black top. The Inveraray Company's funnel was identical, and the little Loch Eck steamer also sported the same attractive funnel livery.

Captain Robert Campbell

The Kilmun steamers were painted in a most attractive livery. Hulls were black, but the underbody was bright green, a welcome change from the all but universal pale pink or salmon colour used in other fleets. The funnel was all-white, as were saloons, and also sponson houses, except on the older ships, where they were black.

Lochlong & Lochlomond Steamboat Company

A painting of the *Chancellor* of 1864 in the Wotherspoon collection shows her to have had a black hull, with pink underbody, and white paddleboxes. Saloons and sponson houses were white, with pale pink panelling. There was a profusion of giltwork at bow and stern, as well as on the paddleboxes, which had horizontal slots. A red funnel with black top, and a burnished copper steampipe, completed one of the most attractive liveries on the firth. The 1880 *Chancellor* was painted in similar colours.

Campbeltown & Glasgow Steam Packet Joint Stock Company, Ltd

A very broad red band on the black funnel of this company divided it into approximately equal sections of black/red/black. Hulls and paddleboxes were black, and boot-topping salmon.

Seath & Steele

The first *Bonnie Doon* had black hull, paddleboxes and sponson houses, with pink underbody, but the second ship of the name was painted green under the waterline. Saloons were white, and the funnel in each case was cream.

Various Owners

The Helensburgh boats were unique in having green hulls, but these became black under later owners after Graham Brymner. Hugh Keith's all-red funnel with thin white hoops was another unusual feature, never repeated on the firth. All-black funnels were quite common at one time, the Duke of Hamilton's and Graham Brymner's steamers wearing this sombre colour. Dumbarton steamers were always characterised by an unusual funnel with a deep white band, dividing it into equal sections in the same style as the Campbeltown Company's ships, although the latter had red bands instead of white. Old paintings show the Dumbarton boats with blue paddleboxes, but this may have been a feature confined to very early ships.

Appendix II

THE CLYDE STEAMER FLEET IN 1888

Argyll Steamship Company, Limited

S.S. Argyll (1886)

Captain William Buchanan
P.S.-Balmoral (1842)
P.S.-Benmore (1876)
P.S.-Eagle (1864)
P.S. Elaine (1867)
P.S. Guinevere (1869)
P.S. Scotia (1880)
P.S. Shandon (1864)
P.S. Vivid (1864)

Campbeltown & Glasgow Steam Packet Joint Stock Company, Limited
S.S. Davaar (1885)

S.S. Kinloch (1878)
S.S. Kintyre (1867)

Peter and Alexander Campbell
P.S. Madge Wildfire (1886)
P.S. Meg Merrilies (1883)
P.S. Waverley (1885)
on charter to Bristol Channel

Captain Alexander Campbell
P.S. Adela (1877)
P.S. Argyle (1866)
P.S. Arran (1867)
P.S. Lancelot (1868)
P.S. Victoria (1886)

Frith of Clyde Steam Packet Co, Ltd
P.S. Ivanhoe (1880)

P

Glasgow & Inveraray Steamboat Co, Ltd
   P.S. Lord of the Isles   (1877)

Hill & Co
   P.S. Cumbrae   (1863)

Lochgoil & Lochlong Steamboat Co, Ltd
   P.S. Chancellor   (1880)
   P.S. Edinburgh Castle   (1879)
   P.S. Windsor Castle   (1875)

David MacBrayne
   P.S. Chevalier   (1866)
   P.S. Columba   (1878)
   P.S. Grenadier   (1885)
   P.S. Iona   (1864)

   P.S. Inveraray Castle   (1839)

Alexander McLean
   P.S. Athole   (1866)
   P.S. Marquis of Bute   (1868)

North British Steam Packet Company
   P.S. Diana Vernon   (1885)
   P.S. Gareloch   (1872)
   P.S. Guy Mannering   (1877)
   P.S. Jeanie Deans   (1884)
   P.S. Lucy Ashton   (1888)

Captain Alexander Williamson
   P.S. Sultan   (1861)
   P.S. Sultana   (1868)
   P.S. Viceroy   (1875)

Appendix III

CLYDE PIERS AND FERRIES FROM 1864 TO 1888

GLASGOW AND UP RIVER
   Broomielaw (North and South Sides)
   Partick Wharf
   Govan
   Renfrew
   Bowling
   Dumbarton
   Dumbarton Old Quay
   Port Glasgow
   Greenock Steamboat Quay

RENFREWSHIRE
   Greenock (Prince's Pier)
   Gourock
   Inverkip (ferry)

   Wemyss Bay
   Skelmorlie

AYRSHIRE
   Largs
   Fairlie
   Ardrossan
   Troon
   Ayr

WIGTOWNSHIRE
   Stranraer

DUNBARTONSHIRE
   The Gareloch
   Row
   Shandon (Balernock)

Rahane (ferry)
Roseneath
Clynder
Barremman
Mambeg
Garelochhead

The Firth
Craigendoran
Helensburgh
Kilcreggan

Loch Long
Cove
Coulport
Arrochar

COUNTY OF BUTE

Isle of Arran
Brodick
Invercloy (Brodick) (ferry)
King's Cross (ferry)
Lamlash
Lamlash (ferry)
Whiting Bay (ferry)
Blackwaterfoot (ferry)
Machrie Bay (ferry)
Pirnmill (ferry)
Lochranza
Lochranza (ferry)
Corrie (ferry)

Isle of Bute
Rothesay
Craigmore
Kilchattan Bay
   (ferry until 1881)
Port Bannatyne

Isle of Cumbrae
Balloch Bay
Keppel
Millport
   P*

ARGYLLSHIRE

Loch Long and Loch Goil
Blairmore
Ardentinny (ferry)
Carrick Castle
Douglas
Lochgoilhead

The Holy Loch
Strone
Kilmun
Ardenadam (Sandbank)
Hunter's Quay

Cowal
Kirn
Dunoon
Innellan
Toward

Kyles of Bute
Colintraive
Ormidale
Tighnabruaich
Auchenlochan
Kames
Ardlamont (Blind Man's Bay)
   (ferry)

Loch Fyne
Tarbert
Tarbert (ferry)
Ardrishaig
Strachur
Crarae
Minard
Furnace
Inveraray

Kintyre
Skipness
Carradale
Carradale (ferry)
Saddell (ferry)
Campbeltown

NOTE: The inclusion of a pier or ferry in this list does not signify that it was in constant use throughout the period, but in each case cited there is evidence to prove that it was used at some point. Skelmorlie was a rare example of a pier which fell out of use, due to the construction of Wemyss Bay close at hand. The Inverkip Ferry service lapsed for the same reason. In some cases piers replaced ferries (as at Lochranza) or tidal jetties and ferries (as at Lamlash), and Keppel (1888) was an example of an entirely new pier opened very late in the period.

Appendix IV

STEAMBOAT DEPARTURES — JULY, 1878

BROOMIELAW

AM	Steamer	Destination
6.45	*Marquis of Bute* or *Athole*	Rothesay and intermediate piers
7.00	*Bonnie Doon*	Partick, Renfrew, Bowling, Prince's Pier, Kirn, Dunoon, Wemyss Bay, Largs, Millport, Ardrossan, Troon, Ayr
7.00	*Columba*	Govan, Greenock, Kirn, Dunoon, Innellan, Rothesay, Colintraive, Tighnabruaich, Ardrishaig
7.30	*Iona*	Greenock, Wemyss Bay, Colintraive, Tighnabruaich, Tarbert, Ardrishaig
7.45	*Glen Rosa*	Partick, Renfrew, Bowling, Dumbarton, Greenock, Gourock, Kirn, Dunoon, Innellan, Rothesay, Kilchattan Bay, Corrie, Brodick, Lamlash (and Whiting Bay MWFO)
8.00	*Guinevere*	Greenock, Dunoon, Rothesay, Kilchattan Bay, Corrie, Brodick, Lamlash
9.00	*Carrick Castle* or *Windsor Castle*	Piers to Lochgoilhead
9.30	*Hero*	Piers to Garelochhead
9.40	*Elaine*	Rothesay and intermediate piers
9.45	*Vale of Clwyd*	Partick, Renfrew, Bowling, Dumbarton, Greenock, Gourock, Kirn, Dunoon, Innellan, Largs, Fairlie, Millport
10.00	*Undine*	Rothesay and intermediate piers
10.20	*Marquis of Lorne*	Rothesay and intermediate piers

10.30	*Carrick Castle* or *Windsor Castle*	Piers to Lochgoilhead
11.00	*Eagle*	Rothesay and intermediate piers
11.30	*Vesta*	Rothesay and intermediate piers
12.00	*Benmore*	Greenock, Kilcreggan, Cove, Blairmore, Strone, Ardenadam, Kilmun
PM		
1.00	*Athole*	Rothesay and intermediate piers
2.00	*Viceroy* (probably)	Piers to Rothesay and Ormidale
2.40	*Sultan* (probably)	Piers to Dunoon
so2.50	*Vivid*	Prince's Pier, Kilcreggan, Cove, Blairmore, Strone, Ardenadam, Kilmun
4.00	*Marquis of Bute*	Rothesay express
so5.00	*Carrick Castle*	Partick, Renfrew, Bowling, Dumbarton, Prince's Pier, Gourock

MWFO   Mondays, Wednesdays and Fridays Only
SO   Saturdays Only

KINGSTON DOCK, GLASGOW — SUNDAY SAILINGS IN 1878

AM	Steamer	Destination
8.30	*Prince of Wales*	Renfrew, Bowling, Dumbarton, Greenock
10.00	*Marquis of Lorne*	Renfrew, Bowling, Dumbarton, Greenock, Gourock, Rothesay
10.30	*Dunoon Castle*	Renfrew, Bowling, Dumbarton, Greenock, Gourock, Largs, Rothesay
PM		
1.30	*Prince of Wales*	Renfrew, Bowling, Dumbarton, Greenock, Gourock

Appendix V

SOME STEAMBOAT FARES OF 1878

	RETURNS	
	Cabin	Steerage
Columba		
Glasgow to Kirn, Dunoon, Innellan	2s 0d	1s 6d
„ Rothesay	2s 6d	1s 6d
„ Kyles of Bute	3s 6d	2s 6d
„ Ardrishaig	6s 0d	3s 6d
„ Inveraray (by *Inveraray Castle* connection)	7s 6d	4s 0d
Lord of the Isles		
Glasgow to Strachur and Inveraray	7s 6d (1st Class Rail)	
(via Caledonian Ry to Greenock)	6s 5d (2nd Class Rail)	
„ Kyles of Bute	5s 0d (1st Class Rail)	
	3s11d (2nd Class Rail)	
Bonnie Doon		
Glasgow to Ayr (Return by Steamer) 'Day'	3s 6d	2s 6d
'Season'	4s 0d	3s 0d
„ Ayr (Return by Rail)	6s 0d	4s 0d
Hero		
Glasgow to Garelochhead	1s 6d	1s 0d
Marquis of Lorne		
Glasgow to Rothesay	1s 6d	1s 0d
Athole		
Glasgow to Rothesay (Saturday Excursion)	1s 6d	1s 0d
Sheila		
Glasgow to Arran (via Wemyss Bay Railway)	5s 3d (1st Class Rail)	
	3s 9d (2nd Class Rail)	
Prince of Wales		
Glasgow to Gourock (Sundays)	2s 0d	1s 6d

Appendix VI

TARIFF ON BOARD
MAGNIFICENT SALOON STEAMER
LORD OF THE ISLES

DAVID SUTHERLAND, *Steward*

BREAKFAST, served leaving Prince's Pier, Dunoon and Wemyss Bay.

Salmon, Steaks, Fresh Herring, Ham and Eggs, Sausages, Cold Meats, Tea and Coffee, Preserves, Jam, Jelly, and Marmalade, &c., Hot Rolls, Toast, Plain Bread, Oatcakes, &c.

2/-

LUNCHEON, served from 10 A.M. till 12 noon.

Soup, Salmon, Cold Meats, Hot Potatoes, Cheese, Oatcakes, Water Biscuits, &c., Pickles various.

2/-

DINNER, served at 12.15 and 2 P.M.

Soup, Salmon, Roast Beef, Boiled Mutton (Caper Sauce), Corned Beef, Roast Lamb (Mint Sauce), Tongue, Fowl, Chicken and Ham, Green Peas, Vegetables assorted, Sweets various, Cheese, Salad, &c.

3/-

TEA, served from 4 to 6.30 P.M.

Fish (Hot and Cold), Cold Meats, Boiled Eggs, Fancy Bread, and Preserves } **2/-**

Plain Tea, Toast, Fancy Bread, and Preserves } **1/6**

Wines, Spirits, Malt Liquors, Aerated Waters, Cigars, &c., all of the Best Quality, and Moderately Charged.

(See Printed Price Lists on Board)

Appendix VII

CLYDE COAST
HOLIDAY ACCOMMODATION

HYDROPATHICS

SHANDON, ON THE GARELOCH. Delightful Residence, sheltered from North and East Wind. Conservatory 165 feet long, richly adorned with flowers. Turkish, Vapour, Sea, and Fresh Water Baths; large Swimming Sea Water Bath. The Mansion stands in its own park, and overlooks the Gareloch. There are extensive Gravel Walks, well sheltered.

Visitors by Helensburgh Railway book to Balernock (Shandon) Pier, adjoining house, by Trains leaving Glasgow 7.30, 10.45 A.M., 4.5 P.M. Several steamers daily from Greenock and Public Omnibus from Helensburgh by 4.5 P.M. Train from Glasgow.

Apply to Manager, West Shandon, by Helensburgh.   (1883)

PHILP'S
GLENBURN HYDROPATHIC,
ROTHESAY, BUTE.

Delightful Residence, Climate Mild. Protected from east winds. Turkish, Salt Water, and other Baths. Finest in Britain. Dr Philp, *Resident Physician.*   (1884)

KYLES OF BUTE HYDROPATHIC
ESTABLISHMENT, PORT-BANNATYNE.
CONSULTING PHYSICIAN—DR. ANDREW J. HALL.
LADY SUPERINTENDENT—MISS MALCOLM.

This favourite Establishment is unrivalled as a Marine Residence. Magnificent Suite of Fresh, Sea Water, and Turkish Baths. The new Turkish Bath is now in operation, and is unequalled in success and excellence.   (1884)

HOTELS

ROTHESAY—BUTE ARMS HOTEL. This Establishment is situated in front of the Pier, and affords magnificent views of the Bay, Loch

Striven, and the Kyles of Bute. Tourists by the "Iona" or the "Lord of the Isles" will find this Hotel one of the most comfortable resting places on the West Coast. CHARLES WILSON, Proprietor. (1878)

ROTHESAY. — THE QUEEN'S HOTEL. Only five minutes' walk from the pier, situated in the centre of the West Bay, away from the noise and bustle of the pier, and the smell of fish and other disagreeable matter arising from the harbour. The extensive alterations and additions to this old-established and first-class Hotel are now completed, including a handsome new coffee-room, the largest in any hotel on the Clyde. The view from the windows and roof of this Hotel is the finest in Rothesay. Billiards, Hot and Cold Baths. Special terms for families. Glasgow to Rothesay one hour and twenty minutes, and from Edinburgh three hours, *via* Wemyss Bay.

WILLIAM WHYTE, Proprietor.   (1878)

ROTHESAY. — House of Rest and Hydropathic Establishment; Christian home comforts; summer terms, from 27s 6d per week. — C. Campbell, Argyll Lodge.   (1884)

Appendix VIII

M I N U T E   O F   A G R E E M E N T
B E T W E E N

The Wemyss Bay Steamboat Company and the Greenock and Wemyss Bay and Caledonian Railway Companies. 1866.

Heads of Agreement between the Caledonian Railway Company on the first part—The Greenock and Wemyss Bay Railway Company on the second part, and the Wemyss Bay Steamboat Company (Limited) on the third part.

It is agreed among the parties as follows—

FIRST   The rates for passenger traffic to remain as at present for one year from the thirty first day of December Eighteen hundred and sixty five.

SECOND   The Railway Companies to allow to the Steamboat Coy. one third part of all rates for all passenger traffic passing to and from Glasgow and Paisley from and to Wemyss Bay and using also the Steamers of the Steamboat Company and one half of all passenger traffic passing to and from Greenock from and to Wemyss Bay and using the said

Steamers and that for the period of one year from the thirty first December eighteen hundred and sixty five.

THIRD   The Wemyss Bay Steamboat Company shall have the exclusive right of through booking with the Railway Companies via Wemyss Bay to Innellan and all places on the Firth of Clyde below Innellan accommodated by the said Steamboat Company and that for one year from the thirty first December eighteen hundred and sixty five.

FOURTH   The pier dues shall be charged at Wemyss Bay for coals used for the Steamers of the Wemyss Bay Steamboat Company for one year from the thirty first December eighteen hundred and sixty five.

FIFTH   The Steamboat Company shall receive one half of the revenue received for carrying mails for the like period of one year from the thirty first December eighteen hundred and sixty five.

SIXTH   Pier dues at Wemys Bay for the Steamers of the Company to be charged as at present for the above period, all other Steamers using the said pier to be charged at the same rate or one penny per passenger for passenger traffic. Declaring that in the event of any of the Steamers of the Wemyss Bay Steamboat Company Limited being taken off and another Steamer substituted therefor no additional charge for pier duties shall be made by reason of the said Substitution unless in so far as the substituted Steamer shall be larger than the one for which it is substituted.

In witness thereof . . .

(Scottish Records Office Ref. GRW/3/121; reproduced by permission of the Controller of HM Stationery Office.)

Appendix IX

FLEET LISTS

The following lists include all vessels believed to have sailed regularly on the Clyde in passenger service during the period 1864-88, with the exception of small steam ferries and ships used principally as cargo carriers. Only those Hutcheson and MacBrayne steamers which deputised frequently on the firth are included. It should be noted that, apart from building and breaking up dates, all information relates to the various steamers during Clyde service within the period 1864-88 *only*.

The following abbreviations have been used:

Cyl.	Cylinder(s)
D.D.	Double diagonal
Diag.Osc.	Diagonal oscillating
lb.	Pounds (per square inch)
N.B.	New boiler(s)
Osc.	Oscillating
P.S.	Paddle steamer
S.D.	Single diagonal
S.S.	(Single) Screw steamer
St.	Steeple

Type	Name	Built Broken up	Builders Engineers	Clyde Owners 1864-1888	Dimensions	Boilers	Machinery	Remarks
Iron P.S.	ADELA	1877 post-1898	Caird & Co Blackwood. & Gordon	Gillies & Campbell	207.7' x 19.2' x 7.4'	Haystack 50 lb N.B. 1887	Ex *Lady Gertrude* S.D. 49" x 54"	
Iron P.S.	ALMA	1855 1865-	Barr & McNab J. Barr	Captain Duncan Stewart	157.3' x 16.2' x 7.4'	Haystack	St. 47" x 42"	
Iron P.S.	AQUILA	1843	Tod & McGregor Do.		121.7' x 16.1' x 7.2'	Haystack	St.	
Iron P.S.	ARDENCAPLE	1866 1888	R. Duncan & Co Rankin & Blackmore	Greenock & Helensburgh Steamboat Co, Limited (1866-1868) J. Russell (1868) John Duncan, Greenock (1868-1869) J. M. Campbell and H. Keith (1869-1875)	150.0' x 16.2' x 6.2' 159.1' x 16.2' x 6.2' (Lengthened 1875)	Haystack 40 lb N.B. 1875	Osc. 2 Cyl. 28" x 36"	Sold off Clyde, 1875
Iron P.S.	ARDGOWAN	1866	Laurence Hill & Co Rankin & Blackmore	as ARDENCAPLE	150.8' x 16.1' x 6.2'	Haystack	Osc. 2 Cyl. 28" x 36"	Sold off Clyde, 1875
Iron P.S.	ARGYLE	1866 1908	Barclay, Curle & Co J. Barr	Captain Duncan Stewart (1866) Wemyss Bay Steamboat Co, Ltd. (1866-1869) Gillies & Campbell (1869-1888)	177.3' x 17.5' x 7.6'	Haystack N.B. 1884	Ex *Alma* St. 47" x 42"	
Steel S.S.	ARGYLL	1886 1893	R. Duncan & Co Muir & Houston	Argyll Steamship Co, Ltd (James Little & Co, Managing Owners)	140.0' x 23.0' x 10.0'	100 lb	2 Cyl. Compound Vertical, 22" & 44" x 30"	
	ARRAN (*See Dunoon Castle*)							
Iron P.S.	ARRAN CASTLE	1864 1866	Kirkpatrick, McIntyre & Co Rankin & Blackmore	A. Watson and W. Brown	220.5' x 21.0' x 7.5'	2 Haystacks		Foundered at sea, 1866
Iron P.S.	ATHOLE	1866 1899	Barclay, Curle & Co Do	Captain Duncan Stewart (1866-1872) A. & T. McLean (1872-1888)	192.1' x 18.5' x 7.8'	Haystack N.B. 1878	St. 48" x 48"	
	BALMORAL (*See Lady Brisbane*)							

	Name	Dates	Builder / Engineer	Owners	Dimensions	Boiler	Engine	Remarks
Iron P.S.	BENMORE	1876 1923	T. B. Seath & Co W. King & Co	Captain Robert Campbell (1876-1884) Captain William Buchanan (1884-1888)	201.2' x 19.1' x 7.3'	Haystack 50 lb N.B. 1887, 1888	S.D. 50" x 56"	Sailed with two funnels for a short period circa 1887
Iron P.S.	BONNIE DOON (I)	1870	T. B. Seath & Co A. Campbell & Co	Seath & Steele (1870-1874)	209.5' x 19.1' x 7.5'	Haystack	S.D. 50" x 72"	Sold off Clyde
Iron P.S.	BONNIE DOON (II)	1876 1913	T. B. Seath & Co A. Campbell & Co	Seath & Steele (1876-1880) Gillies & Campbell (1882-1886)	218.0' x 20.0' x 7.5'	Haystack 50 lb	S.D. 50" x 72"	Sold off Clyde, 1880-82 and finally in 1886
Iron P.S.	BRODICK CASTLE	1878 1910	H. McIntyre & Co Anchor Line	Captain William Buchanan (1878-1887)	207.5' x 21.7' x 7.5'	2 Haystacks 50 lb	Ex Eagle D.D. 38¼" x 66"	Sold off Clyde, 1887
Iron P.S.	BUTE	1865 1878	Caird & Co Do	Wemyss Bay Steamboat Co, Limited (1865-1866)	219.4' x 20.2' x 8.4'	2 Haystacks	Osc. 2 Cyl. 44" x 45"	Sold off Clyde, 1866
Iron P.S.	CARDIFF CASTLE	1844	Caird & Co Do	Henry Sharp in 1866	170.3' x 19.0' x 9.3'		D.D.	
Iron P.S.	CARHAM	1864 1889	A. & J. Inglis Do	North British Steam Packet Company (1869-1871)	141.8' x 20.0' x 8.5'			Sold off Clyde, 1871
Iron P.S.	CARRICK CASTLE	1870 1898	J. Fullerton & Co W. King & Co	Lochgoil & Lochlong Steamboat Co (1870-1881)	192.1' x 18.2' x 7.4'	Haystack N.B. 1877	S.D. 49" x 54"	Sold off Clyde, 1881
Iron P.S.	CELT	1848	W. Denny T. Wingate & Co	Campbeltown & Glasgow Steam Packet Joint Stock Company (1864-1868)	164.8' x 21.3' x 10.4'		St.	Sold off Clyde, 1868
Iron P.S.	CHANCELLOR (I)	1864 1895	Blackwood & Gordon Do	Lochlong & Lochlomond Steamboat Co (1864-1880) Keith & Campbell (1880-1884) Captain William Buchanan (1884-1888)	163.2' x 18.7' x 7.0'	Haystack N.B. 1873, 1885	D.D. 32" x 51"	Renamed Shandon, 1881 Continued to sail as Chancellor for Keith & Campbell during 1880
Steel P.S.	CHANCELLOR (II)	1880 post-1919	Robert Chambers, jun. M. Paul & Co	Lochgoil & Lochlomond Steamboat Co (1880-1885) Lochgoil & Lochlong Steamboat Co (1885-1888)	199.7' x 21.1' x 8.2'	Haystack 50 lb	D.D. 36" x 60"	

Type	Name	Built / Broken up	Builders / Engineers	Clyde Owners 1864-1888	Dimensions	Boilers	Machinery	Remarks
Iron P.S.	CHEVALIER	1866 1927	J. & G. Thomson Do	David Hutcheson & Co (1866-1879) David MacBrayne (1879-1888)	211.0' x 22.2' x 9.3'	2 Horizontal. 40 lb N.B. 1886	Osc. 2 Cyl. 42" x 54"	
Steel P.S.	COLUMBA	1878 1936	J. & G. Thomson Do	David Hutcheson & Co (1878-1879) David MacBrayne (1879-1888)	301.4' x 27.1' x 9.4'	4 Horizontal. 50 lb	Osc. 2 Cyl. 53" x 66"	
Iron P.S.	CRAIGROWNIE	1870 post 1894	R. Duncan & Co Rankin & Blackmore	Greenock & Helensburgh Steamboat Co, Limited (1870-1871) Keith & Campbell (1871-1875)	175.0' x 17.1' x 6.8'	Haystack	Osc. 2 Cyl. 28" x 44"	Sold off Clyde, 1875
	CUMBRAE (See Victory)							
Iron P.S.	DANDIE DINMONT	1866 1901	A. & J. Inglis Do	North British Steam Packet Company	197.2' x 22.5' x 6.9'	2 Haystacks. 40 lb N.B. 1870, 1881	2 Cyl. Diag. Osc. 40" x 60"	Sold off Clyde, 1888
Steel S.S.	DAVAAR	1885 1943	London & Glasgow Shipbuilding & Engineering Co Ltd Do	Campbeltown & Glasgow Steam Packet Joint Stock Company, Ltd	217.8' x 27.0' x 12.9'	Double-ended Scotch boiler. 110 lb	2 Cyl. Compound vertical. 29" & 58" x 42"	
Iron & Steel P.S.	DIANA VERNON	1885	Barclay, Curle & Co Do	North British Steam Packet Company	180.5' x 18.1' x 7.1'	Haystack. 45 lb	S.D. 43" x 60"	
Iron P.S.	DRUID	1857 1880	Barclay, Curle & Co Do	Campbeltown & Glasgow Steam Packet Joint Stock Company (1857-1868)	160.1' x 20.6' x 9.7'		44" x 52"	
Iron P.S.	DUNOON CASTLE	1867 1896	T. Wingate & Co Do	Dunoon & Rothesay Carriers per Duncan Lennox (Manager) (1867-1871) Robert Morrison and others (1871-1874) Henry Sharp (1874-1885) James Hill (1883-1884) Captain Alexander Campbell (1884-1888)	191.7' x 18.2' x 7.5'	2 Horizontal N.B. 1883	St. 50" x 45"	Renamed *Arran*, 1883
Iron P.S.	EAGLE	1864 1899	Charles Connell & Co Anchor Line (first engine) W. King & Co (second engine)	Captain William Buchanan	189.0' x 20.5' x 7.5' 204.0' x 20.2' x 7.5' 219.5' x 20.5' x 7.5' (lengthened 1866)	(1) 2 Haystacks (2), Haystack (1876)	(1) D.D. 38½" x 66" (2) S.D. 50½" x 56" New engine, 1876	

Name	Type	Dates	Builder	Owner / Operator	Dimensions	Boiler	Engine	Disposal
EARL OF ARRAN	Iron P.S.	1860 1872	Blackwood & Gordon Do	Ardrossan Steamboat Company (1860-1871)	140.0' x 18.5' x 8.5'	Tubular	Double Steeple	Sold off Clyde, 1871
EDINBURGH CASTLE	Iron P.S.	1879 1913	R. Duncan & Co Rankin & Blackmore	Lochgoil & Lochlong Steamboat Co	205.3' x 19.9' x 7.6'	Haystack. 50 lb	S.D. 50" x 66"	
ELAINE	Iron P.S.	1867 1899	R. Duncan & Co Rankin & Blackmore	Graham Brymner & Co (1867-1874) Captain Duncan Stewart (1874-1879) Captain William Buchanan (1879-1888)	175.0' x 17.1' x 6.6'	Haystack. 40 lb N.B. 1880	Osc. 2 Cyl. 28" x 44"	
EXPRESS	Iron P.S.	1854 1864	J. Barr Do	Captain Robert Campbell	179.0' x 16.1' x 6.9'	Haystack	St.	
GAEL	Iron P.S.	1867 1924	Robertson & Co Rankin & Blackmore	Campbeltown & Glasgow Steam Packet Joint Stock Company (1867-1883)	211.0' x 23.2' x 10.6'	2 Haystacks. N.B. 1872, 1879 (35 lb)	Osc. 2 Cyl. 45" x 63"	Sold' off Clyde, 1883
GARELOCH	Iron P.S.	1872 1906	Henry Murray & Co D. Rowan & Co	North British Steam Packet Company	180.0' x 18.2' x 6.8'	Haystack. 40 lb	Osc. 2 Cyl. 35" x 54"	
GLEN ROSA	Iron P.S.	1877 1919	Caird & Co Do	Shearer Brothers (1877-1881)	206.1' x 20.0' x 7.5'	Haystack. 50 lb	S.D. 50" x 72"	Sold off Clyde, 1881
GRENADIER	Steel P.S.	1885 1928	J. & G. Thomson	David MacBrayne	222.9' x 23.1' x 9.3'	2 Navy. 95 lb	Compound Osc. 30" & 58" x 51"	
GUINEVERE	Iron P.S.	1869 1892	R. Duncan & Co Rankin & Blackmore	Graham Brymner & Co (1869-1876) Hugh Keith & Co (1876-1884) Captain William Buchanan (1884-1888)	200.3' x 19.1' x 6.8'	2 Haystacks. 40 lb N.B. 1875	Osc. 2 Cyl. 36" x 54"	
GUY MANNERING (See Sheila)								
HEATHER BELL	Iron P.S.	1871 1902	Blackwood & Gordon Do	Duke of Hamilton (1871-1874)	207.7' x 21.0' x 8.8'	2 Horizontals 40 lb	D.D. 40" x 66"	Sold off Clyde, 1874
HERALD	Iron P.S.	1866 1894	Caird & Co Do	James Little & Co (1866-1867)	221.6' x 22.0' x 10.4'	2 Boilers. 25 lb N.B. 1880	Osc. 2 Cyl. 44" x 57"	Sold off Clyde, 1867
HERO	Iron P.S.	1858 1908	T. Wingate & Co Do	A. Watson (1865-1866) G. Ferguson (1866-1871) Malcolm McIntyre (1871-1876) Hugh Keith & Co (1876-1884) Captain William Buchanan (1884-1886)	181.0' x 19.1' x 7.1'	Haystack. N.B. 1868, 1884	St. 48" x 42"	At Bangor in 1864/65 Sold off Clyde, 1886

Type	Name	Built / Broken up	Builders / Engineers	Clyde Owners 1864-1888	Dimensions	Boilers	Machinery	Remarks
Iron P.S.	INVERARAY CASTLE	1839 / 1895	Tod & McGregor / Do	David Hutcheson & Co (1864-1879), David MacBrayne (1879-1888)	158.5' x 20.2' x 9.3', 172.9' x 20.5' x 9.3' (Lengthened, 1873)		St. 50" x 48" (ex-*Tarbert Castle* of 1838)	
Iron P.S.	IONA	1864 / 1936	J. & G. Thomson / Do	David Hutcheson & Co (1864-1879), David MacBrayne (1879-1888)	255.5' x 25.6 x 9.0'	2 Horizontals N.B. 1875	Osc. 2 Cyl. 50¼" x 51"	
Iron P.S.	IVANHOE	1880 / 1920	D. & W. Henderson & Co / Do	Frith of Clyde Steam Packet Co, Ltd	225.3' x 22.2' x 8.3'	2 Haystacks. 50 lb	2 Cyl. Diag. Osc. (1 Crank) 43" x 66"	
Iron & Steel P.S.	JEANIE DEANS	1884 / 1920	Barclay, Curle & Co / Do	North British Steam Packet Company	210.0' x 20.1' x 7.6'	Haystack. 45 lb	S.D. 50' x 72"	
Iron P.S.	KINGSTOWN	1862 / 1886	T. Wingate & Co / Do	A. MacFarlane (1885-1886)	151.0' x 20.1' x 7.3'	2 Haystacks N.B. 1877	D.D. 36" x 36"	Sold of Clyde, 1886 Built as ferry for Irish service
Iron S.S.	KINLOCH	1878 / 1928	A. & J. Inglis / Do	Campbeltown & Glasgow Steam Packet Joint Stock Company (Limited from 1883)	205.0' x 24.1' x 12.7'	Double-ended Scotch 80 lb	2 Cyl. Compound Vertical; 29" & 54" x 42"	
Iron S.S.	KINTYRE	1867 / 1907	Robertson & Co (1) Blackwood & Gordon (2) Kincaid, Donald & Co	Campbeltown & Glasgow Steam Packet Joint Stock Company (Limited from 1883)	184.7' x 22.9' x 11.5'	N.B. 1882	(1) 2 Cyl. Vertical 36" x 30" (2) 2 Cyl. Compound Vertical; 26" & 48" x 30" (compounded 1882)	
Iron P.S.	KYLES	1865 / 1888	Caird & Co / Do	Wemyss Bay Steamboat Co, Ltd (1865-1866)	219.4' x 20.2' x 8.4'	2 Haystacks	Osc. 2 Cyl. 44" x 45"	Sold off Clyde, 1866
Iron P.S.	LADY BRISBANE	1842 / 1891	J. Barr / Barr & McNab	McKellar (1864-1868), Keith & Campbell (1868-1884), Captain William Buchanan (1884-1888)	136.7' x 18.2' x 7.9'	N.B. 1868, 1883, and 1888	St. 47" x 50"	Renamed *Balmoral*, 1869. Survived for many years after disposal as a hulk at Newry
Iron P.S.	LADY GERTRUDE	1872 / 1877	Blackwood & Gordon / Do	Gillies & Campbell	190.0' x 18.0' x 7.5'	Haystack. 40 lb	S.D. 49" x 54"	Lost by stranding at Toward, 1877
Iron P.S.	LADY KELBURNE	1843 / 1869	Barr & McNab / Do	McKellar (1864-1869)	149.2' x 17.4' x 8.0'		St.	Did not sail after 1867
Iron P.S.	LANCELOT	1868	R. Duncan & Co / Rankin & Blackmore	Graham Brymner & Co (1868-1874), Gillies & Campbell (1874-1888)	191.2' x 18.0' x 6.9'	Haystack. 40 lb N.B. 1877	Osc. 2 Cyl. 32½" x 48"	

Type	Name	Year	Builder	Owner	Dimensions	Boiler	Engine	Disposal
Iron P.S.	LARGS	1864	T. Wingate & Co / Do	Wemyss Bay Steamboat Co, Ltd (1864-1869) Gillies & Campbell (1869-1877)	161.4' x 19.1' x 7.9'	2 Haystacks	2 Cyl. Diag. Osc. 36" x 36"	Sold off Clyde, 1877
Iron P.S.	LENNOX	1864 / 1867	Clyde Shipbuilding Co / Rankin & Blackmore	New Dumbarton Steamboat Co	139.4' x 14.1' x 6.5'	Haystack	Osc.	Sold off Clyde, 12/1866; wrecked near Kingstown in March, 1867
Iron P.S.	LEVAN	1866	Kirkpatrick, McIntyre & Co / Rankin & Blackmore	Greenock & Helensburgh Steamboat Co, Ltd (1866-1871) Keith & Campbell (1871-1875)	150.2' x 16.2' x 6.2'	Haystack	Osc. 2 Cyl. 28" x 36"	Sold off Clyde, 1875
Iron P.S.	LEVEN	1864 / 1867	Clyde Shipbuilding Co / Rankin & Blackmore	New Dumbarton Steamboat Co	139.4' x 14.1' x 6.5'	Haystack	Osc.	Sold off Clyde, 12/1866; foundered off Irish coast in March, 1867
Iron P.S.	LOCH GOIL	1853 / 1912	J. Barr / Do	Lochgoil & Lochlong Steamboat Co (1864-1870) George Iron, Clynder (1877-1880) Henry Sharp (1880-1885)	163.9' x 16.5' x 7.1'	Haystack	St. 45" x 42"	Renamed Lough Foyle, 1870. Sailed from Londonderry, 1870-1877. Sold to David MacBrayne, 1885, by whom she was employed thereafter on the Caledonian Canal
Iron P.S.	LOCH LOMOND	1867	A. Denny & Co / M. Paul & Co		129.0' x 16.8' x 6.5'			Sold off Clyde, 1870
Iron P.S.	LOCH LONG	1859	Wm Denny & Bros / Denny & Co	Lochgoil & Lochlong Steamboat Co	150.4' x 15.2' x 7.2'	Haystack	Osc.	
Iron P.S.	LORD OF THE ISLES	1877 / 1904	D. & W. Henderson & Co / Do	Glasgow & Inveraray Steamboat Company	246.0' x 24.2' x 9.0'	2 Haystacks. 50 lb N.B. 1886	2 Cyl. Diag. Osc. (1 Crank) 46" x 66"	
Iron P.S.	LORNE	1871 / c. 1900	A. McMillan & Son / J. & G. Thomson	Captain Duncan Stewart	212.5' x 20.0' x 7.8'	2 Haystacks	2 Cyl Diag. Osc.	Sold off Clyde, 1875
	LOUGH FOYLE (See Loch Goil)							
Steel P.S.	LUCY ASHTON	1888 / 1949	T. B. Seath & Co / Hutson & Corbett	North British Steam Packet Company	190.0' x 21.1' x 7.2'	Haystack. 50 lb	S.D. 52" x 60"	
Steel P.S.	MADGE WILDFIRE	1886 / 1945	S. McKnight & Co / Hutson & Corbett	Captain Robert Campbell	190.0' x 20.0' x 7.1'	Haystack. 50 lb	S.D. 49" x 60"	
Iron P.S.	MARQUIS OF BUTE	1868 / 1908	Barclay, Curle & Co / Do	A. & T. McLean	196.6' x 18.1' x 7.3'	Haystack. 45 lb N.B. 1880	S.D. 48" x 60"	

Type	Name	Built Broken up	Builders Engineers	Clyde Owners 1864-1883	Dimensions	Boilers	Machinery	Remarks
	MARQUIS OF LORNE (See *Victory*)							
Iron P.S.	MARY JANE	1846 1981	Tod & McGregor Do	David Hutcheson & Co (1864-1879) David MacBrayne (1879-1888)	153.0' x 20.2' x 9.3' 165.4' x 20.2' x 9.4' (Lengthened 1875)	Horizontal N.B. 1883	St. 56" x 54"	Renamed *Glencoe* and tranferred to West Highland services, 1875
Iron P.S.	MEG MERRILIES (I)	1866 c. 1912	A. & J. Inglis	North British Steam Packet Company	192.1' x 23.1' x 7.1'	2 Haystacks 40 lb	2 Cyl. Diag. Osc. 40" x 60"	Sold off Clyde, 1868
Iron P.S.	MEG MERRILIES (II)	1888 1921	Barclay, Curle & Co Do	North British Steam Packet Company (1883) Builders (1884) Captain Robert Campbell (1885-1888)	210.3' x 21.4' x 7.2'	2 Haystacks. 50 lb Haystack (after new boiler fitted in 1888)	D.D. 43" x 60"	On Belfast Lough on charter in 1884
Iron P.S.	MOUNTAINEER	1852 1889	J. & G. Thomson Do	David Hutcheson & Co (1864-1879) David MacBrayne (1879-1888)	174.3' x 17.6' x 7.9' 184.1' x 19.0' x 8.3' 195.6' x 18.2' x 8.2' (Lengthened 1869 and 1871)	2 Horizontals 26 lb N.B. 1882	St. 57" x 48"	
Iron P.S.	NELSON	1855	T. B. Seath & Co T. Wingate & Co	A. McKellar (1864-1866) Greenock & Helensburgh Steamboat Co, Ltd (1866-1868)	150.1' x 16.5' x 6.8'	Haystack	St. (ex-*Eclipse* of 1850)	Sold off Clyde, 1868
Iron P.S.	PETREL	1845 1885	Barr & McNab Do	Henry Sharp by 1876	168.6' x 18.0' x 8.4'	Haystack N.B. 1866	St. 54" x 51"	
Iron P.S.	PRINCE OF WALES	1858	Laurence Hill & Co Scott & Sinclair		153.0' x 18.0' x 7.0'	N.B. 1877	D.D. 34" x 42"	
Iron P.S.	ROSNEATH	1866 1890	R. Duncan & Co Rankin & Blackmore	Greenock & Helensburgh Steamboat Co, Ltd	150.0' x 16.2' x 6.2'	Haystack	Osc. 2 Cyl. 28" x 56"	Sold off Clyde, 1870
Iron P.S.	ROTHESAY CASTLE	1865	Henderson, Colbourne & Co J. Barr & Co	A. Watson (1865-1866) Run by Barr & Co after death of owner in 1866 Captain William Buchanan (1867-1879)	208.0' x 19.3' x 7.9'	2 Haystacks N.B. 1870	St. 51" x 48"	Sold off Clyde, 1879
Iron P.S.	SCOTIA	1880 c. 1914	H. McIntyre & Co W. King & Co	Captain William Buchanan	211.2' x 21.8' x 8.3'	2 Haystacks. 50 lb	2 Cyl. St. 45" x 48"	
	SHANDON (See *Chancellor* (1)).							

	Name		Builder	Owner	Dimensions	Boiler	Engine	Notes
Iron P.S.	SHEILA	1877 1913	Caird & Co Do	Gillies & Campbell (1877-1882) North British Steam Packet Company (1882-1888)	205.5' x 20.7' x 7.7'	Haystack. 50 lb	S.D. 50" x 72"	Renamed *Guy Mannering* in 1883
Iron P.S.	SULTAN	1861 1919	Barclay, Curle & Co J. Barr	Captain Alexander Williamson	166.0' x 16.6' x 7.2' 176.0' x 16.6' x 7.2' (Lengthened 1865)	Haystack. 30 lb N.B. 1877	St. 45" x 42" ex-*Wellington* of 1853	
Iron P.S.	SULTANA	1868 c. 1907	Robertson & Co W. King & Co	Captain Alexander Williamson	188.1' x 18.3' x 7.3'	Haystack. 45 lb N.B. 1886	S.D. 49" x 54"	
Iron P.S.	THE LADY MARY	1868 c. 1890	Blackwood & Gordon Do	Duke of Hamilton	173.5' x 20.0' x 8.3'	2 Haystacks. 40 lb	Osc. 2 Cyl. 38" x 45"	Sold off Clyde, 1874
Iron P.S.	UNDINE	1865	Henderson, Colbourne & Co Do	J. & P. L. Henderson (1865-1866) Captain Duncan Stewart (1866-1879)	200.0' x 18.5' x 7.7'	Horizontal Scotch	S.D. 50" x 60"	Sold off Clyde, 1879
Iron P.S.	VALE OF CLWYD	1865 1888	T. B. Seath & Co A. Campbell & Son	Seath & Steele (1866-1888)	186.5' x 18.1' x 7.0'	Haystack N.B. 1869 and 1876	2 Cyl. St. and Diag. on one crank (non-compound) 16" and 49" x 48"	Sold off Clyde, 1881
Iron P.S.	VALE OF DOON	1866	T. B. Seath & Co A. Campbell & Son	Seath & Steele	197.0' x 18.1' x 7.3'	Haystack	St.	Sold off Clyde, 1868
Iron P.S.	VENUS	1852 1875	J. & G. Thomson Do	McKellar (1864-1868) Gillies & Campbell (1868-1875)	159.2' x 17.1' x 8.2'		St.	
Iron P.S.	VESPER	1866 1867	Barclay, Curle & Co J. Barr	Captain Robert Campbell	173.3' x 16.6' x 7.7'	Haystack	St. ex-*Express*	
Iron P.S.	VESTA	1853 1886	J. Barr Do	J. & P. L. Henderson (1864-1866) Captain Robert Campbell (1866-1884) Captain William Buchanan (1885-1886)	162.3' x 16.5' x 6.8'	Haystack N.B. 1875	St. 42" x 42"	Destroyed by fire at Ardenadam in 1886
Iron P.S.	VICEROY	1875 1911	D. & W. Henderson & Co Do	Captain Alexander Williamson	194.7' x 20.1' x 7.1'	Haystack. 50 lb N.B. 1886	S.D. 51½" x 60"	
Steel P.S.	VICTORIA	1886 1900	Blackwood & Gordon Do	Gillies & Campbell	222.4' x 23.1' x 8.0'	2 Haystacks. 50 lb	D.D. 40" x 66"	

Type	Name	Built Broken up	Builders Engineers	Clyde Owners 1864-1888	Dimensions	Boilers	Machinery	Remarks
Iron P.S.	VICTORY	1863 1892	Barclay, Curle & Co J. Barr	Captain Duncan Stewart (1864-1865) Wemyss Bay Steamboat Co, Ltd (1865-1869) Gillies & Campbell (1869-1871) Duncan Dewar (1871-1882) Hill & Co (1882-1888)	176.7' x 17.6' x 6.8'	Haystack N.B. 1866 and 1879	St. 54" x 42"	Renamed Marquis of Lorne (1871) and Cumbrae (1882) Survived for many years after disposal as hulk at Newry
Iron P.S.	VIVID	1864 1902	Barclay, Curle & Co Do	Captain Robert Campbell (1864-1884) Captain William Buchanan (1885-1888)	188.3' x 18.2' x 7.8' 197.3' x 18.2' x 7.8' (Lengthened 1877)	Haystack N.B. 1877	St. 48" x 48"	
Iron P.S.	VULCAN	1854 1879	Robert Napier Do	A. & T. McLean (1864-1872) J. & G. Thomson (1872-1879)	167.9' x 16.3' x 8.1'	Tubular square	Osc. 2 Cyl. 36½" x 42"	Sold to shipbuilders in 1872 for private conveyance of their workmen
Steel P.S.	WAVERLEY	1885 1919	H. McIntyre & Co Hutson & Corbett	Captain Robert Campbell (1885-1887)	205.0' x 21.2' x 7.5'	Haystack. 50 lb	S.D. 52" x 60"	To Bristol Channel under same ownership in 1887
Iron P.S.	WINDSOR CASTLE	1875 c. 1910	T. B. Seath & Co W. King & Co	Lochgoil & Lochlong Steamboat Co	195.8' x 19.0' x 7.2'	Haystack. 50 lb N.B. 1886	S.D. 50" x 54"	

FLAGS AND FUNNELS

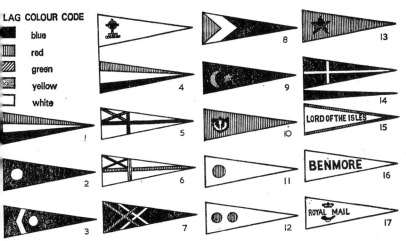

FLAG COLOUR CODE

- ■ blue
- ▥ red
- ▨ green
- ▩ yellow
- ▢ white

1. Captain William Buchanan
2. Captain Robert Campbell (original pennant)
3. Captain Robert Campbell (from circa 1885)
4. Campbeltown & Glasgow Steam Packet Joint Stock Company Ltd. Two flags
5. Glasgow & Inveraray Steamboat Company
6. Lochgoil & Lochlong Steamboat Company
7. David Hutcheson & Co and David MacBrayne
8. Frith of Clyde Steam Packet Co Ltd
9. The 'Turkish Fleet' of Captain Alexander Williamson
10. North British Steam Packet Company
11. Captain Duncan Stewart
12. Hugh Keith
13. Seath & Steele
14. Gillies & Campbell. Two flags
15. Name pennant (Glasgow & Inveraray Company — red lettering)
16. Name pennant (most other fleets—red lettering. An occasional variant was a blue pennant with white lettering)
17. Royal Mail pennant (red lettering and devices)

Q

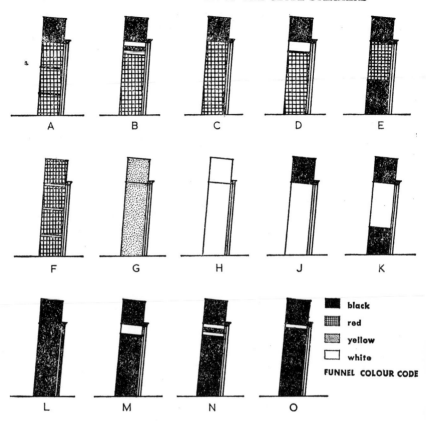

KEY TO FUNNEL COLOURS

A   David Hutcheson & Co and David MacBrayne; A & T McLean

B   Glasgow & Inveraray Steamboat Company; Lochgoil & Lochlong Steamboat Company. The McKellar steamers had a similar funnel, although the shade was reported to have been salmon rather than a true red.

C   North British Steam Packet Company (until 1882); Lochlong & Lochlomond Steamboat Company; Hill's Fairlie and Millport steamers; Henry Sharp (earlier colour)

D   North British Steam Packet Company (from 1883)

E   Campbeltown & Glasgow Steam Packet Joint Stock Company Ltd

F   Hugh Keith's Gareloch steamers

G   Frith of Clyde Steam Packet Co Ltd and (as a cream shade) the Glasgow and Ayr steamers owned by Seath & Steele; the 'Herald,' plying on the Campeltown station; and the Argyll Steamship Co Ltd

H   The Kilmun funnel, associated throughout the period with the Campbell steamers, but in the unusual circumstances referred to in Chapter 3 the *Benmore* sailed with an all-white funnel in 1885 under Buchanan's ownership

J   The steamers of the Wemyss Bay Steamboat Co Ltd, Gillies & Campbell, who later succeeded to the Wemyss Bay trade; Duncan Dewar's *Marquis of Lorne*

K   New Dumbarton Steamboat Co Ltd

L   Duke of Hamilton's Arran steamers; Greenock & Helensburgh Steamboat Co Ltd; Graham Brymner

M   Captain Alexander Williamson's 'Turkish Fleet'; Captain Duncan Stewart; Captain William Buchanan; Henry Sharp (later colours)

N   Shearer Brothers' *Glen Rosa*

O   The *Dunoon Castle* while sailing for the Dunoon and Rothesay carriers

It was common for the steampipes on the funnels of older steamers to be unpainted and polished bright. The miniature chimneys or funnels leading up from the galleys on the sponsons were often painted in the same house colours as the main funnel, or a modified version thereof.

AUTHOR'S NOTES
AND ACKNOWLEDGMENTS

In dealing with the mid-Victorian period of Clyde steamer history a student soon discovers that original documents are exceedingly scarce. In a period when individual shipowners often personally commanded their vessels, when the demands of the law and the Inland Revenue were less stringent, and sheer business 'instinct' counted for much, a steamboat proprietor felt no necessity for maintaining detailed records. In consequence, unlike the case of the railway fleets of later years, little documentary evidence has survived which might throw light on the inner workings of even the larger privately-owned fleets.

I have therefore drawn heavily on newspaper reports for much of the information in the foregoing pages. Fortunately, the workings of Clyde steamers in those years were *news*, and even minor events were faithfully chronicled in considerable detail, so that a fairly comprehensive picture emerges. In addition to recording my appreciation of the help given by the staff of the Mitchell Library, Glasgow, over a period of several years, I have also to thank the editor of the *Oban Times* for permission to examine old files of that excellent newspaper, and Mr W. M. Martin, Librarian of the Royal Burgh of Dumbarton, has also kindly afforded me similar facilities.

I again record with pleasure the most valuable assistance of Mr G. E. Langmuir, himself an author of long standing in this field, for having generously lent several photographs from his collection, and for reading and checking the manuscript, while many discussions with him during the preparation of the book have clarified obscure points. Mr J. F. McEwan has kindly provided notes on the North British route to Helensburgh, for which I am most grateful, while much information of great interest concerning T. B. Seath, the Rutherglen shipbuilder, has come from his grand-daughter, Mrs H. Y. Fleming, of Glasgow.

Mr Alisdair Macdonald has been of great help in preparing the line drawing of the *Iona* which adorns the dust cover of the book, and also several other drawings, while to Mr Ian Shannon I am most grateful for his kindness in allowing me to examine his collection of steamer photographs and for his valued assistance in drawing to my attention a number of excellent subjects. To Mr Shannon also is due the credit for having allowed me to reproduce as an appendix the 1878 menu of the *Lord of the Isles*, now in his possession.

Mr George Barbour, of the Scottish Records Office, Edinburgh, himself a transport enthusiast, has most kindly made available for study the minutes and other surviving papers of the Greenock & Wemyss Bay Railway and the Wemyss Bay Steamboat Company, Limited. Information derived therefrom, and transcripts of Crown copyright records in the Scottish Records Office appear by permission of the Controller of H.M. Stationery Office, for which I am much indebted.

Not least of all, I acknowledge with pleasure the continued encouragement and advice of Mr John Thomas during the preparation of this further venture into the absorbing field of Clyde steamer history.

The detailed research into the period covered in the book has been a great pleasure to me, giving a most enlightening insight into the lives and affairs of the Victorians. If it has done little else, it has made me realise that those much maligned people faced problems as great as any experienced by us, their great-grandchildren, but they met them often in a spirit of optimism far removed from the cynicism of a later generation.

A.J.S.P.

NOTES ON THE PHOTOGRAPHS

Some general remarks on the illustrations may be of interest. The sixties saw the beginning of Clyde steamer photography on an appreciable scale, but one or two vessels continued to escape attention, particularly in the early part of the period dealt with in this book. Nevertheless, most of the ships described were photographed many times and it has been possible to include some pictures of great value. Unquestionably the finest of these have come from the marvellous collection of the late George Washington Wilson, whose superb glass negatives record so faithfully the details of the steamers of a century ago, and I am very much indebted to Mr W. R. McDonald for permission to include several views from the collection, now housed in the University of Aberdeen. From this source, the most outstanding examples are the photographs of the *Hero* and the *Undine*. The former had not been so finely recorded at this stage of her career, and in the case of the *Undine* it is believed that only two other pictures exist of Stewart's handsome flagship. I have preferred to include several full-page illustrations to do proper justice to these views rather than multiply half page pictures simply to cover as many ships as possible.

Messrs Annan's fine old picture of the McKellar steamer *Venus* at Rothesay in 1869 is of fascinating interest, depicting as it does so much of the old harbour and boat yard that has long since been swept away. The approximately contemporary view of the famous *Iona* at Ardrishaig in her first season depicts that long-lived steamer in a guise unfamiliar to any living person, and forms an interesting contrast with later photographs when she had been considerably altered and modernised. Of her superb sister, the never-to-be forgotten *Columba*, so many views were available that a choice proved something of an embarrassment, but Mr Ian Shannon kindly drew my attention to the picture now reproduced from his collection. I know of no other which conveys better the impression of power and majestic grace of that truly wonderful steamer.

In choosing the remainder of the illustrations I have attempted to hold a balance between rare views and pictures of steamers which were well known for many years on the firth. It is hoped that by doing so an accurate impression has thus been given of the Clyde boats of these years. None calls for special mention apart from those above, and the G. W. Wilson view of the *Eagle* at Brodick during the annual fair. This immensely attractive picture gives a fine impression not only of the old Buchanan favourite in her final condition but also of the liveliness of an event which each summer drew large crowds to Arran —a classic evocation of the Clyde steamboat scene of the Victorian summer.

A.J.S.P.

BIBLIOGRAPHY

BOOKS AND BOOKLETS

Duckworth, C. L. D., and Langmuir, G.E. *West Highland Steamers*. Richard Tilling, 1936. Revised and enlarged editions, 1950 and 1967.

Duckworth, C. L. D., and Langmuir, G. E. *Clyde River and Other Steamers*. Brown Son & Ferguson, 1938. Revised editions, 1947 and 1971.

Duckworth, C. L. D., and Langmuir, G. E. *West Coast Steamers*. T. Stephenson & Sons, Ltd, 1953. Revised edition, 1966.

Farr, G. E. *West Country Passenger Steamers*. Richard Tilling, 1956.

Galbraith. Rev Wm. C. *Sixty Years of the Lucy Ashton*. Clyde River Steamer Club, 1948.

Galbraith, Rev Wm. C. *Sixtieth Anniversary of the Caledonian Steam Packet Company, &c.* Clyde River Steamer Club, 1949.

Macdonald, H. *Days at the Coast*. Thomas D. Morison, 1857.

MacLeod, D. *Lochlomond Steamboat Companies*. Bennet & Thomson, 1889.

McQueen, A. *Clyde River Steamers of the Last Fifty Years*. Gowans & Gray, Ltd, 1923.

McQueen, A. *Echoes of Old Clyde Paddle Wheels*. Gowans & Gray, Ltd, 1924.

Paterson, A. J. S. *The Golden Years of the Clyde Steamers (1889-1914)*. David & Charles, Ltd, 1969.

Somerville, C. *Colour on the Clyde*. The Buteman, 1958.

Stromier, G. M. *Steamers of the Clyde*. Nicholson, 1967.

Williamson, J. *The Clyde Passenger Steamer*. MacLehose, 1904.

TECHNICAL

'The History and Development of Machinery for Paddle Steamers'. Paper read to the Institution of Engineers and Shipbuilders in Scotland by G. E. Barr, 1951.

Files of *The Engineer, Engineering, The Marine Engineer* and *Marine Engineering*.

SCOTTISH RECORDS OFFICE, EDINBURGH

Minutes of the Greenock & Wemyss Bay Railway Company
Minutes of the North British Railway
Minutes of the Caledonian Railway
Minutes of the Glasgow & South Western Railway
Working and Public Timetables of the above railway companies

NEWSPAPERS, PERIODICALS, ETC.

The Bailie
The Buteman
The Dumbarton Herald and *Lennox Herald*
The Glasgow Herald
The Greenock Telegraph
The North British Daily Mail
The Oban Telegraph
The Oban Times; and several other Glasgow and Clyde coast newspapers of the period.

MISCELLANEOUS

The Wotherspoon Collection, The Mitchell Library, Glasgow.
Records of the Clyde River Steamer Club, Glasgow.

INDEX

Illustrations are indicated by italic type, and fleet list references by bracketed page numbers

INDEX OF STEAMERS AND
OTHER VESSELS

259

MISCELLANEOUS SHIPS